# SISTERS OF GLASS

# NAOMI CYPRUS

**HARPER**
*An Imprint of* Harper Collins*Publishers*

With special thanks to Rosie Best

Sisters of Glass
 For information address HarperCollins Children's Books, a division of HarperCollins Publishers, 195 Broadway, New York, NY 10007.
www.harpercollinschildrens.com

ISBN 978-0-06-245847-6

17 18 19 20 21 CG/LSCH 10 9 8 7 6 5 4 3 2 1

First Edition

To my daughters:

May you always give each other strength

To fight the battles that matter most

And never let anyone tell you

You aren't powerful

# Part One
## Before the Mirror

# Chapter One

## Nalah

*Thauma activity is hereby forbidden to be practiced within the city limits. Under this regulation, no crafts—medicinal, protective, or otherwise—are permitted to be made or sold. The penalty for illegal Thaumaturgic activity may include exile, imprisonment, or, in cases of extreme misuse, physical alteration or execution. Penalties will be decided at the discretion of the Hokmet.*

*The Thauma are dangerous. They must be contained.*

***Clause 5, "New Hadar Regulations Regarding Thaumaturgic Activity"***

Nalah Bardak bit her lip in concentration as she worked. The heat from the furnace scorched her face, and she twisted her free arm up to wipe a bead of sweat away before carefully drawing the long, hollow steel pole out of the fire. A red-hot bulb of molten glass about the size of her fist clung to the end.

Nalah glanced behind her and paused, rolling the pole

between her hands to keep the glass from dripping off. She waited, listening for footsteps, for her father's voice outside the door.

There was nothing. Nobody was coming toward her father's workshop at the back of the little house on Paakesh Street.

*Good.*

Nalah turned back to the glass, and after one final look out the window to check for spies, carefully dipped and rolled the hot bulb in the flat dish of silver-blue powder that lay on her father's workbench.

"Moonstone for luck," she said quietly, "turquoise for protection."

Adding the dust would imbue the object with only a little magic. Harmless magic. Still, she knew that even this much Thauma work was forbidden, that her father would be as angry as any Hokmet enforcer if he found out. But . . .

But the feeling—the excitement and triumph she felt when the magic took hold—was addictive. She couldn't stop.

Nalah dipped the bulb back into the furnace and turned it to keep the gathered glass smooth. Her father should understand the feeling. He'd spent his whole life doing Thauma glasswork—it was who he was. He'd had to stop when the government made all Thauma work illegal, but you can't just stop being who you are because of some government regulation. She was only twelve years old, but even she knew that.

There was no going back now, anyway. She'd mixed the powders and lit the furnace. The magic was already taking hold, binding to the glass itself, changing it into something *more*.

She pulled the pole out again and began to roll the molten bulb against the marble surface of the workbench, shaping it into a smooth oval, letting it cool just a little. Then she rested the pole on the shaping rail and began teasing and tugging at the glass with her iron tweezers and thin chisel, constantly turning the pole so that her work wouldn't sag. The glass had the consistency of thick taffy, and looked like the boiled-sugar sweets that Mr. Asiz sold in the market. But this glass was hot enough to melt your skin.

Nalah held the image of a bird in her mind, imagined its bright eyes and the proud line of its neck. She could feel the beat of its wings and hear its cry as she tweezed out a beak, shaped the creature's head, and fanned out a chunk from the base to form the tail.

She rolled and pinched and chiseled, and finally there it was: perched on the end of the steel pole, a blue falcon, still glowing faintly from the inside. The bird's aspect was noble, but also a tiny bit playful, its head tilted just slightly to one side.

It was perfect.

Nalah examined the bird with deep affection, and a bit

of the warmth from her chest seemed to trickle down her arm and into her gloved hand—a familiar sizzling sensation that filled her with dread.

*Just calm down,* she thought. *Take slow breaths and it will go away.* This always happened when she got too excited. But she was wearing her father's thick glassworking gloves and was just holding a metal pole. Not glass. It should be fine.

For a moment, it had almost looked like the falcon was glowing from within—as if it were still inside the furnace. But when she looked closer, there was nothing out of the ordinary to see. *Just a trick of the light,* Nalah assured herself.

"All right," she told the falcon, "in you go." She covered the end of the hollow steel pole with her thumb and plunged the bird into a bucket of water. The water roiled for a moment; when it was still, she pulled the bird out and quickly struck the weak point at the base with a chisel. The falcon came away neatly and fell into her gloved hand.

"Got you," Nalah said, and jogged across the workshop to put it into the cooling cupboard. "I'll see you in an hour," she told the bird, which seemed to give her a sideways look, as if to say, *Why so long?* She shut the heavy metal door and set the rusty old clock timer on the table for sixty minutes.

Nalah let out an enormous breath and flopped down into the squashy old armchair in the corner of the room. She tugged off the thick gloves and hooked her legs over the arm of the chair. Her own fawn-colored gloves lay on a side table nearby, where she'd cast them aside when she put on the work gloves. But she wasn't ready to put them back on just yet. Right now she was enjoying the sensation of air on her hands and fingers, which she felt so rarely. *I'll put them back on later,* she told herself.

This was the worst part. Nalah was good at shaping the glass, but she was bad at waiting. She seized a book with a tattered golden spine from the little side table that stood next to the armchair, but even *The Collected Tales of the Great Magos* couldn't hold her interest. Normally, there was nothing Nalah loved more than to escape into the fantastical world of the Magi Kingdom, a fairy-tale land where everything and everyone was bursting with magic. A place where someone like her would be celebrated—not kept secret. But today she was just too excited to concentrate on the stories. She set the book back down.

She stared into space and tried to think about something else: the weather, her father's smile when he'd left that morning, which path she'd take to the market later. But she kept sneaking peeks back at the cupboard. She couldn't wait to to open it up and pull out her latest creation.

Finally, after what seemed like an eternity, the timer let out a metallic *ding*. Nalah leaped from her chair, tugged open the cooling cupboard, and poked her head inside. The bird, its head slightly cocked, looked up at her as she pulled it out, cradling it carefully in her bare hands. It was a perfect, smooth turquoise. Its beak was sharp, and its eyes seemed to regard her with interest. She ran a finger over the bird's smooth, warm neck. It almost felt alive.

"You're so handsome," she cooed.

"Nalah! What are you doing?"

Nalah jumped, spinning on the spot to see her father in the doorway, a basket hanging loosely from his hand. She took a step back, her heart pounding, and her fingers began to tingle.

*No! Not again!*

She tried to breathe slowly and calm her racing heart, but this time, it was no good. A shock of power surged through her body into her hands, like a tidal wave hitting a rock pool, crushing everything in its path.

The precious glass falcon cracked, a line of white snaking down from its eye deep into its chest.

In an instant, her father was at her side, tearing off his coat and wrapping the falcon in its folds. He held it tight for a few breathless moments before he relaxed.

"Are you all right?" he asked Nalah. She nodded, unable to speak.

*I was so close. He was so beautiful. If only I had worn my stupid gloves . . .*

"Nalah, how could you?" her father snapped. She looked up at him and saw the terror in his face morph into anger. "We've talked about this! You infused that with magic, didn't you?"

"No!" Nalah snapped back. The lie was small, but it still tasted bitter in her mouth. "I just wanted to work with the glass—"

"But you know what happens." Mr. Bardak held out the broken falcon, perched in the nest of his rumpled coat. "What if the glass exploded again? You were lucky to get away with a few scars. This time, it could have blinded you! Why would you risk so much for a glass bird?"

"Because I'm bored!" Nalah blurted. It sounded childish, even to her ears. But it was true. "I've read every book in the house eight times," she continued, trying to make her father understand. "I've done all the laundry and washed all the dishes. All I do is walk from here to the market and back, every single day, and I don't have any—"

She stopped abruptly. It was just too sad to say out loud.

"You have friends," her father said, and Nalah cringed.

"Forget it, Papa, all right?"

"But you do, don't you? There are always lots of other kids at the market."

Something inside Nalah cracked, and tears threatened to break through. "The Thauma kids call me No-Luck Bardak," she said flatly. "They think I break everything I touch. And none of the other kids will even talk to me."

Mr. Bardak looked confused. "But I thought you got along with the other Thaumas," he said. "What about Marcus?"

"Oh, well . . . *Marcus*," Nalah said begrudgingly. "How

would you like it if I forbade you to go anywhere or speak to anyone but *Marcus*?"

"What's wrong with young Mr. Cutter?" her father asked.

"Oh, he's fine, I guess," Nalah replied. "He's just such a show-off. It's always, 'I made *this*' and 'I made *that*.' He knows that I can't practice my craft, even without Thauma magic, and it's like he's constantly rubbing it in. He thinks he's so much better than me, Papa—he probably just talks to me out of pity, because no one else does." Nalah crossed her arms and scowled.

Her father dropped his coat and parcels on the table and plopped into the armchair. "I'm sorry," he said, sounding tired. "I know this is hard for you. I wish it could be different, I do. But the enforcers are really cracking down on those who don't observe the new restrictions, arresting anyone even suspected of still trying to sell Thauma crafts. And with your problem—"

"Papa, they don't know that it's a magical Thauma problem—they just think I'm clumsy," Nalah said. "And anyway, there are still people making Thauma crafts. Marcus just told me his dad has him working on a commission for someone in the Hokmet! If I practiced my craft, I might eventually be able to control it better and stop breaking things. I could—"

"No!" Mr. Bardak blurted, with surprising force.

Nalah fell silent, the arguments she'd lined up stilled on

her lips. Her father never yelled at her.

Mr. Bardak took a deep breath. "Marcus's family is rich," he said, his voice controlled now. "They have influence with the Hokmet. We don't. And anyway, it's not a matter of you needing more practice, Nalah. You're not like the others. You're . . . special. But they'd see you as dangerous. They'd take you away from me. They'd—" He stopped himself, and looked away.

Nalah frowned. She didn't feel special. She felt like a freak. Set apart from everyone else because of a power she had never asked for. She'd thought that maybe if she just figured out how to control it, she could make it go away. But now she couldn't even do that. Why? Her father was always a worrier, but this was different. Had something happened?

"After your mother, I can't risk losing you, too," he said with finality. "I'm your father, and you need to trust me. Please, Nalah. Just go to the market and come straight home. Promise me?"

"I promise," Nalah said, suddenly feeling very small.

Her father gave her a weary smile, and then hugged her tight. "I have some errands to run," he said, rising. He pulled her into a tight embrace. "I'll see you later, all right? And please, be careful."

When he had gone, Nalah stood in the workshop alone, the quiet gathering around her once more. If only she were still six years old, and her father and the market were still enough for her. If only things didn't have to change.

But Nalah's strange power was growing stronger every day—she could feel it, like a rising tide threatening to drown her. She wouldn't be able to keep it inside forever.

With a heavy heart, Nalah turned to pick up her gloves from the table. They were made from the thinnest leather her father had been able to find, and as close to the color of her brown skin as he could manage. Nalah appreciated the effort—but sometimes the gloves felt like a brick wall between her and the world. Every time she put them on, she felt a little more shut out.

With one last look at her broken falcon, Nalah gathered up her wares for the market and went to the door. A breeze washed over Nalah as she stepped out onto the street, carrying the scent of New Hadar: jasmine and petrol, cumin and salt from the Hadar Sea, sweat and palm oil. Big black motorcars rattled down cobblestoned streets, honking at one another like angry, sputtering beasts, while on the horizon Nalah could see one of the hulking cargo ships coming in to port. Skirting around the morning commuters in their sedate black robes, Nalah made her way toward the center of the city, where the gleaming white tower of the Hokmet loomed over Market Street like a sentinel.

The New Hadar market had once been teeming with stalls and vendors, selling all manner of wonders. Artisans from all four Thauma clans—glasswork, woodwork, fabricwork, and metalwork—had been proudly represented here. Now the market was reduced to a mere dozen stalls, whose once-legendary artisans had been reduced to peddling useless souvenirs.

Nalah envied the tourists. They could wander down the palm-lined streets, pointing at the old men and women begging for coins, never realizing that many were homeless Thauma who'd once been respected shop owners or artisans, people whose livelihoods had been swept out from under them by a government that feared them. Most of the tourists came from far-off countries and had no knowledge of what really went on in New Hadar with the Thauma population. The Hokmet saw to that.

Nalah, her basket of baubles held firmly in both hands, turned onto Market Street and wove through a crowd of laughing women in pastel pink headscarves and large dark glasses. She glanced up at an ancient, fading sign painted on the side of an abandoned building:

**MASTER AL-HARTHI'S WOODWORK EMPORIUM**

She looked up at the sign on her way to the market every day. Master al-Harthi's emporium would have been as grand and magical as her great-grandmother's glasswork store, but like all the other Thauma stalls and shops, they were both gone now. Nalah's father sometimes said that the glasswork store had been a cave of wonders, where you could buy mirrors that spoke, and chimes that would ring out the time of day whether there was a wind or not. Back when real, powerful magic was common and Thaumas were respected.

After the war, the Thaumas had been blamed for the storms and the earthquakes that had torn fissures through the city. The new Hokmet had preferred electricity to magic. They made sure everyone knew: the wonder-workers were dangerous. Soon, nobody wanted to live near their workshops or use their crafts. And every year, the regulations got more and more strict—until the day that Thauma magic was outlawed altogether.

By the time Nalah was born, her father said, Thaumas had started to seem romantic to those who had never known their true power. Stories of "forbidden magic" drew tourists to New Hadar. The Hokmet made sure that stories were all they would find.

The market stalls were laid out in a horseshoe shape, each one festooned with colorful decorations and bright, eye-catching signage. The merchants sat behind their stalls, the white canvas over their heads flapping in the breeze, and called out their wares to passing customers. Jewelry glittered on tables, embroidered robes and scarves billowed in the breeze, and delicately carved figurines stood frozen in dramatic poses. It was beautiful—but lifeless. Before the regulations, the necklaces would have enhanced the beauty of the wearer, the robes would have changed color depending on the time of day, and the figurines—instead of being frozen—would have danced if music began to play.

Now, all of that was gone.

Nalah gave a skeptical side-eye to a shrill woman who was selling bejeweled veils in lurid colors.

"Morning, No-Luck," the woman sneered when she saw Nalah. Nalah flushed and looked away.

"Hey, you stay away from my stall," said the teenage boy at the next table, leaning protectively over ranks of collectible spoons and thimbles.

Nalah tried to ignore them, but her cheeks burned with the heat of embarassment. If this wasn't the only time she got to really get out of the house and be on her own, she would have stopped coming to the market a long time ago.

She reached her own stall, rolled up the canvas, and shook out the tablecloth. She started setting up the stall with her father's crafts: the glass balls with whorls of color inside, the elegant vases, and finally the little glass animals. There were cheetahs, elephants, ibex, and tiny white rabbits, so detailed that they almost looked alive. Her falcon was nowhere near as delicate as these, but one day . . .

"You're late," said a voice. "I was getting worried. How am I supposed to steal all of your customers if you're not here?"

Nalah was already rolling her eyes as she turned. "Hi, Marcus," she said.

Marcus Cutter was leaning against the edge of his stall,

sipping a glass of cold mint tea. He held a second glass out to Nalah, and she took it with a half smile.

The Cutters were fabric Thaumas. Their stall was draped in scarves and gloves and socks and cushions stitched in every color of the rainbow. Marcus said his great-great-grandmother had come to New Hadar from a land north of Svalberg, a place where it snowed all year round and you could go for months without seeing the sun. Nalah thought Marcus had an overactive imagination, but he did have the Cutters' slightly foreign look, with his green eyes and straight, silken hair the color of sand.

"Want to see my new project?" he asked.

Nalah sighed. *Here we go again. "Look at what I made, Nalah! Isn't it so great?"*

Not waiting for an answer, Marcus fished behind his stall and pulled out a delicate scarlet scarf. One end was embroidered with white flowers and blackthorn twigs. "I'm working with silk now," Marcus boasted. But Nalah could tell it wasn't any ordinary scarf—it was full of powerful Thauma magic. She could feel the power in it, tugging at her.

"Are you crazy?" said Nalah, looking both ways to see if anyone had noticed them. "An enforcer could be watching!"

"Oh, relax," Marcus scoffed. "There's nobody watching. I checked. And anyway, someone at the Hokmet personally requested this scarf." He paused, and she knew he was waiting for a compliment. This was a big moment for him; silk thread was far too expensive to waste on an unskilled craftsman.

*So this was the special commission from the Hokmet,* Nalah thought. *Unbelievable. Nearly a year younger than me, and he's working with silk. Meanwhile, I'm exiled from the workshop. It's just not fair.*

"It's very nice," she said with difficulty.

"I'm using some really exciting techniques," Marcus said. "This is *Class Twelve* stuff!"

Nalah shook her head in disbelief. Marcus definitely wouldn't have been making it if the Cutters weren't so well connected. No Cutter ever ended up on the Hokmet watch list. Her father was right. They had money, which meant they had friends. She reached out to touch the scarf, eager to feel its softness even though she had her gloves on. As she did, one of the embroidered white buds burst into bloom. *Pretty,* Nalah thought. "Hey, Marcus," she said. "What kind of Thauma thread did you use for these flowers?"

"The flowers are just decoration," Marcus said, eyeing some potential customers who were approaching. "It's the silk that's Thauma. Keeps you warm at night and cool in the daytime."

Nalah was confused. She'd just seen the flower bloom when she touched it! "But—"

"Good morning, ladies!" Marcus said to the tourists. "Have I got a treat for you!" He brought his voice down to a whisper, as if telling a secret, and pulled out a stack of folded squares of fabric from under his counter. "Lie-detecting handkerchiefs—scented or color-changing options. Great to have on a first date!"

The tourists tittered and pulled out their coin purses.

Nalah suppressed a laugh and sipped her mint tea. It annoyed her that Marcus had the freedom to skirt the regulations and live the way he wanted. But, at the same time, she admired him for it. Even if he wasn't her ideal friend, Marcus was all right.

The morning wore on, and the lunchtime rush came and went, filling the market with the scents of grilling lamb and stewing spices. As the crowd cleared, an open spot in the market caught Nalah's eye. It was an empty table, draped with a dark gray cloth.

"Have you seen Mrs. Kayyali today?" she asked Marcus.

"Only just noticed, huh?" he said darkly. "Nope, she hasn't been around since yesterday."

Nalah frowned as she picked up one of the vases to wipe away the greasy kebab fingerprints from her last customer. "I don't think I've ever seen Mrs. Kayyali miss a market before. Do you think she's okay?"

Marcus gave a shifty look to his left and right, and leaned closer to Nalah's stall.

"I heard she went to visit her family in Ikhtiyan," he said. "Only, Cassia was talking to the baker, and *he* says Mrs. Kayyali doesn't *have* any family in Ikhtiyan. He says"—

Marcus lowered his voice—"she carved a healing bracelet for a baby, and the enforcers came for her."

Nalah's gaze was drawn across the market to a stall that was selling iced tea and coffee. The vendors were doing a roaring trade—it was hard to believe that only two weeks ago, Kiva Lang had been selling her glasswork from that same spot.

What was it people had said about Miss Lang? *Gone to take care of her sick mother somewhere far to the south.* Or was it the east?

Now the Bardaks were the only glassworkers left in the market. Trade had picked up, but Nalah's father had seemed on edge ever since. New gray hairs were sprouting from his head every day.

*Was it Mrs. Kayyali who had him so worried this morning?* Nalah wondered.

"There's something else, too," Marcus said. "One of the other fabricworkers died last week. It was an accident," he added hurriedly. "That is . . . that's what we were told."

He left that hanging in the air, and Nalah shivered.

"What do you think is really going on?" she whispered to Marcus.

He shook his head. "Maybe just preventing the Thaumas from practicing isn't enough anymore."

Nalah looked around the market again, horror creeping up her spine. Every Thauma who hadn't gone underground was here, just trying to make an honest living. Could the market simply be the Hokmet's way of flushing the remaining Thaumas into the open, so they could pick them off one by one?

She felt her heart start to beat faster, and quickly stuffed her gloved hands into the pockets of her dress.

*If the Hokmet wanted us gone, they would just make a law and banish us from the city,* she reasoned to herself. *They wouldn't resort to killing. There's no need to panic.*

*Not yet.*

Still . . . there were Ephraim and Nasrin at their woodwork stall with their young children playing underfoot, and there was Master Sinali's metalwork gleaming in the sun. There were so few of them now, and here they all were, every Thauma family who hadn't been driven onto the streets or into hiding. Were they all naive to think that working within the regulations was enough to keep them safe?

Suddenly, as she stared at Master Sinali's stall, she realized that someone there was staring back. It was a customer—a tall man in a cream linen suit. He was hefting a large metal box in his hands, and looking straight at Nalah.

*I know that man,* she thought. She was certain that they'd met before, but she couldn't think where or when. He had a perfectly trimmed beard that turned his chin into a sharp black point, and piercing eyes that gazed out from under the shade of his wide-brimmed fedora.

"Hello, dear," said a quavering voice, and Nalah tore her

gaze away from the man to see an elderly woman approaching her stall.

"Miss Masoud!" she said, smiling at the sight of her old nursery school teacher.

Miss Masoud smiled back, but Nalah's heart sank as she saw that her smile was strained, and her eyes looked cloudy.

"How are you, Nalah?" Miss Masoud asked. "And how is your dear father?"

"He's very well, thank you," said Nalah politely.

Miss Masoud nodded and tucked a stray hair back inside her blue headscarf. "I'm so glad," she said. "I have some work for him. It's . . . sensitive."

Nalah's stomach twisted uncomfortably. "I'm sure my father will be happy to make anything you commission, as long as it's permitted by the regulations."

The look on Miss Masoud's face told Nalah this wasn't going to be that simple. "I'm sick," the old teacher whispered. "The doctor can't help me, she says it's too late. I'm—I'm going blind, Nalah."

Nalah's heart sank. Tears welled up in her eyes but she tried to blink them away. "I'm so sorry," she said, feeling like a monster for not saying more. For not *doing* more.

Miss Masoud swallowed. "I know that your father . . . He's a very talented man. Please, I know he could—"

Something caught Nalah's eye: a flash of gold and blue, moving through the crowd.

*Enforcers!*

"I promise you, madam," she said, trying to mask her terror with false cheer, "you won't find more well-crafted glasswork anywhere in New Hadar!" She scooped up a tiny rabbit from the display and held it out to Miss Masoud, shooting a meaningful glance over her shoulder. The old lady froze, spied the enforcers, and then turned back to Nalah, her face paler than before.

Nalah babbled something about how each animal was made by hand, until the enforcers were gone. Her heart was racing, but she tried to keep her voice level as she looked into Miss Masoud's cloudy eyes.

"I wish I could help," she said, her heart aching. "But I can't. My father doesn't make healing orbs anymore. It's too dangerous."

Miss Masoud swayed unsteadily, as if she might faint. "You were my last hope," she said.

Nalah looked down at the rabbit in her gloved hand. "Take this," she said. "Papa still puts a little moonstone in it for luck. It might—" But her teacher had already turned and walked away, disappearing into the crowd.

Nalah took a deep, shaky breath and placed the rabbit back on the table.

It was so unfair. So *unjust*. How could the Hokmet allow this? How could they live with themselves, knowing that the Thaumas could heal the sick? Nalah clenched her fists, her pulse quickening, the anger rippling through her with a prickling energy. How could they force her to stand there powerless, when she could have helped? Just because some cowards had decided that it wasn't *permitted*, that *she* was *not permitted*—

She slammed her hands down on the table, and with a crash, all the trinkets shattered at once. They burst and fell in a million glittering pieces, scattering shards across the tablecloth like stars in a clear sky.

Nalah gave a strangled sob and staggered back from the table.

"Nalah, what the—?" Marcus gasped.

Nalah stared down at her hands, panic rising in her throat. "But I'm wearing my gloves," she said "I—I'm wearing my gloves—how could this happen?"

"It's all right." Marcus held up his hands and approached her slowly, like she was a wild animal. "Just calm down."

"I can't calm down. I can't be here. The enforcers—"

"Excuse me, miss," said a voice, and Nalah nearly jumped out of her skin.

She was certain the enforcers had come to take her away, but the man in front of her stall was wearing a cream suit, not a blue and gold-braided uniform. It was the same man who'd been looking at her from across the market earlier.

She looked from him to the stall full of shattered glass. "I'm sorry," she said, trying to keep her voice level. "I have no inventory right now, sir. There's been an accident."

"Are you all right?" he asked.

"I'm fine. I just need to—"

"You are Mr. Bardak's daughter, yes?"

Nalah stared at him. Was he from the Hokmet, after all?

The man gave her a faint smile. He didn't seem at all concerned to be standing right in front of the scene of a possibly dangerous magical accident. His bearing was upright, calm, and completely confident.

"You seem troubled, young lady," he said. "I'd like to help you. I wish to see your father about a job. I promise, I'll make it worth your while."

Nalah was silent. She felt like every eye in the market was turned on her. Seeing her distress, Marcus stepped in and folded up the tablecloth around the broken glass. "His workshop's on Paakesh Street, sir," Marcus said crisply. "I'm sure he'll be happy to help you with anything that's within regulations. But Miss Bardak's stall is closed now."

He turned to Nalah and nodded toward the backstreets behind them. "I'll clear this up," he hissed. "Get out of here!"

Nalah nodded gratefully, grabbed her empty basket, and took off, leaving the strange man and the broken glass behind. She put her head down and ran for home, her vision blurred by tears.

Nalah sat on her bed, wrapped in a blanket, staring at her hands.

They seemed so ordinary. Soft, brown, with short and slightly dirty fingernails. There were a couple of scars on her palms—but her father said the best Thaumas always had a couple of scars.

How could these be hands that shattered glass without even touching it?

It had started when she was little. Even now she remembered the day that she had toddled into Papa's workshop and got hold of one of his glass animals: a giraffe with a long, elegant neck. She had squealed with delight—and the giraffe cracked in half beneath her fingers, the sharp glass cutting into her flesh. Her mother and father thought it an accident. But then it happened again. And again. Finally, Papa brought her her first pair of gloves. That seemed to work, keeping her accidents to a minimum—until now.

"What's happening to me?" she asked the photograph beside her bed. "What do I do?" Her mother gazed back silently from within the frame. Rina was sitting on the seawall by the beach, her back to the waves and the bright sky, her black hair loose and flying in the wind. She was smiling, leaning back to enjoy the sun on her face.

Sometimes, when Nalah asked her mother for advice, she could almost hear her reply. *Wear your gloves for now, darling,* she would say; or, *You don't want friends who treat you this way*; or, *Your father is only trying to protect you.* But that only worked when the answer was somewhere deep inside Nalah's mind already.

"How can I live in this world if I break everything I touch?"

There was no answer to that.

"I miss you," she said, the words catching in her throat. "I wish you were here." The answer came back clear enough from Nalah's imagination: *I wish that too, love.*

Rina had always been the one who would talk to her about magic, even when Nalah was too small to really understand it. Nalah's father tended to shut down after a little while, as if he thought it was bad luck to talk about it for too long.

There was a knock, and Nalah looked up to see her father at the door. He gave her a sad smile. "Hello," he said. His eyes traced Nalah's gaze to the photo of his wife, and he sighed.

"I'm sorry about this morning," he said softly. "May I come in?"

Nalah nodded and shifted along the bed. Her father stepped into the little room and sat down beside her.

"Look, baba, I know I might seem like I'm being overly cautious," he said. "Maybe even paranoid. But it's just that I can't lose you. You're my life. You know that, don't you?"

Nalah nodded, and then steeled herself for what was coming next. "Papa, there's something I need to tell you," she said. If he was going to be angry with her, she wanted to get it over with now. "Today, at the stall, I—I broke the glass. I broke *all* of it. I was wearing my gloves, but I was so angry. I just put my hands down on the table and it . . ." She swallowed back tears and forced herself to meet her father's gaze.

He sat perfectly still for a long moment, fear flashing in his eyes. But then he took a deep breath and reached out to wrap his arms around her, pulling her close.

"I'm so sorry," he said. "I should have been there. I shouldn't have let you go to the market alone after we argued like that. You were upset—"

"It's not just that," Nalah said, pulling away, shaking her head. "Something's happening to me. It's getting worse."

Her father looked up at the ceiling for a moment, and then took her hands in his. "Nalah . . . you know we're on the Hokmet's watch list, don't you?"

"Of course," said Nalah quietly. "Because of the fire."

It had been years since she'd dreamed of that terrible night, but the memories were still clear—too clear. Nalah remembered the smoke billowing through the house, the flickering flames, and her father screaming. The last images of her mother, who had started the fire in a magical attempt to cure Nalah's illness. There one moment, gone the next.

Mr. Bardak sighed. "We will never truly be free in New Hadar. Perhaps we should try to leave the city. I heard things weren't so bad in the Anong Provinces. Perhaps if we save up some money . . ." He looked around the sparsely furnished room, and Nalah knew he was thinking of what else they could sell. But they had already sold so much. "For now, I don't know if you should return to the market—"

"No!" Nalah exclaimed. "It's the only time I get to go out of the house. This won't happen again. I promise."

"Nalah, it's for your own safety!"

"Papa," Nalah whispered. "Please."

Her father looked pained. "All right. For now. But the minute you feel upset or unwell—you come right home. Understand?"

Nalah nodded, relieved.

"Oh—I brought you something." He put his hand into his pocket and pulled out a small blue object.

"My falcon!" Nalah trembled as Mr. Bardak laid it in her palm, but it didn't shatter.

"I put it through the furnace to seal the break," he said.

Nalah ran a finger gingerly over the bird's chest. She could still see the crack, a faint white line running through the center of the glass, but the surface was perfectly smooth.

"Let it bring you luck," her father said.

Nalah carefully set down the falcon on the table, beside the photograph of her mother. "I hope it will," she said.

"How about a story?" Mr. Bardak asked. Nalah was probably too old for bedtime stories, but she wasn't about to tell him that right now. Right now, she wanted to be taken far away from here, into a fairy tale. She nestled into the crook of her father's arm, and he began.

"There once was a beautiful, faraway kingdom, where the power of the Thauma flowed freely and magic was in everything, from towers to teacups, from the bricks of the palace to the swords of soldiers. And there lived a king—King of the Magi—who had fought a long and punishing war. . . ."

Nalah smiled and closed her eyes. None of these awful things would happen in the Magi Kingdom. In that world, magic was respected and Thaumas were revered for their talents. Even wars could be ended by magic.

Too bad it was all just make-believe.

"And so it was," her father said, "that on the darkest night of a long war, as swords enchanted with Thauma fire clashed before the palace gate, a man appeared before the King. And O, my daughter, what a strange man was this!"

Her father had read the story so many times, he didn't need the book to quote it word for word.

"He had but one eye in his head," Mr. Bardak went on, "and that eye was full of heavenly cloud; it was an eye that saw nothing but divine truth. Cyrus was his name, and he was the Prophet of the Sands. He had traveled far across the war-ravaged land to give a message to the King. . . ."

Nalah felt herself drifting off, while Cyrus's message swirled around in her head. He had promised the king that there would be peace. But peace had come with a heavy price.

*Tell me the price*, she thought. *I will pay it. Anything . . . if we could only live in peace. . . .*

But how could they live in peace, when at any moment Nalah's power could reveal itself and ruin everything?

# Chapter Two

## Halan

*I have seen the future, and it is shattered.*

*They say that the weapon can unknit reality and forge a new kingdom, free from war. They do not know how close they are to the truth.*

*I go now to warn them, to stop them. I only pray they will listen.*

*If I fail, you may look for me in another world.*

*Cyrus, Prophet of the Sands*

A warm breeze ruffled the feather of the calligraphy pen in Princess Halan's hand. She paused in her work of copying out Thaumaturgic symbols from the book at her elbow and turned her face toward the window, glad of anything that disturbed the air in this stale, stuffy room.

Lord Helavi had long ago covered every wall in his study with shelves, and lined every shelf with books, and now books were stacked in teetering piles on the floor, and on his desk, and even on the windowsill. Still, between the spines of *Thaumaturgtic Theory* and *A History of the Great Thauma Families*, Halan could see down into the palace courtyard.

It was busy at this time of day, after the long, hot noon, when the sun was starting to sink toward the Sand Sea and there were shadows in the kingdom again. Guards in black scale mail stood by the walls, keeping in the shade. A man in green robes held a scroll and gestured widely as he directed carts across the yard. They were laden with goods from the city and from the farmlands beyond the Great Delta Lake. All of them places Halan had never seen.

*When I'm queen*, she thought, the calligraphy pen drooping in her hand, *I'll travel, just like Father does. When I'm queen, they won't be able to stop me. I'll see my whole kingdom—the lake and the mountains and the Sand Sea.*

Halan's gaze was drawn to the entrance of the stables. A boy and a girl were standing on either side of one of her father's great black horses, washing the dust from its coat. The two stable hands were grubby and their clothes were patched and poor, but even they had the freedom to go beyond the palace walls.

Halan's mother often said that the royal family had to make sacrifices for the kingdom, and for their own safety. Halan just wished they would let her make that choice for herself.

The horse neighed and tossed its mane, throwing droplets of clear water across the face of the boy. He recoiled with a shriek, and the girl stifled a fit of giggles in the sleeve of her sand-brown tunic. Then the boy carefully bent down and soaked his rag with water. Halan watched as the boy tossed it and hit the girl square on the top of her head. She squealed and threw the rag back, water splashing on them and the horse alike, both stable hands dissolving into laughter.

Halan's smile widened, and then faded.

*But who will come with you on your grand adventure, once you're queen?*

The stable hands might be poor, but they had their freedom, and they had each other.

Halan had servants, teachers, guards. Dozens of them. But friends?

For even just one true friend, Halan would give all the treasures of the kingdom.

A wet sensation on her wrist made her look down, and she realized that her pen had left an inky black smear across the parchment, changing the word "fire" into an illegible squiggle.

Halan didn't bother trying to change it. Lord Helavi would know it was an accident—and even if he didn't, it wasn't as if he'd correct her, or even notice. He was still standing in front of his beloved chart of the Thaumaturgtic Wheel, intoning the lesson with all the charm of a croaking sandgull.

"As the Glassworkers' glass flows like water, so their

connection is to the element of water. And so the heat of the Metalworkers' forge connects them to the fire of life. . . ."

*And Fabricworkers with air, and Woodworkers with earth. I already know this, Lord Helavi.* He wasn't an old man, but he spent so much time studying arcane history that he didn't seem to remember what had just happened in reality—like the fact that he'd taught the princess this same lesson several times already.

"No Thauma, no matter how powerful, can master the craft without many years of study and practice," he went on, in his thin and reedy voice. Everything about him was thin, from his drooping mustache to his threadbare yellow robe. She found herself watching him with fascination.

*When will he stop for breath?*

"Thauma techniques are closely guarded by the great Thauma families, who both practice and restrict the teaching and use of their crafts. Untrained or unregulated Thauma activity can be very dangerous to the safety of the people and the stability of the kingdom, especially if it creates so-called Wild Thauma objects without any restriction on who can pick up and use them," he said, and *finally* drew a breath.

*Easily fifteen seconds. Perhaps twenty.*

"The great families are, of course, the noble families of the Magi Kingdom. They are the chosen people whose inborn powers helped to raise the kingdom back to peace and prosperity after the war, making them the rightful rulers of the land. The commoners—all nonmagical folk—need the leadership of the Thauma. Without us, there would be anarchy in this land. Those of the royal line have always been born as powerful Thaumas."

He paused and looked up, seeming to remember that Halan was in the room. His face flushed.

Halan almost felt sorry for him. It wasn't his fault she was . . . *defective.*

He cleared his throat and continued, trying desperately to save face. "That is, the Tam family are Metalworkers and Fabricworkers, and the queen's great-great-grandfather was something of a legendary Glassworker."

*I've definitely heard worse*, Halan thought. Sometimes, when people found themselves talking about the royal family's abilities around her, they got caught in a loop of stuttering, or asked to be excused on some urgent and obviously made-up business. Once, one of the younger guards actually ran away from her rather than finish a sentence that would have made reference to her powers. Or rather, her *lack* of powers.

Halan clenched her fists. She just wished that everybody would stop pretending. She knew what some of the nobles said behind her back: How could a princess without any magic ever be allowed to take the throne? No other child of Thauma parents had ever been born bereft of powers. It was unheard of. That is, until Halan came along.

*Lucky me*, Halan thought bitterly.

Out in the courtyard, a bell sounded. Halan glanced out the window and saw the guards in the shadow of the wall jolt to attention. Her heart began to beat faster. *The changing of the guard—it's time.*

It was time to work the only magic that Halan knew. Strategy and manipulation.

*If this is going to work, I've got to get moving,* she thought. *Sorry, Lord Helavi.*

"What about the Fifth Clan?" she asked. She'd asked the same question several times before, and she knew exactly what her forgetful old teacher would say.

"Oh," said Helavi, his hands gripping the wooden rod he had been using to point at the chart. "Yes, such a fascinating legend."

"I heard there once was a Thauma line so powerful they could manipulate any material with just a touch," Halan prompted. "Is it true?"

"Oh, no, certainly not," Lord Helavi said firmly. "It is a tale much loved by the common people, but it is merely superstition. In all the histories, there is no proof there ever was such a clan."

For a moment, Halan thought he was going to stop there, and she gritted her teeth, uncertain whether to push him. But then a faraway look came over Lord Helavi's face, and Halan relaxed.

"Still," he said, "I can understand why the people find the stories so compelling. How could the clan command such immense power? Where did they go, and why is there no trace of them? Imagine, Princess, having the ability to control many elements, not just to craft magical objects, but to manipulate almost any material by touch alone! For commoners without any powers at all, it must be—"

Halan seized upon the moment like a cat pouncing on an unsuspecting mouse. *I've got you now!*

She rose to her feet, glaring at her tutor and trying to make her lip wobble. "How *dare* you?" she cried. "Compare me to a commoner? Is that how you see me? A powerless commoner?"

The pointing rod in his hands snapped. "I-I-I apologize, Your Highness, most humbly!"

"I think I've had enough lessons for today," Halan snapped. She saw the relief pass over his face, and then he bowed so low he almost banged his forehead on the desk in front of him before dashing from the room.

Halan walked to the door and looked out. Apart from the hem of Lord Helavi's yellow robe vanishing around the corner, there was no sign of anybody in the passage. No guards. No escort.

She counted to ten before she allowed herself to smile.

*It's not easy*, Halan thought with a touch of pride, *moving around the royal palace unobserved—especially when it's your own palace*. But she could always count on Lord Helavi to stick his foot in his mouth when prompted, ending her lessons early and giving her time to explore. It was too risky to do it often, but sometimes Halan couldn't help herself. Despite all her finery, despite the servants who waited on her hand and foot and the nobles who tripped over themselves to please her, she still felt like a bird in a cage.

A pretty cage. But still a cage.

Sometimes she needed to get away, even for just a few minutes.

There was no hope of disguising herself from the people who lived in the palace. They'd known her all her life. There was also no time to go back to her room and change out of her golden gown.

But there was a window—a small and precious sliver of time when the guards were changing their positions, her noble escorts were busy, and the dusty back stairs from the libraries to the laundry were deserted.

*I would trade every jewel I own for a shadow cloak*, she thought as she hurried down the stairs. But no, using Thauma objects was something beyond her, and always would be. And even though she had feigned offense when Lord Helavi spoke about the "powerless" commoners, even though she'd been hearing the whispers at her back her whole life, she'd be lying if she said it didn't hurt.

Because it still did. Every time.

The cloud of soap-scented steam that escaped from the laundry as Halan opened the door blew the dark thoughts from her mind. The room was a cavern of sandstone, with a high-vaulted ceiling that collected and funneled the steam from six huge tubs, each swirling with hot water and fabric of a different color. At the side of each tub, four or five young servants with their hair covered in gray headscarves stirred the laundry with long wooden staffs.

Halan ducked inside and seized a plain cotton shawl from a wooden rack beside the back door, where it had been draped until it could be taken for drying. It felt damp across her shoulders, but it covered her gown so that she didn't glimmer as she made her way around the edge of the room, toward the tub where the rising steam was tinted blue.

She slipped alongside the tallest of the servants, a girl a few years older than Halan. The girl had a smear of blue dye across the bridge of her nose. Halan leaned casually on the edge of the tub and grinned at her.

"Hi, Ester," she said.

The tall girl turned, saw Halan, and almost dropped her wooden staff into the blue water.

"Princess!" she exclaimed. Halan winced and pulled the shawl more tightly around the neckline of her gown. "Sorry, Halan," Ester whispered. "I just didn't expect you. How did you get in here without being seen?"

"I have my ways," Halan said, a little smugly.

She risked a look at the other servants, who were stirring and prodding the fabric in the tubs nearby. The only one who was paying them any attention was a young girl, perhaps seven years old, who was staring openmouthed at Halan. Halan raised a finger to her lips. The girl's mouth shut abruptly, and she went back to stirring as if her life depended on it.

"Anyway," Halan went on, "you haven't been on duty upstairs for so long! I thought I'd come and see you instead."

Ester smiled and tucked a stray curl of hair back inside her headscarf. "Are you going to get in trouble?"

"Only if somebody finds out where I went, and I'm not going to tell them." Halan shrugged.

"You're terrible," Ester joked, shaking her head. "Such unseemly behavior, consorting with the commoners!"

Halan smiled. Ester was the only one of the servants brave enough to talk and joke with their princess. Halan worked hard to seem breezy and casual around Ester, to put the laundry girl at ease. But in reality, every time Halan came here, she wanted to spend hours talking, talking, talking, until her throat was raw. The truth was, Ester was the closest thing to a real friend Halan had. But Halan knew that she and Ester could never *truly* be friends outside the laundry.

Halan leaned over the edge of the tub and watched a pair of loose indigo silk pants circling the whirling pool. "They won't let me visit the city, but they can't stop me talking to who I like in my own palace! Let's just pretend that I'm nobody, all right?"

"If you were nobody, you'd have to grab a staff and

do some work," Ester teased, prodding the pants as they swirled past. "How are all our noble visitors getting along? Have they eaten every last plum in the palace larder yet?"

"I think my mother might be going a little crazy trying to keep them busy," Halan said. "You should see the way some of the country lords behave. They're always showing off, trying to prove they're richer and more powerful than the others."

"I know," Ester said darkly. "Believe me, you haven't seen the worst of it."

Halan flushed and drew the shawl tighter around her shoulders again. "Anyway, palace gossip is always the same: someone's marrying someone for their Thauma armory, someone's plotting revenge for being insulted at dinner. It's like a game. Everyone's always planning three moves ahead. I want to know something *real*. Like, what's going on with you and Armsman Lajani?"

Halan grinned and waggled her eyebrows at Ester, but the tall girl sighed.

"Very little is going on with me and Pedram, if you must know. The captains keep the guards so busy. I'm starting to worry he'll take up with one of the girls in his legion just to have a girlfriend he actually gets to *see*!" She laughed, but Halan could see the worry in her face.

Halan hesitated, running her fingers along the damp edge of the tub, making the warm blue water dribble down the sides. Halan had an idea. She felt a little bad, because she didn't want to manipulate her only friend, but she was desperate.

Then, trying to look as though the thought had just occurred to her, she asked, "Why not simply go to him while he's working and steal him away? It'd be so romantic! I bet Pedram would love that. Oh!" Halan said, "I know. The grand feast is tomorrow, and two days after that all the nobles will finally leave. Everything will be so much more relaxed when they're gone, I bet you and Pedram can just slip away somewhere that night and nobody will even notice."

She held her breath, staring into the water. Ester didn't say anything for a moment.

Halan's stomach felt heavy with guilt. She hated to use her friend this way, but being trapped in the palace was driving her crazy. She had to get out, even for a little while, and this was the only way she could think of to do it. Besides, she *was* helping Ester and Pedram get together, so it wasn't that selfish . . . was it?

"Do you really think it would be all right?" Ester said under her breath.

Halan tried not to sigh with relief. "Definitely," she said. "Trust me. I've snuck around these halls long enough to know."

Ester stared into the water a minute longer, and then a big, pretty grin spread over her face.

"I'll do it!" she said. The next thing Halan knew, Ester's

arms were around her shoulders and the laundry girl was hugging her tight. Halan stiffened, despite herself, not quite sure how to respond. Ester pulled away. "Oh, sorry, Your Highness."

"No, it's—it's nice!" Halan said, feeling her cheeks turn hot. Awkwardly, she leaned in and Ester hugged her again, squeezing tight for a second before letting go. It *was* nice, but unwanted tears sprang to Halan's eyes, anyway. The hug only served to remind her how rare it was for her to feel close to someone, which made her feel even guiltier. "I—I'm sorry," she said quickly. "I have to go."

Dashing the tears from her eyes, Halan slipped out through the back door to the laundry, and up the dusty stairs. She was in such a rush that she walked right into the black, steel-scale armor of a palace guard.

"Your Highness!" said the guard, stepping back quickly and dipping his head. "I am so sorry, Princess. Are you all right?"

"I'm fine, Captain . . ." *Oh gosh, what is his name?* Halan was sure she knew it. He was one of the friendlier guards, sometimes willing to stop and talk, usually ready with a smile. *Bardak*, that was it. Halan drew herself up haughtily, hoping that the guard wouldn't dare to ask what she was doing alone in this part of the palace.

"Captain Bardak. I must be off, the . . . ah . . . queen is waiting for me."

"Of course," said Captain Bardak, stepping back. But as

Halan made to move past, he reached out and put a hand on her shoulder. "Wait," he said.

"Yes, Captain?" Halan tried to sound casual, but her heart was thumping. *Please don't figure out that I shouldn't be here. If my mother knew...*

"Just be careful, Your Highness. I am not sure you should be walking alone in these halls."

Halan stared at him for a moment, puzzled by his seemingly genuine concern. Then she straightened, squaring her shoulders and putting on an air of confidence. "Certainly, Captain. I assure you that I'm fine."

The guard let go of her shoulder and stepped back to a respectful distance. Halan walked away, turning through the first arch she came to and finding herself in the Sun Garden. She stepped lightly across the lush grass, weaving between the huge mirrors that filled the small courtyard with reflected light. When she reached the other side and stepped into the shade, she turned and looked back, but the guard was gone.

"Princess Halan, thank goodness. Lady Amalia was starting to . . . *worry*." Halan's handmaiden, Lilah, stood at her door, wringing her hands. Lady Amalia was Halan's prison guard—er, governess—and she never let the princess have any fun.

"I'm sorry if you got in any trouble," Halan said.

Lilah had gone back to unfolding and hanging up the

many-layered robes of silver that Halan guessed she would be wearing that night. "Not at all," said Lilah. "Are you ready to dress for dinner?"

Halan sighed and nodded. Lilah hurried around behind her to unlace the back of her day gown. Halan kept still, despite the urge to try and help—the last time she tried, it only ended with the two of them tangled in lengths of ribbon, and Lilah hadn't even laughed.

The problem with Lilah, Halan thought, watching her work in the dressing mirror, was that she knew her place. And you would need the strength of an elephant to pry her out of it. Lilah reported directly to the queen, and that's where her loyalty lay. She was no help to Halan at all.

Well, not with her secret plans, anyway.

Halan had to admit that Lilah had dressing her down to a fine art. She draped and wrapped the layers of silver cloth over and around Halan, seeming almost to form a robe out of thin air, like she was commanding the fabric to do her bidding. Next, she draped silver chains around Halan's neck and wrists, and pinned her silky black hair up with tiny silver stars. In the flickering candlelight, the princess sparkled like a glass moon.

It was so boring.

Halan tried not to be ungrateful. She felt pretty. It was . . . *nice.*

But nowhere near as nice as Ester's hug.

She thought of the package, still tied up in its parchment,

in the trunk by the bed. The colors burned bright in her memory.

But they weren't for today. They had to wait.

"Thank you, Lilah. It's lovely."

Lilah gave her a rare smile. "You're welcome, Princess. Of course, we shall have to do something special for the grand feast tomorrow. Are you looking forward to it? I hear there will be dancing."

Halan thought about the feast, and her smile widened.

The first part of her plan was in place. At the feast, she would secure the second part. And then . . .

She'd heard that out in the city, there were marketplaces that sold clothes and food and crafts and even animals from all over the world. She'd heard that there was music on every corner, a constant drumbeat so that the people couldn't help but dance in the streets. She'd heard that around the Thauma royal workshop district, the ground itself was so steeped in magic that people saw visions and heard voices from other worlds.

"I am," she said. "I'm looking forward to it very much."

# Chapter Three

## Nalah

UNCONTROLLED THAUMA FIRE KILLS YOUNG MOTHER
*A workshop fire claimed the life of a young mother yesterday afternoon in the Thauma Quarter. Mrs. Rina Bardak was attempting a piece of complex metalwork, which she intended to use to heal her young daughter, when a fire broke out in her workshop, taking Mrs. Bardak's life and almost destroying several neighboring homes. In the wake of this tragedy, Minister Tantawi has proposed stricter restrictions on the use of Thaumaturgy. Mrs. Bardak leaves behind a husband, glassworker Amir Bardak, and their daughter, Nalah."*

*From the* New Hadar Herald

Nalah tugged her dress down over her head and shoved her feet into her sandals, yawning. Today was a new day. She pulled her gloves on, though she wasn't sure how much difference they would make, and as she was wriggling her fingers to stretch out the leather, she heard voices downstairs.

One was her father's. She didn't recognize the other one—at least, not at first.

*It's that man from the market!* She hardly dared to hope—it had been months since the last time her father had taken a commission. It would be much more profitable than the market baubles. As long as it was legal . . .

She hurried downstairs, but froze a few steps from the bottom as she saw her father crossing the kitchen toward the front door, his face a storm cloud.

"Get out of my house, Zachary," he barked.

The tall man, again wearing his cream linen suit, followed him at a leisurely pace, looking around at the small room as if he was in no hurry to leave.

That's when Nalah realized who the man was. *Zachary Tam.*

Nalah remembered him now, all in a rush. He was the rich man who lived in the old mansion up on the hill, who had come to visit so often when she was small. When her mother was alive. They must have been friends.

He looked very different now, which was probably why Nalah had so much trouble recognizing him at the market. She remembered him being a scruffy, hairy figure who was always bringing some new and exciting Thauma artifact with him. She'd been delighted, but her father had always seemed to be grinding his teeth when Tam was around. Nalah hadn't understood why until this moment: Tam had been bringing them contraband, and her father had been afraid they would be caught.

Nalah was fairly certain Tam never got caught. From the cut of his suit and the way he stood in the Bardaks' kitchen, as if he owned the place, he was still a rich enough man to buy his way around the regulations, probably even more easily than the Cutters.

"Out," Mr. Bardak snapped, turning around and seeing that Tam had slowed to a stop. "How dare you show up here, after all this time? I meant what I said back then. You are not welcome in this house."

Nalah frowned. Tam had stopped coming after Rina died, but not *right* after. He'd visited a few more times, in those horrible days when the sun couldn't pierce the gloom and the house had been full of soot and sadness. She was sure that, despite everything, he and her father had been friends. But then there'd been an argument, and suddenly Tam's visits ended.

"Listen to me," Tam said in a placating voice, holding his hands up in a gesture of peacemaking. "I only want to help you."

"You've done enough of that," Nalah's father said.

"Please, Amir," Tam urged. "Let's not pretend. You're struggling. Anyone can see it. There's no shame in that, but you're a fool if you don't take what I'm offering you. You and Nalah deserve better than this."

"So, you've come to make a charitable donation?" Mr. Bardak sneered. "What's the matter, guilty conscience starting to get to you?"

"I'm not here to patronize you," Tam said. "I'm offering you work."

"Well, you can take your work and—" Mr. Bardak began, but then one of the wooden steps creaked under Nalah's weight, and he and Tam looked up quickly. Nalah winced as they spied her on the stairs.

*Oops.*

Tam's eyes locked with Nalah's. His eyebrows quirked and a curious smile played across his lips.

"Why, hello, Nalah," he said. "Nice to see you again. It's been a very long time since I was in this house. You probably don't remember me—"

"I remember," Nalah said. "Now, I remember."

"Nalah, go to your room," her father said quietly, without taking his furious gaze off Tam's face.

"No, let her stay—this concerns her too, after all." Tam pulled out one of the old wooden chairs and sat down at the kitchen table, as if he hadn't even heard Nalah's father telling him to leave.

Nalah felt emboldened by Tam's wish to include her. "What's the job?" she asked, coming down the stairs. She felt her father's disapproval like a blast of heat from the furnace, but she kept her eyes fixed on Tam.

Tam smiled and reached into his jacket pocket, pulling out a slender wooden box and a folded sheet of paper. He swept aside some empty mugs and a bowl of tangerines, and unfolded the paper.

"I need you to re-create this mirror."

Nalah stepped a little closer. A mirror didn't seem like such a terrible request. They were glassworkers after all.

The mirror drawn on the paper was beautiful in its simplicity, but the measurements along the sides of the picture said it was enormous, as tall and wide as a man. Mirrors were hard to get right—a tiny bit of warp in the glass and the image would be completely distorted.

"And," Tam continued, "I need this to be a part of it." He slid the box toward Nalah. Mr. Bardak snatched it from the table, opened it, and then put it back down.

"No," he said.

Nalah reached out and gingerly turned the open box so she could see. Inside was a shard of mirrored glass, like a lightning bolt. It glittered, sparks of blue and green and pink opalescence flashing across its surface as it moved.

*Thauma magic.*

"It's beautiful," she whispered.

"It's completely illegal," her father added. "And Mr. Tam knows that perfectly well. I don't know what this thing does, Zachary, and I don't care. This box alone could get all three of us thrown in jail, or worse. Now I want you to take your contraband out of my house and—"

"Ten thousand dinars," said Tam.

"—don't come . . . back," Mr. Bardak finished, weakly.

*Ten thousand?* Nalah stared at Tam, at the beautiful

shard in the box on the kitchen table, and then up at her father, trying to communicate her thoughts with her eyes. *For that amount we could leave this city. Start a new life in the provinces. We could be safe there, free to practice our magic.*

For the first time in her life, Nalah realized, she wouldn't have to hide her powers—she could embrace them.

"No," said her father again, though now there was sadness in his voice. "And don't think of raising the price, either. There's no amount of money that will make me touch that thing. Nalah and I will get by. I will not risk our lives for you."

Nalah felt her shoulders sag. She glanced at Tam and found him looking at her with a quiet, calculating stare. A shiver crept up her spine. It was strange—she didn't remember feeling unnerved by him when she was younger. He had always seemed so cheerful, such a good friend to her parents. Perhaps she just hadn't understood the danger he posed.

"Such a shame," he said, folding the paper and slipping it back into his pocket. "I know I haven't been a good friend to you recently—I thought if we worked together on this, we would both benefit. But I understand. You must do what you must do. But if you reconsider . . . you know where to find me."

He stood and walked out of the house without looking back.

Nalah and her father watched him go. "Papa, I really think—" Nalah began, as soon as the door had closed.

Her father held up a hand. "I know what you're going to say," he said, sinking into a chair at the table. "But I can't."

"But it's just one job, Papa," Nalah pressed. "What if you stayed inside the whole time and just worked on the mirror? Then as soon as you were done, as soon as we got the money, we could leave the city and never look back."

"Please," her father said. "Stop."

"But, Papa . . . my accident yesterday. It must have cost us so much. We need this. And if we had a new life in the country, I wouldn't have to hide anymo—"

"Nalah." Her father interrupted. Then he paused, looking up at the ceiling.

Nalah's skin prickled. She knew that look. He was preparing himself to say something, something she wouldn't like.

His eyes, wide and wet, returned to hers. "Sweetheart, we don't have to run away. I'm giving up glasswork. For good."

Nalah gaped at her father. It was as if he had told her he was giving up breathing. "You can't! How will we live?" *You've already given up your magic—how could you give up your craft, too?*

"Far more easily," he said with a wry smile. "I have a job interview this afternoon at the factory. It's just ordinary work, hard work, but at least it's still a kind of craftsmanship. We can sell the house—if we don't need the workshop, perhaps we can move somewhere the roof doesn't leak. Wouldn't that be nice?" He glanced at his watch and abruptly stood up again. "I have to go—the interview."

He gripped Nalah's shoulders and planted a kiss on her forehead.

"We don't need Tam, baba. We don't need his money or his illegal Thauma work. Things will get better for us, you'll see." He grabbed his coat and headed for the door. "I'll see you this evening. Please . . . be good."

Nalah forced a smile and waved, but when he was gone she sat down heavily at the table and stared into space.

*Give up the workshop?* The place where her mother and father used to work together, creating beautiful, useful things? Where Nalah's earliest memories were forged, memories full of wonder and pride at her parents' talent and passion? It would be even harder than giving up magic—the thing that defined their family, made them special, made them who they were.

How could Father just throw it all away?

*Maybe he can turn his back on being a Thauma,* Nalah thought, *but I can't.*

Trying to get her mind off things, she started to move the mugs, thinking to wash them up, if she could get the tap to work today . . . and froze. There, behind the mugs and the bowl of fruit, was a slender wooden box.

"Oh no," Nalah whispered.

Tam must have left it there by accident.

Her father would have a heart attack if he knew Tam had left a shard of contraband Thauma mirror on his kitchen table! She had to get rid of it. She picked up the box and flipped it open, gazing again at the iridescent surface of the glass. It was truly amazing work. She could feel the magic in it, pulsating, like a drum beating in her head. It was intoxicating. It drew her in, its rhythm pulling her toward it like a snake charmer's song. She wanted to touch it. She knew she shouldn't, but she couldn't help herself.

Nalah slid a finger down the surface of the glass. The drumbeat grew louder, and then—

*The drumming merged with the sound of the crowd that thronged the bright space. A woman in purple danced and swayed in time to the beat. Colored fabrics blew in the hot breeze. The shifting crowd parted and closed again over a view of white dunes rolling away into the distance, as far as the hazy horizon. Nalah could smell smoke, Thauma smoke, that slightly sweet scent that made sparks dance on the back of her tongue—*

She dropped the box onto the kitchen table, where it fell closed with a slap. Panting, Nalah pressed her palms together and held them to her chest, trying to contain the wild beating of her heart.

*I didn't break it,* she told herself. *It's all right. I didn't break it.*

But what *was* that? A vision? But of what?

As soon as she'd caught her breath, Nalah felt the shard pulling her in again, calling out to her. And against all reason, despite the fear that clutched her heart after she'd seen that strange vision, she wanted very much to pick up the box and hold the shard in her hands. It was calling out to her, and she desperately wanted to answer.

*I have to get this thing out of here,* Nalah thought, *now.*

She would take it back to Tam. It was dangerous, but Nalah felt certain that letting it remain in the house with her was even more dangerous. She couldn't wait for Father to get back. He might destroy it rather than return it to Tam. And Nalah couldn't let that happen.

This thing, whatever it was, needed to be protected. She knew that, though she couldn't think why.

She tried to look on the bright side—perhaps Tam would give her a reward. At least that would be something. Father might refuse the man's money, but that didn't mean Nalah had to.

She wrapped the box in a shawl and dropped it gingerly into her canvas bag before setting off to walk to the mansion on the hill.

All the way up the steep road that led out of the city, Nalah felt like she was being watched. Every shadow between the buildings looked like an enforcer. She knew she was probabaly being paranoid, and yet . . . she was farther from home now than she had been in years.

It was a huge relief when she finally climbed out of a

green tunnel of drooping palm trees and found herself in front of the largest house in New Hadar. It was a once-grand, opulent home, its stone walls sagging under the weight of years. She could imagine a great king once lived here, though now its walls were covered in vines, and its windows were either shuttered or so dirty she couldn't see inside. All around and under it, she could see the crumbled remains of the old city that New Hadar had been built upon.

Clutching her bag, she took a deep breath and knocked on the imposing wooden door.

A moment later the door opened, and Zachary Tam stood there, an expression of polite surprise on his face.

"Hello," Nalah began, feeling suddenly awkward.

"Nalah—I didn't expect to see you so soon. How delightful. Won't you come in?"

"Oh, um. All right." She stepped into a cool, empty courtyard and waited for Tam to shut the door before she patted her bag and said, "You forgot your . . . You forgot it. At our house."

"Oh my," Tam's hands flew to his pockets. "Thank you for bringing it back! Please, come in. You must be parched after walking all the way up here."

Tam led her through a door into a long corridor, and Nalah hesitated, gazing up at the walls in shock.

The corridor was lined with Thauma metalwork. There were curved scimitars fanned out and pinned to the walls, their blades humming with energy. There were helmets on plinths, and a chain mail shirt that glimmered with an inner light. She turned to look at it, and found her fingers itching to pull it on.

"These things," she breathed, hardly daring to speak above a whisper. "They're all illegal."

"Of course," said Tam casually, as he pushed through a door at the end of the hall. Nalah followed, and found herself in an enormous, rather dusty kitchen. Tam opened a freezer and pulled out a tray of cherries frozen in a sticky-looking juice.

Nalah sat down at the table and took one. It was incredibly sweet and refreshing. Before she could take another, she suddenly remembered why she was there. She removed the box from her bag and slid it across the table to Tam, who had sat down across from her.

Tam laid his hand on the box and looked up at Nalah, studying her. "I'm so glad it was you who brought this back to me," Tam said at last. "There is so much of your mother in you. I wonder, have you done much glasswork?"

Nalah blushed, both at the comparison to her mother and at the reference to glasswork. "I'm . . . not really supposed to," she said.

A slow grin crossed Tam's face. "Ah, but that's not a 'no,' is it?"

Nalah looked away, but found herself smiling. "I've done a little. I'm quite good," she added, feeling boastful. "But you saw how Father is."

Tam's eyes flashed. He took a frozen cherry and gave

it to her with a conspiratorial wink. "I certainly did. It's a shame, though. I sense such talent in you." He looked thoughtful for a moment, and then stared at Nalah as if an idea had just struck him. "Would *you* make my mirror for me?"

Nalah nearly choked on her cherry. "Me? I've never done anything like that before." She clasped her gloved hands tight in front of her, visions of shattered glass swirling through her mind.

"Please. I'll double the fee."

*"D-double?"*

*Twenty thousand dinars. We could run all the way to Svalberg if we wanted.*

"This piece means so much to me. It's an heirloom, you see. It's all I have left of my family. Perhaps your father doesn't believe you have the power, Nalah, but I do. Even if you fail—at least you'll have tried."

He slid the box back across the table toward Nalah.

She shouldn't. It was illegal, and worse, her father would kill her if he found out. Still . . . no one had ever trusted her to make such a complicated piece of glasswork before. And she knew she could do it. Could prove that her power was more than just a curse. That it could create—not just destroy.

Once again, she could hear its intoxicating song, calling out to her.

She looked at it for what felt like a very long time.

***

"Nalah! There you are, thank the stars!"

Nalah stopped cold on the road back to town. Had someone seen her leaving Tam's mansion? But it was only Marcus Cutter, hurrying toward her, a basket piled with folded cloth pinned under one arm.

"Where have you been all morning? I thought you might have, you know, *gone to visit your relatives*," he said, his eyes widening meaningfully.

"Oh, no, I was just running an errand for Papa, fetching supplies and such." She shrugged her shoulder and the slender wooden box in the bottom of her bag shifted. She gave Marcus what she hoped was a casual smile.

"Oh, right, I see." Marcus nodded. "You've got a bit of something red, just there." He tapped at the corner of his mouth. Nalah flushed.

"Cherries," she said.

"Did you stop at a café for lunch? Here . . ." Marcus fished in his bag and tossed her a handkerchief. Nalah wiped her mouth gratefully.

"Thanks! I did, I stopped at the café by the acacia tree. I was in a hurry, so I just bought a handful of cherries. And speaking of hurry, I ought to get home. Papa will be waiting for me." She wiped her mouth again and pulled a face. This corner of the handkerchief smelled of peppermint, so strongly it made her eyes water. "Anyway, I'll see you tomorrow, probably," she said, handing the handkerchief back.

Marcus took it and stuffed it into his pocket. "Sure," he

said slowly. "I'll see you tomorrow."

"Bye!" Nalah said, forcing herself to give him a cheerful wave as she hurried away. She hated to lie, but it was necessary. Marcus would understand, if he knew. Not that he, or anyone, could ever know.

*I'll tell Papa when I'm done, for better or worse. He might be angry at first, but then I'll hand him the money, and it will all be okay.*

She smiled as she thought about what they could do, where they could go. How they could finally be free.

*I'm going to save us both.*

# Chapter Four

## Halan

*In the chaos after the end of the war, after the destruction of the Year of Storms, the survivors emerged from the rubble to restore the kingdom. With their newly intensified powers, the noble Thauma families assumed leadership over this new world and began to rebuild in their own image. It was those Great Thaumas who wove, forged, carved, and shaped the Magi Kingdom we know today. It was the greatest display of magic ever seen: the four clans supplied water and sustenance, rebuilt the city, and made a new way of life. The common folk were glad to have the firm hand of the noble Thauma to guide them into a bright future, where Thaumaturgic activity was restricted to those who knew best how to wield it, for the safety of all.*

*Legend has it that the Fifth Clan went into exile after the war, but all true scholars understand this as further evidence that they never existed. After all, they would have been most able to help rebuild the kingdom. Where would they have gone at such a time, and why?*

**Lady Fulvia Helavi, A History of the Magi Kingdom**

Halan stood in the middle of her room in her undergown, feeling like the eye of a storm. She wasn't sure how servants always found so many things to do on these big occasions. She was only one, relatively small, princess—how many women could it take to put a dress on her?

"If you would raise your chin just a little, Your Highness," said Lilah, holding up a glass bottle with a long spout. The bottle was filled with swirling, gold-flecked oil. Halan obeyed—and remembered to hold her breath just in time. Lilah uncorked the bottle, and misted gold perfume across Halan's neck and shoulders. Halan blinked against the musky scent of jasmine and sandalwood.

When her eyes stopped watering, she could see two of the other servants opening chests and drawing out her best robes, the ones she always wore on these occasions.

Halan drew herself up to her full height, trying to project a sense of command. "No, not those, Lilah. I shall wear the gown and jewels presented to me by Master Eshaq the metalworker on his last visit to the palace."

Lilah looked surprised, but she bowed low, and fetched the parchment-wrapped package from the chest. As Lilah unwrapped it, Halan heard her intake of breath. She guessed what her handmaiden was thinking: *Really? This?*

Lilah unfolded the gown carefully, and two of the other servants held it up between them.

The base layer was a white skirt, which flared as it

moved, and a matching white vest. Over the top flowed layers of red, orange, and yellow Thauma silk. They waved and fluttered like a living flame, even though there was no breeze. Lilah reached into the package and held up a necklace of polished metal shards that shone like a rainbow on the surface of an oil slick.

"Your Highness," said Lilah carefully, "you know the king doesn't approve of such . . . such *flamboyant* garb. If you would like to wear color tonight, perhaps I could fetch a nice lavender?"

"My father will not be at the feast," said Halan, drawing herself up as regally as possible. "In fact, he isn't even in the kingdom. How can he object to a gown he will not see?"

Lilah still hesitated. Halan saw her glance at the other servants, as if consulting them, and felt a little affronted. It was *her* dress, wasn't it? And wasn't she the princess? True, this may have been the first time that Halan the Powerless ever exerted a little bit of force, but there was a first time for everything.

Halan felt her resolve begin to wither under the gaze of the servants, but she resisted the urge to back down. *Stand your ground*, she told herself.

"If my father is angry, he will be angry with me, not you." she said, addressing all of the servants at once. "So if you would rather leave than obey my orders, please do so."

One of the eldest women carefully put down the pair of silver slippers she had been holding, bowed deeply, and left.

Halan, trying to disguise her shock, watched the woman go. "Anyone else?" she asked, making an effort to keep her voice even.

None of the other servants moved. "Your wish is our command, Princess," Lilah murmured, though she didn't meet Halan's eyes. The bustle in the room resumed.

Halan nodded, and prepared herself to be dressed. *One step closer to my goal*, she thought.

A few minutes later, Halan smiled at her reflection in the mirror. She stood on a pedestal, half hypnotized by the rippling colors of her gown and the flashing metal at her throat. Lilah had brushed her hair into a shiny black curtain, and one of the other servants had drawn lines of kohl around her eyes.

She looked like a living, slowly undulating flame. It was beautiful. It was *perfect.*

This evening was going to be everything she had hoped; she could feel it.

But Halan's smile froze on her face as she saw, in the reflection over her shoulder, the door to the room open and a figure step inside.

It was Queen Rani: her mother.

The servants immediately stopped what they were doing, turned to the queen, and bowed low. Halan didn't move. She gave her mother a small, hopeful smile. *Don't I look pretty?* But the smile wasn't returned. Halan wondered if the chill in her mother's eyes would extinguish her fiery dress.

"Thank you all," said the queen. "I wish to speak to my daughter before the feast. Please leave us."

Halan sucked in a deep breath, trying to steel herself for the conversation that she knew was coming. Trying to salvage some of the rare excitement and happiness she'd felt just moments before. She watched in the mirror as the servants scurried out. When they had gone, Queen Rani closed the door and silently sat down on the foot of Halan's bed.

"Will you face me, Halan?" she asked.

Halan didn't want to. Somehow, it felt safer to talk to her mother through the mirror—the same way that, on the few occasions she had something to say to her mother, it was easier to ask Lady Amalia to pass on a message. She just felt more comfortable with *something* in between them.

But she guessed that being rude would be a bad idea right now, so from her place on the pedestal, she turned and looked her mother in the face.

Queen Rani's eyebrows twitched as she took in Halan's dress. The queen herself was dressed in a gold-edged lilac silk coat that was tied with black sashes at her waist, and a lilac headdress crowned with a circlet of gold. She looked like she always did—regal and stiff, like a statue who'd been brought to life and wasn't entirely happy about it.

Halan stood up straighter and tried not to fuss with the silk overlay of her gown. *It was a gift from a Thauma master, on a royal occasion*, she thought. *I dare you to forbid me to wear it.*

But, as always, Halan was wrong about what her mother was thinking.

"I met Lord Helavi in the library yesterday afternoon," the queen said. "When you should have been in your lesson."

"Oh?" Halan replied lightly, not trusting herself to say anything more.

"He threw himself on my mercy, as soon as he saw me," her mother went on, pinning Halan with a sharp stare. "He was so sorry for offending you, he seemed convinced I might have him arrested."

Queen Rani paused. Halan tried not to squirm.

"So, where did you go, once you had got rid of poor Lord Helavi?" the queen asked.

"Nowhere," said Halan at once. "I sat in his study and read. Then I left and went for a walk in the Sun Garden. I didn't go anywhere else."

"You knew that Lady Amalia would be there to join you when your lesson was finished," her mother said. "Why didn't you wait?"

"I forgot," said Halan.

Queen Rani sighed. "It's for your own protection, Halan. Nobody knew where you were! If something had happened—"

"What could happen?" Halan interrupted. "This is the

palace, there are guards everywhere!"

"Well, apparently not," her mother replied, "because none of them saw you again until dinner! If the rebels—*Don't* roll your eyes at me, Halan!"

Halan hadn't meant to. She clenched her fists at her sides. "Mother, there are no rebels inside the palace walls."

"You don't know that!" Queen Rani exclaimed. Her shoulders sagged, as much as they could in the stiff silk coat. She spoke slowly, as if speaking to a five-year-old. "They hate your father, do you understand? They would do anything to hurt him, including hurting you, and I can't guarantee your safety if you give your protectors the slip whenever you get bored."

"You can't keep me in here forever!" Halan insisted. "When I'm queen, I'll need to know the world outside my own palace, won't I?"

"When you're queen," her mother countered, "you won't be able to keep shaking off your responsibilities like this."

"*What* responsibilities?" Halan asked indignantly. "You know Lord Helavi's not teaching me anything useful."

"Well, if we *could* teach you metalworking or glassworking, we *would*," the queen snapped.

Halan reeled back. She felt like she'd been slapped.

Then the queen seemed to realize what she'd said. Pain deepened the permanent crease of worry between her brows, but it was too late. The words stood between them like a wall.

To hear those hurtful words from servants or nobles was one thing. But to hear it from your own mother was devastating. Up till now, it had only caused Halan pain. But something new was happening inside her. She was getting angry.

The queen took a deep breath. "If you had your own power, we could give you more freedom. I know it's not fair, but it's just the way it is. You're twelve years old, Halan—you are still a child. Without power, you're defenseless."

"I am not defenseless," Halan said, through gritted teeth. She hated when people spoke about her like she was a helpless kitten, just because she didn't have magic! She got to her feet, her cheeks burning, her voice rough and full of emotion. "I am not . . . *nothing*! I have my wits, Mother, I can look after myself. I'm not *broken*!"

Queen Rani's eyes sparkled with tears, just for a moment; then she blinked and they were gone. "Never accuse me of thinking nothing of you, Halan. Every waking hour, I . . ." She got to her feet and turned away from Halan. When she turned back, the emotion had drained from her face. "It doesn't matter," she said. "You will be protected. Whether you like it or not."

*That's right*, Halan thought. *Go back to being a queen—you're much better at that than at being a mother.* She opened her mouth, tempted to say it aloud. But then there was a tentative knock on the door, and it opened just far enough to let Lilah look in, her face creased with discomfort.

"My queen, the feast is beginning," she said quickly, and then ducked back out and shut the door again before Rani or Halan could reply.

Halan took a deep breath and forced herself to paste on her brightest, most insincere princess smile.

"Shall we go, Mother?" she asked. "We shouldn't keep our guests waiting. That's what's important, isn't it?"

Queen Rani didn't reply. She simply left. Halan trailed after her, allowing her elbow to be taken by one of the guards waiting outside her rooms, only just registering the surprise on the guards' faces as they looked down and saw the wonderful dress. Their reactions should have made her happy, but all she felt inside was empty.

She stared at the back of her mother's head as they were escorted down the halls.

*I just don't want to end up like you.* The thought caught Halan off guard and she felt sick for even letting it cross her mind. But it was true.

Queen Rani had no friends. She had subjects and servants, nobles who scraped and bowed for her favor, a daughter she looked at with more fear than love, and a husband . . .

Well, Halan guessed they must love each other, but sometimes it was difficult to tell.

But Queen Rani had no friends. She was too busy, too important, too far above everyone to have friends. And already Halan was feeling a little too close to becoming just like her. *I won't let it happen,* Halan reassured herself. *I won't.*

Halan thought that her mother must be as lonely as she was—but unlike Halan, Queen Rani seemed happy in her cage. Halan had long ago given up hoping that her mother would ever reach out to her. *You'd think that we'd find comfort in each other. But no . . .*

The golden doors to the banquet hall opened slowly. A buzz of conversation flowed over Halan, and then died away as she and the queen stepped inside, flanked by guards. Halan watched the crowd of nobles inside the hall—a sea of colorful robes, glass and metal shining in the shifting light from the floating light orbs above their heads. They rose to their feet, every face full of polite respect or fear or excitement, before every head bowed toward the queen and her daughter—the powerless heir to the throne.

Halan scanned the crowd as she followed her mother to the raised platform at one end of the hall. She was looking for one noble guest in particular. She found herself genuinely smiling as her gaze finally rested on the tight black curls and slightly protruding ears of a boy of sixteen. He was wearing a dark gray coat with no sleeves and a glinting silver sword, held at his side by a thin chain.

*Lord Soren Ferro. You don't know it, but you're about to skip ahead several moves in the intrigue game tonight.*

"Welcome, Lords and Ladies of the Magi Kingdom," said the queen, opening her hands, bidding them all to raise their heads and look at her. "And thank you for gracing our palace with your company and extraordinary talents. It has been a pleasure to receive you. I hope you return to your noble houses all across the land . . ."

*As soon as possible,* Halan thought.

". . . full of inspiration, with many new friends and trade agreements, and with wonderful stories to tell of our great city. Now, eat and be merry, and let the demonstrations begin. To the king's health!"

"The king's health!" chorused the nobles.

Queen Rani sank gracefully toward the floor and settled herself on a pile of gold-embroidered cushions. Halan followed her, more hesitantly—the ability to sit down without looking behind you was a queenly gift she had not mastered yet.

The servants brought out trays of food and began setting them in front of the guests: cured meats, spice bread, steaming bowls of stew, saffron rice, and fresh green salads arranged to look like blossoming flowers.

Some nobles moved to serve themselves, but others hurried toward the platform, clutching boxes and bags and strange-shaped objects wrapped in parchment. One woman was even dragging a small cart laden with a lumpy, canvas-covered object as tall as Halan.

Halan ducked her head to hide her smirk as they all tried to look casual while getting ahead of their competitors in the line to approach the queen. Elbows were sneakily thrown into ribs; one lord took a shortcut around the back of a cushion circle and cut off at least three others; the woman with the cart ran over someone's foot. *It must be a myth that the nobles are more civilized than the peasants,* Halan thought. *I can't imagine a more cutthroat bunch than this.*

When a civilized line had finally formed, Queen Rani nodded to Steward Osaya, who raised her voice over the hubbub of chattering nobles.

"A demonstration by Lady Artaz, woodworker," the steward declared, and stepped aside for a woman with gray hair that had been braided and woven into a high bun.

"Your Majesty, Your Highness," she said, bowing to Rani and Halan and holding out a wooden box. "I present to you the finest work of my family, a masterpiece of Thauma excellence." Lady Artaz opened the lid. For a moment, nothing happened. Then a small wooden head appeared, pyramid ears flicking back and forth curiously. Carved black eyes blinked, and a little nose stuck out of the box as if sniffing the air. Lady Artaz reached in and placed the animated wooden kitten on the platform.

Halan couldn't help smiling as she reached out a hand and the kitten warily padded over to her, its paws *tap-tap-tap*ping on the sandstone floor. It opened its mouth and let out a meow that sounded like creaking wood. Halan let it climb over her leg and into her lap, and petted the smooth carved place behind its ears.

"Very nice, Lady Artaz," said Queen Rani. The elderly woodworker's creased brown face flushed with excitement at the compliment, and she bowed low again before she was ushered away.

Steward Osaya scooped the kitten out of Halan's lap. Halan let it go with a sigh, and caught Queen Rani giving her a wary but pleased nod.

*I know. I can't accept any gifts, or I'll have to accept them all. I know that.*

Still, she hoped the kitten would be kept somewhere it could be seen, not hidden away in the royal Thauma collections where nobody but her father ever went. A little creature like that would be good at keeping her company on lonely afternoons.

After Lady Artaz, there was Lord Hosan the glassworker and his chandelier of glowing white lotus flowers. Then there was Lady Khora the metalworker, with a tiny box containing five iron nails that could hold a ton of weight each. Lord after lord and lady after lady approached the platform. They brought wooden bowls that filled themselves with figs, embroidered silks where birds flitted between the folds and sang sweet songs, magical glass eyes that could restore the sight of the old or injured. There were plenty of weapons, too. A metalworker brought out an evil-looking spiked ball on a chain that could be enchanted to swing at a chosen target. A woodworker brought sharp darts that would home in on anyone wearing a particular color.

Another metalworker brought forward a silver circlet and placed it on the head of a trembling servant. The spice bread in Halan's mouth seemed to lose its taste as she watched the lord touch the circlet, gently, and the servant cry out in unbearable pain and crumple to the floor, clutching at the metal around his head. The lord let his servant free at once, and the man got to his feet and gave her mother a shaky bow. But Halan still felt unsettled enough to slyly spit the spice bread into her cloth napkin. *I know we must defend the Magi Kingdom against the rebels,* she thought. *But is such violence truly necessary?* She wasn't sure how her mother could keep the same polite interest on her face for the magical weapons as she could for Lord Drozani's glass choir.

"It's just a shame that Lord Osha couldn't aim his clever little darts by name, or have them sense thoughts," said one of the lords, a man with a single eyebrow like a giant black caterpillar sleeping above his nose. He was standing close to Halan, just to the side of the platform, and didn't seem to realize she could hear every word. "We wouldn't have any trouble with rebels then."

"You'd have the king destroy any citizen who even *thought* of attacking us?" the lady at his elbow asked. To Halan's dismay, she didn't seem shocked—in fact, she laughed. "It's an idea!"

"Did you hear they attacked the Adulla family's workshop? Or they tried to," the lord scoffed. "What sort of idiotic rabble attempts to attack Thauma metalworkers?"

"I heard the rebels had Wild Thauma weapons," said the lady, pulling her purple shawl tighter around her shoulders, making the little bells on the ends of its tassels jingle. "I intend to tell the king as soon as he gets back, he *must* try harder to root out the Thaumas working with the rebels. If Ironside is able to make enough Wild weapons—"

"I'm not convinced that Ironside even exists," the lord said. "What is he? A traitorous noble? An upstart commoner with some Thauma heritage? Or maybe just a scary-sounding name on some inflammatory pamphlets."

*Ironside,* Halan thought. It wasn't the first time she'd heard the name mentioned around the palace. Some nobles spoke of the mysterious rebel leader with scorn and derision, but others feared the specter of a Thauma secretly arming the angry rebellion. She'd even seen some of the servant children playing games together, one pretending to be the bloodthirsty Ironside, the others falling before his sword. Halan wondered how much of it all was gossip, and how much was true.

"Well, the rebels must have someone with connections working with them," the lady continued. "Where else would they get Wild Thauma weapons? Anyway, apparently they attacked the Adullas' workshop because they believed that was where the king was making the Dust."

Halan shivered. She knew there were rebels outside the palace walls. A few dangerous malcontents who were determined to hurt the noble Thaumas, as her father had explained to her—mostly out of jealousy, because they had no powers of their own. Sometimes Halan would hear that there had been an attack or a riot, but the attackers were always repelled. The guards had Dust, and a pinch of the magical Thauma powder would knock out a large man instantly.

Halan had heard about Ironside before, but not that Wild Thauma was finding its way into rebel hands. Lord Helavi had taught her that unlike regular Thauma objects, which have magic in them to restrict their use to other Thaumas, Wild Thauma could be used by anyone. That made it very valuable to the rebels, and very dangerous to the nobility. Hoping to eavesdrop a bit longer, Halan pretended she was staring out a window and craned her head toward the speakers.

The lady shrugged theatrically, making her bells jingle again. "All I can say," she said to her companion, "is that either someone has made a lot of Wild Thauma work very quickly, or someone has been removing the tethers from stolen work. Either way, it seems they have a Thauma with them. A *talented* one."

"Well," said the lord, raising his glass to her, "long life and good health to the king, eh? I'm sure that once he roots out the traitor, he'll make an example of him. King Tam runs a tight ship. He won't allow this rebellion to go on much longer."

The two of them wandered off, still talking, but their words were lost to Halan as they moved farther away from the platform.

She stared into space for a moment, her heart racing. Was this why her mother had been so scared for her? If the rebels who wanted to kill her father truly had a Thauma on their side, did that mean they'd soon be making weapons like the ones that had just been shown here? Halan's stomach turned as she pictured the mysterious Ironside placing the torturous silver circlet on her father's head. The world outside the palace suddenly seemed darker and more dangerous than she'd imagined.

*Am I making a mistake?*

Her thoughts were interrupted by the first ringing notes of a simple melody played on a Thauma dulcimer. The musicians were warming up their instruments, which produced haunting, dreamlike sounds that no traditional, nonmagical instrument could produce. The drumbeat began: at first a gentle tapping, and then a more intricate rhythm.

The servants were clearing away the food now, and several of the young guests rose, hand in hand, and headed for the area of mosaic floor that served for dancing. A singer stood there, dressed in simple black, with her arms, midriff, and feet bare, swaying in time to the music.

The dancing began, and Halan took a deep breath. Dancing was for the commoners and the young nobles—

an activity for royalty to witness, not participate in. It was too free, too uninhibited for a stately princess like Halan, who had her reputation to think of.

At least, that's what everyone had always told her.

*It's time I took my life into my own hands.*

She stood up and stepped lightly down from the platform, without waiting for an escort or looking back at her mother. She could see the faces of the noble guests—jaws dropping, shocked glances being thrown—and the odd whispers being exchanged. *They can't believe I'm bold enough to do this. I can hardly believe it myself.* Still, none of them tried to stop her.

The guards fell in behind her, but she didn't look at them, either. She headed right toward the side of the dance floor, where the dashing Soren Ferro was already standing with other young nobles. He bowed to a girl in a long, draping headscarf that covered half her face in sparkling blue lace, and he took her hand.

Then he saw Halan coming.

"Princess," he said, and the other young nobles turned hurriedly and bowed to Halan.

"Lord Soren, may I invite you to join me in a dance?" Halan said, forcing herself not to blurt it out, to take her time, as if she had only just thought of it and had not made a beeline right for him.

"Oh!" Soren said, clearly surprised, before seeming to remember his manners. His face relaxed into its usual wry, charming expression. "Of course, Your Highness. I would be most honored."

Halan glanced at the girl in the blue scarf. Even with half of the girl's face covered, Halan could clearly see the disappointment in her eyes. A dance with Soren Ferro was something many of the girls would have fought over—but this was the princess, after all. The girl immediately bowed her head and backed away.

*Well done,* Halan thought. She had never heard of a royal princess dancing among the people, let alone asking the boy of her choice, but Soren was taking it remarkably well. *That's why I chose him.* Soren was popular with everyone at the palace—the old liked him for his polite, kindly manner, and the young—particularly the young women—liked him for his wit and boyish charm. He was handsome but not overly so, and his light brown eyes, though friendly, held a cunning sharpness, like the eyes of a hawk on the hunt. He was exactly what Halan needed.

As Soren linked his arm with hers and they stepped onto the dance floor, she saw him smiling at her. Halan felt her cheeks grow warm. It was almost as if they were truly friends, sharing some funny little secret. *I guess this is what it would feel like to have friends outside the palace.*

Well, good. If he liked this, he would *love* what she was going to ask him next.

"I'm afraid I don't really know how to dance," Halan

said. "But I think I've seen you dance with every young person here, so I'm assuming you can show me."

"I'd be delighted," said Soren, taking one of her hands in his. He spun her gently one way, and then the other, holding up his free hand as if he were balancing a plate on it. Halan tried not to trip over her skirt. She mostly succeeded. "I must say, Your Highness, I'm flattered—and impressed."

"That I decided to dance?" Halan grinned. "Or that I picked you?"

Soren grinned back and spun her once again. "The former, of course. But I should have known you were feeling rebellious when you first walked in wearing that dress," he said. Halan glanced over his bare brown shoulder at the platform where her mother was still sitting—and saw her covering her eyes with one hand.

Well, Queen Rani might be embarrassed, but Halan wasn't. She knew all the nobles were whispering, but for once she didn't care. She was going to have her moment, and no one was going to take it from her.

"It was made for me by Master Eshaq, from the north," she told Soren.

"It's very modern. It suits you."

Halan blushed with pleasure. "You should know, my lord. You are always so well dressed. Do you buy your clothes in the city?"

"Sometimes," said Soren. "You'd be amazed what you

can find in the bazaar—trinkets and baubles, mostly, but I enjoy them."

"I would love to see it," she said. *Slow down, don't frighten him off now.* She paused while she concentrated on turning a tricky step without falling over, and then lowered her voice. It was time to get to the point. "Soren, I need you to help me."

There was a small pause.

"I'm trying," Soren said wryly. "I can't help it if you royals all have two left feet."

"I want to visit the bazaar," Halan said, ignoring his joke. "You know that we nobles hardly ever get to have any fun—imagine how much worse it is for me! I'm basically a prisoner here. But I have a plan to get out for a little while and see the city. The thing is, I can't do it without your help."

Soren's face was impossible to read.

"Your father says you're not supposed to leave the palace," he said finally. "He'd have my head if he found out I snuck you into town."

"My father is away, and I don't intend to tell him."

"He has good reason to forbid you. It could be dangerous."

"It won't be if you're with me."

The tone of the music changed. The drums beat more softly, and the singer began a new phrase, something about moonlight in the desert. Halan was glad of the slower pace.

She faced Soren, looking up into his eyes with what she hoped was an unshakably determined expression.

"I *will* see the city for myself," she said. "If you don't take me, I'll just have to ask someone else. Who would you recommend I trust with my safety?"

Soren didn't answer. His expression had turned deadly serious.

"I've taken care of everything," Halan went on. "I can get away. Please! All I need is a horse and a friend to show me around."

"Which one am I supposed to be?"

Halan stared at the young man's face, waiting for the real answer to come. Soren looked down at her, and smiled again—but it wasn't a sarcastic smile this time. "As you wish, Princess," he whispered.

Halan's heart soared.

*It's really happening.*

Her plan was working.

*I'm finally going to see the real world! For one night, I'll be free.*

# Chapter Five

## Nalah

*I have always striven, in my work, to make mirrors that do more than simply reflect life. Instead, I hope that when someone looks into my glass, they see a side of themselves—a side of life—that they have never seen before.*

***Xerxes Bardak, World-Renowned Glassworker***

Nalah stood at the top of the stairs, swaying. She had already turned around on the spot seventeen or eighteen times, hung upside down from her bed with her head dangling, and lightly wet her forehead with rainwater from outside her window.

She descended the stairs, with some genuine difficulty, and headed out to the workshop.

"Papa?" she called weakly.

"Good morning," came her father's voice. He was inside, taking jars off a shelf and writing something down in a ledger.

Nalah's heart sank. The jars contained his ingredients—the gems, sand, and silica that glassworkers were still allowed to keep in their workshops. He was taking stock for the last time, preparing to sell up and close the workshop.

"I don't feel well," she said, and it was true. She needn't have bothered with spinning and hanging upside down to make herself look ill—the sight of her father giving up his craft was sickening enough. "I don't think I can go to the market today."

Her father put down his pen and looked over at her with concern. "Of course you can stay home, baba. I'll go. I need to talk to Mr. Caron about giving up the stall, anyway."

Nalah hugged him tight and buried her face in the soft, worn cotton of his shirt.

She hated lying to her father, but she hated the idea of a future without magic, without glass, without freedom, even more.

After Mr. Bardak had gathered up the last of their stock and headed off to the market, Nalah opened the closet where her father kept his tools. She pushed aside the thick apron and the heavy gloves, and lifted out the headband with the black glass visor. Those were just his ordinary tools. She was going to need something a bit more *extra-ordinary*.

She ran her fingertips over the old wood at the bottom of the closet, tapping and pushing until she found the loose board. It lifted out easily. Behind it there was an old metal box about the length of Nalah's arm. She wriggled it out and laid it on the worktop, tugging at the lid. It gave an unpleasant, rusty screech, like a final protest, before it opened.

Inside were an ordinary-looking, red leather-bound book and a soft brown pouch. Nalah picked up the book. Strangely, she remembered it being more impressive than this. There was almost no need to hide it in the closet—the Hokmet would never know it was Xerxes Bardak's famous *Technical and Magical Aspects of Thauma Glasswork* unless they looked inside and saw her great-grandfather's name on the first page. Along with her regular bedtime stories, Nalah remembered her father telling her all about their famous ancestor, whose leadership and glassworking abilities were so great that the tales about him sometimes veered into the mythical. In the days leading up to the Thauma War, he had been both an inspiring speaker for peace and a man who could make seeing glass eyes for the blind and mirrors that reflected only the truth.

Papa had once told her that his grandmother swore Xerxes had been able to work wonders with more than just glass. But that was impossible. Everyone knew that. Even if a Thauma's parents came from two different clans—as Nalah's did—the Thauma would inherit the talent from only one of them, usually the father. No, it wasn't true. It was just another nice story to help her sleep at night—the idea that there was once someone in her family who had been free to practice his craft and speak his mind.

Nalah moved the book aside and emptied the contents of the pouch onto the worktop. The tools inside were small, fine things made of silver, now tarnished, and dusty glass: a pair of pliers, some pointed calipers, an eyepiece that swiveled to swap between two magnifying lenses.

There was no putting it off any longer. She took out the shard of mirror and laid it on the workbench in front of her, careful not to cut herself on its razor-sharp edge. The splintering rainbow sheen never seemed to keep still, even when Nalah held her breath and there was no movement anywhere in the workshop.

She leaned down to peer at the shard, using a pair of tongs to carefully turn it over and over. If this were an ordinary mirror, she would need to make the glass sheet first and then paint the liquid metal onto the back—but was that how this one had been made? With a bit of luck, Great-Grandpa Xerxes would have something to say about magic mirrors.

Nalah turned the shard glass-side-up and screwed the eyepiece into her eye to study it. When she swiveled to the second lens, the shard seemed to vibrate, as if it were about to shatter. Nalah jerked away from the worktop, almost toppling off her stool—but the shard lay still and unbroken.

"What is that?" she wondered aloud. Curious, she fished the cobalt-blue glass falcon out of her pocket and looked at it through the eyepiece. It seemed to be vibrating too, though only very slightly. She could see pulsating blue and silver streaks across its surface: the moonstone and turquoise she'd used to imbue it with the powers of protection and luck. She couldn't help grinning to herself—Xerxes's lens could see her magic. That meant it was working!

"I might actually be doing the right thing," she told the falcon. "Your luck has to rub off on me sometime, right?"

She looked through the eyepiece at the mirror shard once more, studying the particular streams of color and shapes that flitted across its surface. "Green-yellow, spitting like a firework . . . ," she muttered, alternating between looking through the lens, writing down what she saw, and searching through Xerxes's book. "Lavender-purple that looks like ink in water. Bright white, hard to look at—"

She read her notes, then the page in the book, and then her notes again.

"Got you," she whispered. She'd found a match.

"Transcendent Glass," read the title at the top of the page.

"All magic objects bend reality," the first line began.

> *But uniquely among glassworks, Transcendent Glass allows the user to see beyond reality. A mirror or bowl of Transcendent Glass is a powerful, dangerous thing that must be kept safe from those who would use it unwisely. I fear that looking too long or too often into what lies beyond our world may damage the fabric of reality.*

*I include here the active ingredients, and a theoretical method for creating Transcendent Glass—yet this is for academic purposes only. Any glassworker considering making a Transcendent Glass object should be utterly certain of its intended use before attempting such a thing.*

Nalah sat back, a long breath whistling between her teeth.

Perhaps this was a mistake.

What exactly did Zachary Tam plan to do with the mirror when it was finished?

Nalah remembered learning of the Thauma Wars, when the Thauma had fought each other for control over the country, maybe the whole world. In the stories, there were Thauma objects so powerful they had to be destroyed, or hidden. It was because of what happened in that very war that a new war emerged: the war against the Thaumas themselves. Nalah had read that the men who led the clans in battle had been arrested and sentenced to death by a group of nonmagical folk—men and women who'd been caught in the crossfire. It was those same angry, bitter people who eventually established the Hokmet and, little by little, erased Thauma magic from the land.

Suddenly Halan wondered if, in this case, the Hokmet might be right. Perhaps using Thauma magic to make this mirror was dangerous. Too dangerous.

But Tam had been a friend of her mother's, and was clearly an expert in Thauma artifacts. Surely he would know better than to use the mirror as a weapon? And if it was only an heirloom, something to keep hidden in his house like all the rest, there was no harm in it, was there?

"What do you think?" she asked the falcon.

The falcon's slightly tilted head looked back at her. It felt like it was saying, *I think you can do this.*

"I dunno, it depends what you're up to," said a voice.

Nalah whirled around, her heart in her throat.

Marcus Cutter was standing in the doorway to the workshop, his arms folded.

"What are you doing here?" she demanded, blocking his view of the worktop, hoping he wouldn't see the book or the shard of glass. "Why aren't you at the market?"

"Really? Why am *I* not at the market?" Marcus smirked.

"I'm busy. I'm sick. I couldn't risk it after yesterday," Nalah blurted out. Then she cringed.

"You just told me three different things," Marcus said. "I don't need a magic handkerchief to tell you're lying to me. Not this time."

"What?" Nalah frowned.

Marcus came into the room, and Nalah tried to shift so that she would keep herself between him and the shard. "Yesterday. You said you went on an errand for your dad and stopped at a café. You remember how the handkerchief I gave you stank of peppermint?"

"Oh," said Nalah, as it all became clear. She wanted to kick herself. "A lie-detecting handkerchief. 'Great to have on a first date'—or for spying on your friends," she added bitterly.

To her surprise, the smug look on Marcus's face faded. "Hey, *I'm* not the one who's sneaking around," he said. "I just wanted to know what you were up to. Maybe I can help."

"You can't," Nalah said desperately. "I'm sorry I lied. But you have to go. I'm fine, but this could be . . . trouble."

"Oh, *trouble*? Well, now I'm definitely not going anywhere," said Marcus, thrusting his hands into the pockets of his trousers. "You know how much I love trouble."

"You can't help me," Nalah said again.

"Well, someone needs to. You look like you've been through a sandstorm."

Nalah reached up and touched her messy hair self-consciously. "Go away, Marcus!" she growled.

"Fine," Marcus said with a shrug. "I guess I'll just tell your father about this little project you're working on the next time I see him."

Nalah glared at him. "Why, you . . ." She clenched her fists at her sides, helpless in the face of this nosy, meddlesome boy. "Why can't you just leave me alone?"

"Because," Marcus replied in a low voice, "I think you're already alone too much."

Fury rose inside Nalah. But he just looked at her with

those puppy-dog eyes and she felt her anger deflate. She sighed, and let her fists relax again. Maybe he was right. The mirror was a big project; it might not be the worst thing to have an assistant. Even if it *was* Marcus Cutter. "Oh, all right," she said. "But you have to promise me you won't tell Papa, or *anyone.* I could get in deep trouble." She glanced down at the mirror shard again, moving out of the way so that Marcus could see it too. "Not to mention, there's a chance I could destroy reality."

"Cool," Marcus said, his eyes glinting.

A few hours later, Marcus and Nalah were strolling along the promenade, looking out across the beach toward the jewel-blue Hadar Sea. Nalah pulled her headscarf closer around her face and blinked in the glare of the afternoon sun, wishing she had a pair of sunglasses. She shifted the basket on her arm and made sure its contents were covered with the blanket.

"Here?" Marcus said, adjusting the hat he'd borrowed from Mr. Bardak's closet. "Really?"

"Right here, according to Great-Grandpa Xerxes," said Nalah. She lowered her voice. "He said the best place to find cryptocrystals and heliothysts near New Hadar was on the beach at its widest point, where the palace ruins line up with the Fissure. The palace isn't there anymore, but look." She pointed up to the hill where Tam's mansion stood, then down at their feet, where a great crack ran deep through the pavement and vanished into the sand of the beach. "This is it. I'm certain."

"Well, at least it's a nice day for a 'picnic,'" Marcus said.

There were a few other people on the beach, mostly couples walking arm in arm or snuggling together on chairs or blankets and looking out at the sea. And here she was with Marcus.

*Oh, yuck*, she thought.

Nalah wondered if any of the beachgoers were actually enforcers. They didn't always wear their uniforms so they could blend in undercover. Would they patrol the beach, like they supposedly guarded the mines and the forests, to prevent Thaumas from gathering materials?

Nalah led the way down onto the beach, to a spot where she felt she was right in the center of the area Great-Grandpa Xerxes had specified. She and Marcus spread a blanket out, and Nalah sat on the edge of it.

"All right. You keep watch," she said, fishing in the basket and pulling out an empty jar, a trowel, and Great-Grandpa Xerxes's silver eyepiece. "I'm going to . . . make a sand castle now. Tell me if anyone's coming."

"See? You did need me, Bardak," said Marcus, settling down beside her with his face to the city and pulling a peach from one of his pockets. Nalah stuck her tongue out at him. His smug face was even worse when he was right.

She filled the jar with sand and tipped it out to make a sand castle tower, for the look of the thing. Then, when she was certain nobody was watching, she scooped up a tiny amount of sand on the trowel, spread it to form a layer only one grain thick, and then bent to study it through the eyepiece.

Through Great-Grandpa Xerxes's lens, the sand glowed and the grains seemed to dance. No wonder he'd recommended this stretch of beach. Nalah risked a look along the sand through the eyepiece, seeing the whole thing shimmer like a belt of stars between the land and sea.

On her trowel, she quickly separated the dim, unmagical shards of rock and seashell from the glowing crystals, and then she started trying to sort them by the color of their glow or the weird effect they had on her vision.

The sand was quartzite, the kind that made up most of the sand in the kingdom. Perfect for making glass, and able to carry magic, but not special in itself. Then there were small amounts of red rose quartz and garnet, and tiny specks of turquoise, zircon and olivine, spinel and sillimanite.

And there was the heliothyst, sparking like a badly wired electrical connection. There were only three grains of it in the whole trowelful of sand.

Using her tweezers, Nalah transferred all three tiny specks into the empty jar, and then sat up, her back already aching.

"This is going to take a while," she said under her breath.

"Did you find some?" Marcus turned and squinted into

the jar. "Is that it? It just looks like sand to me."

"It *is* sand." Nalah rolled her eyes—but secretly enjoyed the fact that, for once, Marcus didn't know everything. "Sand isn't one thing, it's a hundred thousand different things."

"And how much do we need to collect, again?"

"Two full jars. Of each crystal."

Nalah and Marcus both looked down at the three grains of sand.

"You're right," Marcus said. "This *is* going to take a while."

*Melt the heliothyst and cryptocrystal together. Keep the mixture in a covered crucible. Melt down the base quartz. Add the mixture. Incantation. Remelt. Keep the temperature steady. . . .*

"Nalah? Nalah, wake up."

Nalah blinked and sat up, trying to focus on her father's face. The past day and a half had flown by in a blur. She'd been up all night sorting the jars of sand that she'd carried home from the beach. Then she and Marcus had gone back that morning and spent the whole day doing the same thing. Her shoes, her hair, even her fingernails were full of sand, and her eyes hurt. If she never returned to the beach for the rest of her life, it would be too soon.

But she had two jars of heliothyst and two jars of cryptocrystal.

She was ready.

"Hi! Sorry, I'm awake," she said.

Nalah picked up her spoon and hurriedly swallowed the last few mouthfuls of her soup, feeling vaguely guilty that she'd let it get cold. Great-Grandpa Xerxes's instructions for forming the Transcendent Mirror were circling her mind like seagulls. They sounded so simple, but the consequences for getting any step wrong—shattering at best, a possible tear in the fabric of reality at worst—were steep.

"You're really not feeling well, are you?" Her father reached over and squeezed her hand. "Did you sleep at all last night?"

"Not much," she admitted.

Mr. Bardak cleared both their bowls from the kitchen table and started washing them under the dribbly tap. "Maybe I should take you to the doctor," he said.

"No, Papa, I'm sure it's nothing," Nalah said quickly. "I'll feel better tomorrow, you'll see."

Her father turned and gave her a long look. Nalah attempted to look sick enough not to have to go to the market in the morning, but not *so* sick she had to go to the doctor. She had no idea if she was doing it right, but her father smiled.

"All right," he said. "Well, I'm off to bed. Try to get some rest."

"I will, Papa," Nalah said. "I'm just going to find my book. I'll put the lamps out and be up in a minute."

Her father planted a kiss on the top of her head and went up the stairs, his footsteps heavy and slow. Nalah watched him go.

*Everything will be better tomorrow, Papa.*

She should start work at once. She had to study Great-Grandpa Xerxes's instructions again, and double-check that the ingredients were prepared—

*Tap, tap. Tap-tap-tap!*

Nalah jolted awake, disoriented for a second. She must have fallen asleep again. The clock read midnight—and there was someone tapping on the window. A face, pale in the moonlight, looked in.

With a sigh of relief, Nalah opened the door, and Marcus stepped in.

"Are you ready?" he asked, with the cheeriness of someone who had actually slept in the last two days. It was irritating, but even so, Nalah found herself grinning back at him, a glowing-hot ball of anticipation forming in her chest. Then she pressed her hands together and tried to breathe slowly. If she lost control and zapped the Transcendent Glass with the power she'd let loose on the market stall . . .

Well, she wasn't sure what would happen, but she guessed it would be bad.

Nalah put out the lamps in the kitchen before they went into the workshop, so her father wouldn't know she was still awake. Unless he checked in her room, or looked out of the back window and saw the light from the workshop, or came downstairs . . .

But there was no time to dwell on the possibilities. She had a job to do.

She lit the furnace and Marcus helped her pump it with the long-handled bellows until it was burning red-hot. They brought the ingredients and laid them on the work-top in a neat row.

Nalah cracked her knuckles. Then she poured the jars of heliothyst and cryptocrystal into a crucible, careful to shake out every last white grain. She needed to melt down the magical and nonmagical ingredients separately in two different crucibles, and then mix them together. That was the tricky part. If she hadn't done her measurements correctly, the two components wouldn't meld, and she'd be left with a cloudy, nonmagical mess rather than the makings of a Transcendent Mirror. Once the mixture was ready, she'd pour it into the frame and let it cool. At least, that was the plan.

Taking a deep breath, Nalah pulled the black glass visor on and flipped it down over her face. "Let's do this," she said. "And remember to shield your eyes," she told Marcus. "I don't want to have to explain to your mother how she ended up with a blind weaver for a son." In the gloom, she saw him cover his face with a scarf.

She grabbed the first crucible with the long iron tongs and placed it in the furnace.

The magical grains melted in moments, faster than anything Nalah had ever seen before. They flowed together into a molten circle of pure white, almost too bright to look at even through the black visor.

Nalah slid the ceramic lid onto the small crucible quickly and left it in the furnace while she melted down the ordinary quartz in a second, larger crucible. It took much longer, and soon Marcus had stripped off his jacket and was mopping his brow with the scarf he'd been using to cover his face.

"Is it always this hot?" he complained.

Nalah smirked. "It's a furnace."

When the quartz was finally ready, white-hot and free from bubbles or grains, Nalah rolled her shoulders and seized the first crucible in her tongs.

"Okay. I'm going to pour," she said. She shifted her grip three times, to be absolutely sure she had it. She didn't want to think about what could happen if she spilled the magical mixture on the furnace coals.

*Smoke, and her father screaming her mother's name in the darkness—fire tearing through the house as he carried Nalah to safety—*

She shook the memory from her mind and tried to focus. *I can do this. I* will *do this.*

She slid the ceramic lid from the smaller crucible, trying, even with her visor down, not to look directly at the sparkling light fizzing off the white surface. Then she tipped the contents into the larger crucible of molten quartz.

*"Light of the stars,"* she began, reciting the incantation she'd memorized from Great-Grandpa Xerxes's book. She gasped as she heard a strange, chiming echo in her own voice. Her heart beat strong and steady. She thought she could feel her blood flowing through her veins. *I'm doing it!* she thought excitedly. *"Burn bright, burn through me,"* she continued. *"Light up this glass with your power."*

The magical mixture of molten heliothyst and cryptocrystal swirled through the quartz, staying separate, like oil mixed with water. Nalah stirred it with the long steel pole and held her breath, feeling her heartbeat pulse in her fingertips. Why weren't they melding? Had she done something wrong?

Then, suddenly, the whole mixture flared like a multicolored firework, the sudden light almost blinding. Nalah shrank back, her heart pounding. Next to her, Marcus yelped.

But after the initial burst of light, the brightness faded. Nalah risked a peek inside the crucible, and her heart soared as she saw the mixture was complete. It shimmered and glowed, casting sharp rainbow reflections around the workshop as she pulled the crucible out of the furnace.

"Marcus," she said, hardly daring to speak above a whisper in case she disturbed the magic somehow, "the frame."

"It's right here," Marcus said. He grabbed a suede cloth and wiped it one more time across the silver surface of the large oval sheet mold that Nalah had found in the back of the workshop. The shiny back would mean she didn't have to silver the glass herself. The shard of the old mirror was inside, pressed against the top of the frame.

"Stand back," Nalah said. She lifted the crucible with difficulty and poured the sparkling liquid into the frame. It spread out to fill the frame, as if it knew, somehow, exactly what shape it was meant to be. It swallowed up the shard, and after a moment Nalah couldn't see where it had been. The surface glimmered with the same rainbow sheen that the shard had, and the depths seemed just as strangely deep.

Nalah pulled off the visor and stared at the surface, pride and wonder mingling in her heart. "I did it," she breathed.

Marcus was looking at the mirror, wide-eyed, and Nalah wondered if it was calling out to him, as the shard had done to her. "I'll take the message to Tam first thing in the morning," Marcus said, when he finally tore his gaze from the mirror. "He can pick it up after your dad's gone to work."

Nalah nodded dumbly. As the exhilaration ebbed away, her fatigue returned. She smiled at Marcus, aware that her eyelids were drooping. "Thanks, Marcus. You've been a big help."

"I know," said Marcus airily, and left.

Nalah yawned, but knew she shouldn't fall asleep again. She should wait until the mirror was cool, and then hide it behind the cooling cupboard.

Nalah stared at the mirror, and after a little while she carefully reached out, wearing the heavy gloves, and touched its surface lightly with Great-Grandpa Xerxes's silver tweezers. A tiny chime rang out and kept on ringing so long and quietly that Nalah couldn't quite tell when it had stopped.

It was finished.

She slid the frame off the worktop and leaned it against the wall. The mirror was taller and wider than she was, but it still felt strangely light. She sat back down to search the reflection for any imperfection or distortion—

But in the mirror, a different girl looked back at her.

Different, and yet the same.

It was Nalah's own face, only there was kohl around the girl's eyes and a golden sheen across her cheeks. Her brown skin was a little lighter than Nalah's, like she didn't get much sun, and her hair was sleek and shiny as obsidian. She was wearing bright white satin, and silk the color of flame was draped across her shoulder.

She looked . . . not happy, but not sad, either. She looked determined.

Then Nalah blinked, and the vision was gone. The girl in the mirror now had Nalah's normal face, clean except for the smudges of soot, her hair unbrushed and pulled back in a hasty knot at the back of her neck. Her plain cotton tunic peeked out from underneath the heavy glassblowing apron.

Nalah leaned back against the worktop, staring at her own, true reflection. *Another vision*, she thought, *just like when I touched the shard*. What was this mirror that she'd made? What did it do? Another yawn gripped her, and she collapsed onto a stool. She couldn't start thinking about that now. Tomorrow the mirror would be gone, and they would have money to leave New Hadar.

*Tomorrow is the beginning of my new life.*

Nalah woke with a start.

*I fell asleep!* she thought, annoyed with herself. *I can't believe I fell asleep!*

She opened her eyes and saw herself, reflected in the wide surface of the Transcendent Mirror, still perched on the stool where she'd fallen asleep. She saw the workshop bathed in early sunlight—and her stomach dropped.

Her father was at her side, holding her shoulder and looking from the real Nalah to the mirror Nalah and back.

"Nalah," he said, his voice raspy and strangely hollow. "What have you done?"

Nalah's heart beat hard and she clasped her hands in her lap, glad she had never taken off the heavy gauntlets. She felt like crying, shock and guilt swarming around her head, but she forced herself to take a deep breath before she answered.

"It's for Tam," she whispered. "I made his mirror."

Mr. Bardak shook his head, staring at the mirror in

disbelief. In the reflection, Nalah thought his face looked drawn, older than it used to.

"How could . . . ?" he began, and his hands squeezed Nalah's shoulders. "It's so beautiful, Nalah. You did this? It's amazing."

Nalah looked up at him, hardly daring to hope that he had already forgiven her. But within moments, the wonder in his eyes changed over to anger.

"How could you *do* this?" he growled. He stepped away from Nalah, away from the mirror. "Don't you understand how dangerous this thing is? Don't you understand that if the enforcers knew, they would *kill you*?"

"I do understand," Nalah said, her voice growing stronger. "But what else was I supposed to do? Just stand by while you gave up your craft forever? I couldn't let you do that! Tam left the shard here by accident, and when I took it back to him, he said he would double the price. With that kind of money, we can run away and live somewhere where we won't have to hide! He said he believed in me," she added, and put a hand proudly on the mirror's frame. "He said I had the power to do it. And he was right."

"*Tam*," her father spat, like the name tasted bitter in his mouth. "First my wife, now my daughter—"

"What?" Nalah exclaimed. Her father waved his hand as if to bat away the question, but Nalah got up from her stool and faced him. "Papa, what do you mean, first your wife?"

"Zachary Tam," said Mr. Bardak, through his teeth, "is

responsible for what happened to your mother. Oh, it was an *accident*, it's true. An accident that would never have happened if Tam hadn't put the idea into her head."

"What idea? How could it be Tam's fault?"

Mr. Bardak pinched the bridge of his nose and sighed. "When you were little, you were sick. You know this. You know that the metalwork your mother did that night cured you."

Nalah nodded silently.

"You were born with a weak heart. The doctor said that when you got bigger, you wouldn't have been able to walk. That you would be tired all the time. But you would have *lived*," he added fiercely. "You would still have been our daughter, we would have loved you and taken care of you. *Together*. And then Tam came along, with his wild theories and his illegal metalwork. He showed your mother some kind of legendary formula, and he was certain she could do it—that she could cure you."

"And she did," Nalah said quietly.

Her father nodded. "And it killed her."

Nalah reeled. Her skin prickled and stung. Was he saying that Rina's death was *her* fault? She could see the regret in her father's eyes, and she knew he didn't mean it—but he had said it, hadn't he?

She should change the subject. She should tell him she was sorry, point out that as soon as the mirror was in Tam's possession, they would be fine. But something inside her refused, like a cart wheel getting stuck in one of the Fissures.

"But she did it," she said, her voice a little louder than she intended. "Mama was a genius, you always said that. And her death was an accident! At least Tam didn't want her to hide from her talents. He believed in her, just like he believed in me—and he was right about both of us! All you've ever done is try to hide me away from the world, but I'm trying to help us survive and be free. When have *you* done that?"

As soon as the ugly words left her mouth, she was filled with regret.

But it was too late. Mr. Bardak's face creased with grief and he looked away. Nalah folded her arms, pressing her hands to her sides, feeling like the guilt might pour out through her fingertips and shatter every pane of glass on Paakesh Street.

"My mirror," said a voice.

*Oh no!* Nalah thought. *He's early.*

Nalah turned to see Tam in the doorway to the workshop, his eyes wide as he stared into the Transcendent Mirror. "You did it. Nalah, you are a true wonder."

"Zachary!" Mr. Bardak snarled. "How *dare* you come into my house and trick my daughter into doing your dirty work, after what happened to Rina?"

Tam, his expression perfectly impassive, blinked at Mr. Bardak. He reminded Nalah of a sand lizard—he had that kind of stillness. "I apologize if Nalah didn't tell you about our agreement," he said. "Did she also not tell you that I'm offering twenty thousand dinars for that mirror?"

"Yes," said Mr. Bardak. "But it isn't for sale."

"What?" said Nalah. "But it's illegal, you don't want it in the house!"

"No, I don't," said her father. "But don't you see, if we go along with this, we'll be *dealing* in illegal Thauma work, and that's even *more* illegal than having it in the first place! We have to destroy it."

"No!" Nalah exclaimed, thinking of everything she went through to create it. "You can't!"

She looked back at Tam, hoping he would say something—anything—to change her father's mind. But he said nothing. He had stepped into the workshop and was walking toward the mirror, as if in a trance, as if their argument wasn't relevant to him at all. Tam stood in front of the mirror, regarding his reflection for a moment. "It really is perfect," he said softly. "You have done something incredible, to re-create it so beautifully."

Despite everything, Nalah flushed with pleasure. Never before in her life had someone seen her Thauma talents as a gift rather than a curse. It felt wonderful, but that feeling turned to confusion as she watched Tam begin doing something to the mirror. He was touching its surface, drawing strange, swooping lines across it.

"What are you doing?" Nalah asked.

Tam didn't answer.

"Tam, *stop*!" Mr. Bardak snapped. "I forbid this!"

Tam laughed softly, and began to speak under his breath. Nalah couldn't make out the words, but she heard the chiming echo in his voice, just like she had heard in her own voice when she'd made the mirror. "*Light*," she thought she heard him say, and "*many sands*." He was speaking an incantation! But why?

Suddenly a hot breeze stirred Nalah's hair, and the mirror began to change. Light spilled through it, yellow-warm like a sunbeam. Nalah tried to look into the mirror, but she couldn't see her reflection anymore. There was *something* there, a suggestion of shapes, but it was too bright to make out.

"Nalah," said Tam, "I need your help with something. Come here."

Nalah hesitated, the back of her neck prickling with suspicion.

"It's all right," he said, his voice soothing, the way you'd speak to frightened animal. "It's something very special. Let me show you." He reached out his hand to her.

Nalah, feeling enthralled by the light and his words and the magic of the moment, began inching toward him, curiosity pulling her forward.

But then she saw him reaching inside his jacket for something. Something that glinted silver in the light pouring forth from the mirror. It was a knife.

Nalah recoiled just in time, and he missed catching hold of her by an inch.

"No!" Her father barreled into Tam, seizing his arms. "Don't you dare hurt her! Get away from my daughter!"

"Unhand me, Bardak!" Tam yelled, "You have no idea what this is all about!" He twisted in her father's grip, driving his elbow back into his belly. Mr. Bardak doubled over and Tam turned and brought his fist up in a swing that caught Nalah's father across the temple, making him stagger. His knees bent and he fell to the floor.

"Papa!" Nalah said. She wanted to run to him, but Tam was reaching for her again, so she scrambled onto the worktop behind her and grabbed the first heavy thing that came to hand—the big pair of glass-cutting shears.

"I command you to come to me," Tam snarled.

"Never!" Nalah brandished the shears in front of her. "You lied to me!" she yelled. "You used me! Why? What do you want from us?" The light from the mirror was starting to dim now, its warmth starting to fade. She couldn't feel the hot breeze anymore. Tam glanced behind him, and when he looked back at Nalah, his face was twisted with anger.

"I don't have time for this. You force my hand, girl." He bent down and hauled her father to his feet.

Nalah cried out "No!" and lunged for Tam, but it was too late—Tam had shoved Mr. Bardak backward, toward the mirror. Nalah's father fell against it—no, not against it. *Through it.*

In an instant, he had vanished into the pool of light.

Tam stepped through after him, and turned back, weirdly half in and half out of the mirror, to smile at Nalah.

"You want to see him again? Find the way to open the door, and follow me."

He ducked his head into the mirror, the shining surface closed over him, and he was gone. Nalah dropped the shears with a clang and dived after him, but instead of going through, her hands slammed into a solid surface.

The light inside the mirror flared, and then died.

Nalah stared up at the smooth glass. The mirror was just a mirror once again. Nalah was left alone in the workshop, staring at her own wild-eyed reflection.

"No!" she screamed, but her reflection only screamed back. She let out a strangled cry of rage and grief and fear.

*What have I done?*

# Chapter Six

## Halan

*During the Thauma War, many of the great families feared kidnap or assassination by their enemies. Although the aftermath of the War brought peace to the Kingdom, no King ever slept completely soundly without a way to escape should his enemies rise up against him. If tensions should flare between the Clans, or if the city itself should revolt, the royal family of the Magi Kingdom would be able to evade capture.*

*For this reason, many passages were preserved or reinforced during the rebuilding of the palace.*

*Lord Susa*, The Palace of the Magi

Halan lay in the darkness, trying to relish the comfort of her bed—its silky sheets, the thick, cool pillow under her head. She wasn't succeeding. All she wanted to do was throw back the blanket and jump out of bed, but she forced herself to stay put, eyes closed, not moving a muscle.

She heard the faintest of footsteps, and the tiny creak of the door opening.

Halan tried to breathe evenly.

*I'm asleep. Look at how asleep I am.*

After a moment, she risked opening one eye a sliver, just enough that she could see torchlight from the corridor illuminate the figure who stood by her bed.

Queen Rani had been all smiles and serenity that afternoon, when the last of the visiting Thauma clans had finally left the palace. She had waved them off with a graceful laugh, as if she didn't have a care in the world.

Halan had thought that her mother must really be happy, at least a little bit. It was her mother's job, as the queen consort, to entertain and keep the peace among the nobles, and Halan suspected there was more to it, behind the scenes—politics she couldn't grasp because she had never been allowed to see, intrigue that went beyond dances and marriages and whose Thauma power was stronger. It must have been a relief to get rid of them all.

But now, as the queen stood alone in the dark and looked at her sleeping daughter, her face was a mask of worry.

Queen Rani had watched Halan with the same frightened expression for as long as Halan could remember. It was almost as if Halan was in some kind of danger, hanging by her fingernails from a cliff edge, instead of being King Asa Tam's beloved daughter, living in a palace, surrounded by guards and servants devoted to keeping her safe.

Halan resisted the urge to feel sorry for her mother, for whatever pain she was enduring. *Not tonight*, Halan told herself. *Tonight is all about me.*

As usual, Rani stayed a few minutes, looking at Halan. Then she turned and left, closing the door behind her.

Halan counted to a hundred, slowly.

Then she grinned.

She threw back the blankets and slid out of bed, adjusting the clothes she'd gone to bed in: loose black tunic and pants, leather breastplate, and black sandals. The breastplate was a little bulky, but she figured she should wear it just in case she ran into any trouble. She dug into her bedclothes to find the hooded cloak, and fastened it around her neck. It had all been "borrowed" from the laundry, over the last few months. She had been planning this for so long, and now she was actually doing it.

She went to the door and opened it carefully, looking left and right to make sure she wasn't seen. But there were no guards on these rooms at night—the Thauma door at the bottom of the stairs would only admit the royal family and a few approved servants.

That was what made the plan so perfect.

Still, she shouldn't allow herself to get too careless. If she was caught, her parents would probably set a guard right outside her bedroom for the rest of her life.

She hurried down the hall, holding her breath and stepping lightly as she passed the queen's chambers. Her mother would probably still be awake, but Halan couldn't hear anything stirring behind the ornate green-painted door. She kept half an eye on the door as she carried on down the silent corridor.

"Halan?"

Halan's heart leaped into her throat.

*No!* her mind screamed at her. *I've been planning this for so long! No one is supposed to be here!* Trying to keep her face relaxed, she turned to face the person who had spoken. He was coming around the corner, a tall, graceful shape in billowing red robes.

"Father!" Halan said. It truly was a joy to see him again. She only wished he hadn't come back tonight. She pasted a smile on her face and subtly drew the cloak closed over the leather breastplate. "You're home!"

"My darling!" said the king, his face breaking into a sunny smile. He opened his arms wide. Halan barely hesitated for a split second before she rushed to him. He hugged her tight, then looked down at her with his eyebrows raised. "What on earth are you wearing?"

Halan swallowed and tried not to panic; she could feel her heart stuttering in her throat.

"Such darkness," her father went on. "Why all this black? You hardly look like a royal princess at all!"

Halan took a deep breath. "I don't know." She shrugged, as if the cloak was something she'd just found at the back of her wardrobe instead of having stolen it from the laundry. "It was so dreary here when you were away. I wanted my clothes to match my mood." Halan held her breath as she waited to see if her father would swallow the lie.

The king's expression melted and he placed a hand on Halan's cheek.

*Thank goodness.*

"You're a sweet child, Halan. Tomorrow, you can put on your most sparkling golden robes—in fact, I insist. My business abroad is finished, and everything is going to be all right from now on. No more rebels and criminals in our city. No more war. The Magi Kingdom will be a paradise, my dear." He paused, thoughtful. "At least, I hope to make it so."

"I'm sure you will," Halan said, a genuine smile pushing aside the fake one. Her father was such a dreamer, always talking about how he was going to improve the kingdom. She was sure that whatever had him so excited, it was going to be wonderful.

"In fact," her father said, taking Halan's hand in his, "in a few days I will have a surprise for you. A gift. Something you have always wanted."

Halan looked into his eyes. They seemed different, somehow. There was a fire in them that she'd never seen before. "You really did do something great, didn't you?"

If he had found some way of ridding the city of crime, of making peace with the rebels, then perhaps he would finally allow her to leave the palace. Her father was always promising that one day she would be able to travel as much as she liked, without any fear of being attacked. Could it be that he would actually keep his word?

*Maybe, but I can't wait around for that.*

King Asa lifted his finger theatrically to his lips. "All will be revealed soon. Now, I must get to bed. I've traveled a very, *very* long way. You should get some sleep too—you'll need your energy in the next few days."

"I will. I just want to get a breath of air."

He nodded and headed down the corridor toward his own rooms.

Halan walked around the corner and immediately stopped, catching her breath.

That was too close.

She loved her father, and she wished she hadn't needed to lie to him. But he would never in a million years have allowed her to do this, and she *needed* to do this. If only for a little while, if only this once. She *had* to prove that she could take care of herself out there in the real world. Not to anyone else—but to herself.

She ducked through a door and into a room filled with strange, bulky, looming shapes: the room where the servants stored furniture and decorations that weren't on display.

The door closed behind her, and she was plunged into utter darkness. A creaking noise came from the murk, and a tinny metallic voice began to sing. Halan froze, until she realized it was only an enchanted music box, activated when it sensed a presence in the room. Steeling herself, she continued picking her way through the crowded room.

Finally she came to the tapestry hanging on the far wall. Making sure there was no one else about, she pulled the tapestry aside, revealing a narrow, dark tunnel hidden behind it. She felt cool air on her face, and carefully made her way into the secret passage.

"Thank you, Lord Helavi," she muttered, "for one lesson that actually turned out to be useful." When she'd expressed an interest in the architecture of the palace, he'd been only too happy to bring her every book and scroll he had on the subject. She'd had to sit through a lecture on sandstone and seem interested the whole time, but it had been a small price to pay. Some of the secret passages were common knowledge, but others were only hinted at in cryptic clues left by historians. Halan had put her mind to deciphering them.

It took a while, but she'd done it.

The passage sloped steeply downward and smelled of old stone. It felt a little damp, but the floor seemed to be clear as she walked through the dark, keeping her hand on the stones of the wall to her right. A little way down she heard a squeak from the darkness and suppressed a shriek, but carried on. *So what if there are rats?*

Halan had never actually seen a rat, but she'd heard about them from Ester. Huge, scurrying things with sharp, biting teeth. Her hand along the wall started to tremble.

"I'll have you know, I am your princess," she said into

the gloom. "Out of my way."

It probably made no difference to the vermin, but it made her feel better, anyway.

Suddenly the passage leveled out and started to grow a little lighter. She could see her way now, though she couldn't work out where the light was coming from until she reached a place where a small hole had been made in the roof. This had to be right under one of the courtyards, because moonlight poured in, and it hit a series of mirrors set into the walls, bouncing the dim, gray light around the passage.

At last, she came to a short flight of steps leading up to an ancient trapdoor. Taking a steadying breath, she climbed the steps, braced her shoulder against the trapdoor, and pushed.

The moonlight outside was as bright as a Thauma lamp after the dim tunnel. Halan blinked and peered around, trying to get her bearings as she climbed out. She was alone, right at the edge of the lush, cultivated palace gardens, sheltered from sight by tall palm trees. In front of her there was a clear view down to the city.

She sighed. It seemed so much closer than from her tower window. She could see fires twinkling; torches moving between the low, pale houses; bright lights in the city squares. She couldn't wait to see it all even closer.

"Your Highness," said Soren's voice. Halan turned, and found him waiting on a nearby path, the reins of a beautiful gray stallion held in one hand. Behind him there was a guard post. It was empty and dark. Halan imagined that Ester and the guard she fancied were snuggling somewhere together in the dark, just as she'd planned them to be.

Soren bowed to her. "Your adventure awaits, my lady," he said.

Halan couldn't hold back a huge smile.

She and Soren rode down the road to the city together—Halan, in front of the young lord, holding on to the horse's saddle. To her left, the great darkness of the Sand Sea seemed to swallow even the moonlight, but as they descended the hill the sea itself was hidden from view by houses, workshops, warehouses, and tall, sand-battered acacia trees.

The city was alive with activity, even at this late hour. Men and women strolled through the streets, laughing or talking or arguing with each other; others wheeled carts or worked on the houses. It made sense, Halan reasoned. It was better to do such heavy work through the cool night rather than struggle through the blazing sun.

They passed a few citizens on horses or in carts, but most of the people were on foot. There were even some children still out playing in the streets, urchins who huddled in little groups over games of marbles or chased each other in and out of alleyways.

She could hear music—a little like the music for dances at the palace, but much louder, much more raucous. She found herself tapping on the saddle in time to the beat. Behind her, a chuckle resonated in Soren's chest.

"We should leave Balthazar here and go on by foot," he said, and dismounted in one smooth movement. He tied Balthazar's reins to a post beside another horse, which was black and scrawny. The two horses sniffed each other curiously as Soren helped Halan down from the saddle.

Halan let the hood of her cloak fall down onto her shoulders, eager to take all of it in. It wasn't as if any of the citizens would recognize her—she rather doubted that even the guards who patrolled the city would know her face in a crowd. She let Soren lead her down a side street, looking up in wonder at the washing strung between the roofs to dry, the colored fabric blowing in the soft night breeze.

They emerged into a square filled with people and smells and noise. Halan felt her jaw drop and tried to contain her excitement, but she couldn't help turning to Soren, her hands clasped to her chest.

"A bazaar!" she whispered. "This is amazing! I want to look at *everything*!"

Soren laughed again, and took her hand. They walked into the crowd, ducking and weaving to make their way from one stall to another. Halan took a deep sniff of the scent wafting from a cart that sold spiced meat on skewers, each slice glazed in a different bright color. She saw a man take a big bite out of the meat and choke on the fiery taste, laughing even as his eyes started to water. Beside that was a stall where fabrics in every color and texture lay in giant rolls, and next to that was a stall full of wooden and metal jugs, and then one full of sticky-looking pastries. A woman bought a tray of bright orange sugar twists and walked away, sucking on her fingers. Halan and Soren passed by metal braziers burning wood that gave off flickering, rainbow-colored flames and the distinctive smell of Thauma smoke.

Just as Halan was taking it all in, two shabbily dressed men wove drunkenly past, yelling at each other, though she had no idea what about. Their anger struck a dissonant chord that was at odds with the otherwise cheerful atmosphere in the bazaar. Halan was relieved when they disappeared into the crowd, allowing her own cheer to return.

"There are so many things to see," Halan said. "What's that?" She pointed to a table where a strange, crude metal statue of a man sat on a chair.

Soren looked where she was pointing. "That's an automaton," he said. "A Thauma machine that plays games of chance if you drop a coin into its palm. They say you can win your money back, but not really. The games are rigged," he added under his breath.

Halan frowned. "But that's not fair."

Soren laughed again. "Out here in the real world, you'll find that 'fair' is . . . relative."

Halan nodded and walked on, though she cast a glance back at the automaton and frowned harder as she saw an elderly man, his clothes ripped and dirty, settle into the seat opposite the statue and drop a coin into its hand. Didn't he know that he probably wouldn't get his money back? Somebody ought to warn him.

"Lady, look out!" Soren put an arm around Halan's shoulders and pulled her aside. She tripped over the slightly overlong ends of her trousers as she tried to duck out of the way of something that flew over their heads and crashed to the ground behind them. It was a glass bottle. In front of them, a woman laughed, her mouth wide enough that Halan could see she only had two teeth. Soren helped Halan get her balance and quickly led her away.

Halan walked on, shaken. Underneath the party atmosphere in the bazaar, she was beginning to sense a thin layer of tension—a mixture of anger and sadness that she hadn't expected. *It's okay,* she assured herself. *You're just not used to seeing regular people outside the palace. Here they don't have to cover up their emotions like the nobles do. This is probably totally normal.* She tried to relax and enjoy herself.

They went over to a stall where a big lady in a Thauma cloak that shifted colors as she moved was playing the dulcimer, and a strange-looking boy with bright red hair was making a whole chorus of wooden puppets dance and sing along with the music. Halan clapped her hands, forgetting the poor old man and the toothless woman as she tapped her feet.

She grinned at Soren, and squeezed his arm.

"Is it everything you hoped for, my lady?" Soren asked her. His face seemed strangely serious, as if he was deeply pondering the question.

"Yes," Halan said. "It's wonderful. It's so . . . *real.*" She breathed in, the scents of food and smoke and dirt and sweat all mingling together. She saw smiling faces in the crowd, but she saw other things, too, things others might easily have missed. A gaunt, hollow-eyed woman crumpled in a corner, ignored. A young girl, thin as a rail, stealing a handful of figs from a cart while no one was looking. A large, muscled man, gripping a scimitar at his side, his eyes scanning the crowd.

Soren squeezed her arm, dragging her attention away from the sights before her. "I'm glad you like it. And the night is still young. I promise you, by dawn you will have seen enough of this city to last you a lifetime."

Halan nodded and smiled, trying to ignore the annoying little voice in her head. It had started whispering to her just moments ago, repeating a single sentence over and over again. Words she desperately didn't want to hear.

*You shouldn't have come.*

# Chapter Seven

## Nalah

*A famous sculptor once said: "We Thaumas do not take raw materials and change them into a magical object. The object was there all along, waiting to be set free. We simply open the door."*

*Xerxes Bardak,* Wonderworkers: A History

*What have I done?*

It was a constant refrain, repeating over and over in Nalah's head as she stared at the mirror that had swallowed up the only person who truly loved her.

"Father!" Nalah yelled, louder and louder, not caring who might hear. "Father, I'm sorry! Please, tell me what to do!"

But the Transcendent Mirror showed her nothing but her own reflection.

Nalah raised a fist at herself, rage and hatred rising up like a full moon tide. She hated Tam, she hated the mirror, and she hated the girl in the mirror for thinking she knew what she was doing, for ignoring Great-Grandpa Xerxes's warnings, for putting her father in danger.

*How could I be so stupid?*

Her heart thumped, and as she glared into the sparkling rainbow-sheened glass, she thought that she saw the sparks in the glass gathering around her hand.

Nalah exhaled and stepped back. She forced herself to lower her fist, and the effect faded. Her heart slowed.

She couldn't risk breaking the mirror. It was the only means of getting her father back.

*Find a way to open the door,* Tam had said.

"Tam tried to grab me," Nalah breathed. "Wanted to hurt me, it seemed. But why? Why take Papa? Just to get me to follow? Is it a trap?"

It didn't matter. Nothing mattered, except getting her father back.

"Hold on, Papa, I'm coming," she whispered.

What had Tam written on the mirror, before it opened? What were the words he'd been chanting? Nalah wanted to kick herself for not paying more attention. She almost raised a finger to try to mimic his movements, then froze.

*This is Transcendent Glass. If I draw the wrong symbol, say the wrong words . . . What was it Great-Grandpa Xerxes said about unknitting reality itself?*

Nalah spun on her heel and lunged at the worktop. The copy of *Technical and Magical Aspects of Thauma Glass-work* was still there, in its unassuming red leather cover.

She turned to the page on Transcendent Glass and read it twice.

But there was nothing about doors. Nothing about people stepping into the glass or using it to travel—just that warning about not looking too long or hard into what lies beyond our reality. Nalah tried not to think about what would happen to someone if they actually went *through* it.

"Come on, Great-Grandpa. *Help me.*" She flicked through the book again, more and more desperately, reading every word of every recipe until she had "sillimanite" and "heliothyst" dancing in front of her eyes.

With sweating palms and shallow breaths, Nalah pulled down every book from her father's small collection on glasswork and scanned every page—but there was no hope in her heart. These were just recipes for harmless charms and luck magics; it was no surprise that they didn't hold the secrets of the universe.

Still, there *was* a strange little glimmer of hope. The more Tam's last words echoed in Nalah's head, the more she felt it.

He wanted her to follow him, so he must think that she *could* find the way.

Nalah could think of only one other place to look for answers: Zachary Tam's mansion on the hill.

She dropped the leather apron and gloves on the floor and left the house without looking back. The last time she'd walked to Tam's house, she'd been jumping at shadows, seeing enforcers on every corner. This time, she wasn't afraid. She knew perhaps she should be, but there simply wasn't time for that. The Hokmet would surely have questions for her if they knew, but imprisonment, death, even torture held no threat for her right now.

If the answers to her questions were not in Zachary Tam's house, if she wasn't smart enough to figure this out, she might never see Papa again.

She began to run. Just as she turned off the main street, she heard a voice.

"Nalah! Hey, Nalah!"

*Marcus.*

She stumbled to a stop and turned around to see him running toward her. "I was coming to see if everything went all right . . . ," he said, his words trailing off as he came closer. "Where are you going? Did Tam not turn up?"

"He came," Nalah said numbly. "He's gone. He took my father."

Marcus's eyebrows furrowed in confusion. "What do you mean, he *took* him?"

Nalah shook her head, afraid to say more. She looked around—there were no enforcers on the street, but there were people. A woman pushing a baby in a black carriage threw them a concerned look and hurried on. Nalah reached up and tried to smooth back her hair—it was wild and tangled, and there was sand in it.

She grabbed Marcus's hand. "We're going to Tam's

house. I'll explain on the way."

Marcus looked down at his hand in hers, and Nalah could have sworn she saw him blush. But then he simply looked up at her and nodded silently. Marcus could be annoying, but she trusted him. And it was a relief not to be doing this alone.

As they climbed the road under the bending trees, she told him everything. Dumbstruck, Marcus stared at her.

"It sounds crazy, but that's what happened," she said. "I have to find a way through the mirror. There must be a clue at Tam's house."

They reached the top of the hill, and the huge, tumbledown house came fully into view, looking so much more menacing than it had just a couple of days ago. Nalah was making for the front door when Marcus pulled her back.

"Wait—look!" Marcus said, pointing at one of the windows.

Nalah squinted at the grimy window and saw it—a shifting shadow moving inside the house. "Who could it be?" Nalah wondered. "Tam's gone!"

"A servant, probably," mused Marcus. "He must have *somebody* helping him keep up such a huge house."

Nalah tried to breathe evenly as her mind raced. "We can't turn back now," she whispered. "We'll have to get in without being seen."

At the back of the house, the bushes and palm trees grew tall and wild, but there was a cleared path like a green tunnel to a peeling white door. Nalah crept up and peered into the tiny window at the top of the door. She let out a relieved breath.

"It's the kitchen! I've been here." *It was here Tam convinced me to make the mirror,* she thought, as she gingerly turned the handle and pushed open the door. She could almost see herself, sitting at his table, eating his stupid frozen cherries, and she longed to yell back through time: *Don't do it! He's lying to you!*

She shook off the feeling and beckoned to Marcus. "There's no one here. Let's go!"

They stepped out into the corridor full of Thauma metalwork, and Marcus's intake of breath seemed to ring off the polished surfaces.

"Don't touch anything," said Nalah quietly.

"Don't worry," said Marcus, shrinking a little as he passed a display of gleaming silver swords. "Who knows what any of this stuff is enchanted to do?"

They hesitated at the door to the main hall, and Nalah listened as hard as she could.

There were footsteps coming from the end of the hall. Nalah ducked back and pressed herself against the wall, dragging Marcus along with her.

"Kith?" called a young man's voice. "Are you down here?"

Nalah's heartbeat rang in her ears. *Don't come in here,* she prayed. *Please don't.*

"In the tapestry room, Javid," came the reply. An older, female voice. The footsteps drew closer—two pairs, converging on the hall by the front door.

"I finished Mr. Tam's bedroom and the library," said the boy, Javid. "Do you think I should just look in on the east wing study? It's been a whole week, and—"

"What did I tell you about the study?" said Kith, stern.

Javid paused, and Nalah thought she heard the sound of a foot scuffing on the wooden floor. "Mr. Tam said not to enter it," the boy mumbled.

"*Under any circumstances*," Kith reminded him. "Mr. Tam was quite clear. What if he had some dangerous Thauma artifact in there, and you went blundering in?" She tsk-tsked. "A little dust will do no harm."

"Sorry, Auntie Kith," said Javid. "I just thought—"

"If you're so keen to dust something, come and help me with the silver," Kith said.

Their footsteps and Kith's voice faded, until there was the sound of a door clicking shut.

"East wing?" whispered Marcus, with a grin.

"East wing," said Nalah, nodding. If Tam's secret was kept anywhere, it was most likely in this forbidden study. She took a second to orient herself—the sun set over the Hadar Sea, so east must be the opposite direction from the bay. "Upstairs and to the right," she said.

They crept as quietly as they could down the corridor until they found a grand, curving staircase. Nalah sped up, feeling exposed in the open, airy hall. At the top of the stairs they turned right. Nalah took one side of the corridor and Marcus the other, and they opened every door they came to.

Nalah's first was the library—not the room she was looking for, but her eyes went wide at the number of ancient tomes on Tam's shelves, and she noted where it was in case she needed to come back. Next was a bathroom, with a claw-foot tub. Then a room that made Nalah's heart leap in her chest. As she opened the door, the air stirred the glass chimes hanging from the ceiling. Every shelf was full of glass. Vases and cups, glass eyes, mirrors. The ringing sound vibrated around the room, almost below the level of her hearing, harmonics dancing together.

*If only Father could see this!* she thought, and then, a split second later, the memory hit her like a hot ball of lead to the stomach.

*But Father is gone.*

She bit her lip angrily at the thought that Tam could visit this room anytime he liked, and keep it safe from the Hokmet, just because he was rich. He thought he could do anything—including kidnapping her father. Well, he wasn't going to get away with it. Not this time.

"Nalah," said Marcus, from a little way down the corridor. "Pretty sure this is it."

Nalah closed the door on the room of glass and hurried over to join him.

This was definitely Tam's study. Every other room had been scrupulously clean and well organized, but not this one. Books and papers were piled haphazardly on a desk of black wood. A cracked-leather armchair sat in one corner, surrounded by more papers. The window was open, and along with the hot, petrol-and-jasmine smell of New Hadar, a little gang of buzzing flies had come in, and were circling lazily in the air.

Thauma artifacts lined the shelves. They were labeled, but didn't appear to be sorted in any way—a wooden figurine of a woman danced next to a glass orb that glowed with dark, shifting colors and a pair of golden rings that seemed to be vibrating gently.

In one corner, a large, empty frame stood propped up against the wall. Nalah went over and lightly touched the wood. Could it have held the original Transcendent Mirror? But where were the other pieces? And how was the mirror broken?

"You check out the desk," said Marcus. "I'll look on the shelves. Maybe there's a key, or a secret safe or something."

Nalah nodded and went to the desk, wondering where to start.

What would her father do?

*Don't rush*, he'd say. *Take it slow. Look at everything. That way you won't miss something important.*

His voice was so strong in her imagination that she had to pause, her face turned slightly away from Marcus, to blink away the tears.

She began to move the pieces of paper and the books, checking each one before putting it aside.

At first glance, a lot of the papers seemed to be notes on the properties of Thauma objects—nothing about doorways or Transcendent Mirrors.

After ten minutes of searching, Nalah found herself gazing at a metal vase. It was delicate and beautiful, with spiraling stripes of copper and silver worked into the surface. The single white lily perched within seemed too fresh to have been here for a week or more. As Nalah looked closer, she realized there was no water. The lily was simply floating, held up and kept alive by magic alone.

At the base of the vase was a yellowing card, folded once, with a picture of a lily drawn on the front. She picked it up and unfolded it.

*To Zach,* it read, in looping handwriting. *For when you forget to go outside!—Rina xx*

Nalah stared at the short message, her mouth agape.

"Rina," she whispered. When Marcus turned and frowned at her, she added, "My mother gave him this." *How could she have been so wrong about him? He was her friend!*

Marcus's eyes widened.

"She must have made it herself." Nalah longed to touch the lily, to feel the bit of her mother's magic that the vase kept within, but she resisted the urge. The last thing she wanted was to break another part of her family. She had already broken so much.

Instead she picked up the book that was on top of the pile. Something heavy clattered loudly onto the floor, making Nalah jump. It must have been balanced behind the books. Nalah bent down beside the desk and picked it up.

It was a sheathed dagger. Obviously Thauma work—its sheath and handle were made of stone, and were tightly locked together with iron clasps. Nalah looked around on the desk and on the floor for a label, but she couldn't find one.

She knew she should leave the dagger alone, but something tugged at her, urging her to draw it out. As if in a trance, Nalah unclasped the sheath and pulled out the blade.

It was made of obsidian. *Volcanic glass,* Nalah thought. *Forged in the hottest fires in nature.* She remembered something about it from Great-Grandpa Xerxes's book, some section she'd read while searching for answers about the mirror. Thauma-crafted obsidian was incredibly powerful. Nalah's thumb reached up from the handle and gently touched the flat of the blade.

Marcus vanished.

Nalah stumbled back, reaching out to steady herself against the windowsill—but her hand passed right through it. What was happening?

All around the room, things looked different. The flies

were gone. And in the leather armchair in the corner of the room, his nose buried in a book, was Zachary Tam.

Nalah stumbled back, stifling a scream.

He looked much more like the way Nalah remembered him from his visits when she was little. The neat, pointed beard was gone, replaced by a bushy, unkempt one. His clothes were rumpled and threadbare. There was a little less weight on him, and a lot less poise. He was hunched over the book, talking to himself, scribbling notes on a piece of paper.

Behind him stood the Transcendent Mirror, whole and unbroken in its original frame. Nalah expected to see herself reflected in its surface, but she was shocked to see an empty room instead. Gingerly she reached out and tried to touch the windowsill again. Once more, her hand passed through as if she was made of nothing but smoke.

*I'm not really here,* she concluded. *Is this the past? Or some kind of vision?*

Nalah's eyes widened as a movement over Tam's shoulder caught her attention. The Transcendent Mirror was rippling, like a sheet in the wind. Nalah smelled Thauma smoke, and the mirror began to glow, warm yellow sunlight spilling out into Tam's study, just like it had in her father's workshop.

Nalah watched in horrified fascination as Zachary Tam completely failed to notice the magic happening right behind his back. The surface of the mirror pulled apart like a veil, and something began to emerge—two brown hands, then a body, and a face. A *familiar* face.

Nalah took a step back before she remembered that she wasn't really there.

The man was dressed in a flowing silk robe the colors of a sunset, a perfect gradient from bright gold at his feet through pinks and oranges to deep, dark blue at his shoulders. On his head he wore a glimmering golden turban, studded with gems.

It was Zachary Tam. *Another* Zachary Tam. The same man who'd eyed her from across the marketplace. Who'd strolled through her father's workshop like he owned the place, stroking his pointed, neatly trimmed beard.

"*What?*" breathed Nalah.

Nalah's jaw dropped as the puzzle pieces fell into place in her mind. The Zachary in the chair was her mother's friend, the reclusive collector who had fallen out with her father. But it was this new man—*this* Zachary Tam—who'd asked her to fix the mirror. The man who she'd just seen step lightly from a mirror exactly like the one she'd made.

The new Tam, in his resplendent robes, reminded Nalah of a prince from her favorite illustrations in *The Collected Tales of the Great Magos.* He looked down at his shabby twin in the chair, and his eyes glinted.

He pulled something from the sleeve of his robe, something long and sheathed in stone. Nalah shivered. It was the dagger. The same one Nalah gripped in her hand.

He silently unclasped the sheath, raised the blade above his head, and brought it down into the back of the old Tam's neck.

Nalah yelped and threw her hands over her mouth. The rumpled man didn't make a sound. He spasmed once and fell forward off the chair onto the wooden floor, the papers by his feet scattering like a flock of startled doves.

The new Tam shook the knife, and several drops of blood slipped off the obsidian blade as easily as the blade had slipped into flesh. He raised his hands, staring at them, as if waiting for something to happen.

Then, impossibly, his eyes began to glow.

The glow crept over his skin, making it shine like polished brass. He laughed—an ugly sound—and then suddenly his expression changed from a look of triumph to one of pain. His hands clenched and he doubled over with a moan. The light filled the room in a blinding flash. Nalah shielded her eyes.

There was a thunderous booming noise, loud enough to break glass. And that's what it did.

Nalah looked up just in time to see the Transcendent Mirror shatter into a hundred thousand pieces and blow out of the frame like a breath of air on a freezing night.

Then, as suddenly as they'd appeared, the light and the glass and the body of Zachary Tam were all gone, and Marcus was back in front of her, his eyes full of fear.

"Nalah, wake up!" he was saying, his face pale. "Wake up! Talk to me!"

"I-I'm okay," Nalah stammered.

"What happened? You picked up that dagger and then you were in some kind of trance!"

*How do I explain?* Nalah looked from him to the obsidian blade in her hand. She quickly sheathed the dagger once more and set it back on the table.

"I saw something," she said after a moment. "I saw Zachary Tam. Actually, I saw *two* Tams. And one of them killed the other with this very knife!"

Marcus gave her a skeptical look. "Are you sure it wasn't some kind of hallucination?"

"I don't think so," Nalah said. "It seemed so real! It's almost like the knife was showing me the last moments of a life it took away." She walked around the desk and stood in the middle of the room, staring at the armchair and the place the mirror had been. There was a thick rug on the floor right in front of it.

*That rug wasn't there in the vision.*

On a whim, she reached down and tugged it aside. What she saw on the floor underneath made her stomach turn. The floorboards were stained with something dark and brownish. *Blood.* A fly zipped past Nalah's ear and she waved it away.

"Is that what I think it is?" Marcus said, covering his mouth with one hand.

"Yes." Nalah looked around the back of the chair. The leather was studded with glinting pieces of broken glass, each one no bigger than her thumbnail. "He must've swept the floor and gotten rid of the body."

Marcus shook his head, bewilderered. "How did you know?" he asked.

"I told you," Nalah answered. "The knife showed me."

Marcus walked to the desk and hefted the dagger, waiting. But nothing happened. "Huh," he said, disappointed. "Why did it work for you and not for me?"

"I don't know," Nalah admitted, her stomach fluttering uncomfortably. Why did she suddenly feel like something important was happening?

"Do you think it's because of your . . . you know . . ." Marcus looked pained.

Nalah knew he was talking about her uncontrollable powers. Her *problem*. But she hadn't made these objects; she'd only touched them. Surely touching something couldn't awaken powers that it didn't already have! But what other explanation was there?

"Okay, so let's say what you saw *was* real," Marcus began. "You're telling me that there are two Zachary Tams, and one murdered the other right here in this room? How can there be two? Are they twins?"

"I—I don't know," Nalah said again. "They would have to be, wouldn't they? But it was the one who took Papa who was the killer. He somehow walked through a mirror just like the one I made and stabbed the old Tam. Then he started glowing, and the mirror exploded." She paused. "I guess now we know how it got broken."

Marcus was silent for a moment, staring at the empty frame. "You know what? That actually kind of makes sense," he said.

Nalah stared at him. "*Does* it?" she said. "Please explain it to me, then, because I'm beginning to feel like I'm losing my mind."

"Think about it." Marcus walked around the study. "Tam—the one we met—he was desperate for you to make that mirror. He offered you riches beyond your wildest dreams. You saw him come through the mirror in the vision, but then the mirror broke. He needed you to re-create it so he could go back through it again. It was his only way home!"

Nalah frowned. "Home? What home?" And Nalah finally asked herself the question she should have asked the moment she watched Tam and her father vanish through the mirror: What was on the other side? "Is the mirror just a passage to another part of the world?" Nalah suddenly remembered the way the other Tam was dressed—that he reminded her of a prince from one of her bedtime stories. Tales of a magic kingdom, far, far away. "Or . . . could it be something else?" she wondered. Her heart filled with dread.

"Does it matter?" Marcus asked.

After a moment, Nalah shook her head. "No. It doesn't matter what's on the other side—I'm going."

They resumed their search, with even more vigor now. Illuminating as her vision had been, it hadn't helped her figure out how to open the mirror for herself. As she scanned the desk, something caught her eye. "In the past, everything on this desk was arranged just the same," she noted. "Except for this." She picked up a book from the top of a pile.

It looked ancient, its spine broken and its pages singed. When she turned back the cover, the book fell open to a certain page marked by a thin, rectangular piece of glass.

The words were handwritten in purple ink, in letters so small Nalah almost had to press her nose to the page to read them. There were notes scrawled in the margins; little diagrams and things that looked like scraps of Thauma recipes. And on the right side of the page, she saw a series of strange symbols. They looked almost like someone got bored and was just doodling little squiggles on the page. Nalah's eyes almost passed right over them, but for some reason she felt like she'd seen these designs before. Curious, she lifted a finger and began tracing one of the little squiggles in the air.

Suddenly she realized why they looked so familiar. She'd seen Tam drawing those same designs on the surface of the mirror.

"I think I've found it!" she said, squinting at the words

beside the symbols. "Tam must have needed to research how to activate the mirror too—he knew I'd find the answer because he left it right here! It says: *Way of light . . . kingdom of many sands.* This is definitely the incantation!"

She grabbed a sheet of paper and a pen and began to scribble the words and symbols down carefully. Then she gestured to Marcus, and they made their way discreetly out of the mansion, narrowly avoiding the two servants, who were finishing up the cleaning. But as they went, something was niggling at Nalah. It made sense that Tam needed the mirror to get back to wherever he came from—but why did he come here in the first place? What was the purpose of old Tam's murder?

Nalah tried to clear from her mind the dozens of questions that tugged at her. None of that mattered now. Only one thing did. *Focus, Nalah. Focus.* She began whispering three words, over and over again, like a mantra.

"I'm coming, Papa."

An hour later, Nalah stood before the Transcendent Mirror, which gleamed in the light of the sunset filtering in through her father's workshop window.

Nalah felt as prepared as she thought she ever would. Her hair was tied up in a messy braid, and Great-Grandpa Xerxes's eyeglass was in her left pocket, while she'd slipped her cobalt-blue falcon into the right. She found herself running her gloved fingers over and over the place where her father had fixed the crack in its chest. If ever she needed a little luck, it was right now.

She'd thought of bringing some kind of weapon, but the most she had was a kitchen knife, and something about Tam's gem-studded golden turban and the cold pleasure in his eyes as he killed his twin told her that a simple kitchen knife wouldn't do much good against someone like that.

*Will I ever make it back here?* She looked around the little workshop and swallowed hard. The old chair, the little side table, the walls hiding their smoke stains beneath so many layers of whitewash. She was leaving it all behind.

She turned to Marcus and swallowed. "Marcus, thanks for helping me," she said. "If anyone asks where Papa and I have gone . . . well, you know what they say when a Thauma goes missing. Invent us a relative in the Anong Provinces or something."

"Excuse me?" Marcus folded his arms, as if she'd said something shocking. "You think I'm going to let you vanish into a potentially magical mirror world without me?"

"What?" Nalah exclaimed. Helping her break the law was one thing, but would he really leave behind everything he knew to help her find her father?

"Marcus, this whole thing is incredibly dangerous!" she said. "You've still got family here—what about your parents, your grandmother?"

Marcus shrugged, but his eyes didn't leave hers. "We'll

be back soon, won't we? Besides, we're Thaumas, we have to stick together."

She met his eyes, and they stared at each other for a long moment before Marcus looked away. "Anyway," he added, the smug tone returning to his voice, "you'd probably get yourself killed over there. That's why I've got to go, to keep you out of trouble."

Nalah rolled her eyes. "Uh-huh," she grumbled. *Same old Marcus.* She unfolded the piece of paper where she'd copied out the magical symbols and the incantation. "I guess I'm never going to get rid of you, am I?" she said, her mouth betraying her with a smile.

Marcus shook his head. "Face it, Bardak," he said, flipping a lock of blond hair from his eyes. "You need me."

"I need you like a camel needs fleas," she replied with a huff.

But inside, she was glad.

Nalah took several deep, steadying breaths, pulled off her glove, and raised her hand to trace the symbols onto the glass, going slowly so that her hand wouldn't shake. Each of the symbols glowed and sank into the mirror like a stone into deep water.

*This is it.*

"*Way of light,*" she intoned, and she could feel the chiming harmonics of the glass, singing the words along with her. "*Open the door to the kingdom of many sands. Let me cross over the void.*"

The surface of the mirror rippled and glowed, and the warm golden light fell on Nalah's face. The wind stirred her hair and she could smell the sweet Thauma smoke again, and something like the scent of old books. She reached back for Marcus, and he took her hand.

*No going back now.*

And, taking one last deep breath, she stepped forward and into another world.

# Chapter Eight

## Halan

*We will rise.*

*We will not, cannot, be controlled through fear or hatred, for we have hope. Those who greedily hoard their power will find it slips through their fingers like sand.*

*We are free. We are wild. We will rise.*

*—Ironside*

*Revolutionary pamphlet, confiscated on the streets of Magi City*

Halan felt like one of the honeybees in her mother's garden, weaving happily from flower to flower. She was drunk on the atmosphere of the city, going from one stall to another through the bazaar, enchanted by everything. She allowed the noise and the color and the music of the world around her to drown out the worried little voice in her head.

She was probably just being foolish, anyway. Did she really think that everything in the city would be perfect? It was naive. She needed to stop being so paranoid and enjoy the fruits of her labor. After all, who knew when she'd be able to do this again?

Soren trailed after her with a watchful eye, occasionally steering her away from rough spots in the crowd, but more often simply looking on with an indulgent smile.

"Oh, these are lovely!" Halan exclaimed as she came to a stall where silver jewelry was draped on deep blue velvet cushions. Each piece was unique, inlaid with colored glass—a twisting emerald palm tree here, a leaping golden cheetah there.

"You have beautiful eyes, lady," said the jewelry maker. Halan felt both flattered and self-conscious. She was often complimented at the palace—but this was different. How could she ever know if a servant or noble was telling the truth, or just trying to appease the future queen? This man might only be trying to sell her something, but at least he wasn't *obliged* to be nice to her.

The jeweler held out a brooch. "I believe that this piece would complement their color perfectly."

The brooch was a piece of dark amber carved into the shape of a rose and accented by a thorned bronze stem. It felt warm to the touch, as if sun-kissed. There was something about its delicate simplicity that was so charming—it wasn't at all like the flashy, expensive pieces that filled her jewelry boxes back at the palace.

"It's beautiful," Halan said, and fingered the coins she'd "borrowed" from Lady Amalia that were in the sack tied at her hip. She'd return the unused portion tomorrow—her governess would never be the wiser. She felt thrilled at the prospect of using them—for all her royal baubles, she'd never once bought something for herself. "How much?" Halan asked the jeweler.

"For such a lovely lady as you," he said, "only twenty coppers."

Halan was surprised. "Are you certain?" she asked. "It must be worth much more than that."

The jeweler's eyes twinkled. "Perhaps one day you can repay me with some other kindness." He handed Halan the brooch.

Halan hardly knew what to say. "Thank you, sir," she managed, and pulled out the correct number of coins. "I'll treasure it."

As she walked away from the stall with Soren at her side, Halan looked down at the amber rose and felt happier than she had in her whole life. She felt as if her kingdom was opening up to her, embracing her as its future queen. One day she would return as herself, and tell them all about this night, and they would love her for walking among them as an equal—

And then, in a split second, the rose was gone. She spun around and saw a little boy with a mop of black hair and big dark eyes dancing away from her.

She flushed, appalled that a child would do something so criminal. "Give that back!" she commanded, but the boy just shook his head and ran.

"Stop, you little thief!" Halan yelled. Her heart pounded in her chest—she'd never raised her voice like that in her life! Adrenaline raced through her. She wasn't going to let him get away with her brooch, the symbol of her freedom, the only proof of her adventure!

The next thing she knew, she had taken off after the boy, her feet slapping the flagstones in their borrowed black sandals. She heard Soren at her heels, urging her to stop, but she didn't look back.

The boy was heading deeper into the city, away from the bazaar. *Bad idea,* she thought smugly, putting on a burst of speed. She'd watched the servant children playing from her window for so long that she'd learned a thing or two about chasing someone. *You should've run into the crowd!*

She zigzagged after him, through ever-smaller side streets. She was out of breath now, her legs burning with the effort, but every inch of her focused on not losing the thief. But the boy was too far ahead. She wasn't going to catch him.

Then a figure stepped out from a doorway and grabbed the boy by the collar. It was a guard, wearing a steel helmet and a black leather breastplate much like the one Halan had on under her cloak.

*Aha!* Halan thought triumphantly. *Serves you right. You'll have to give my brooch back now.*

But when the boy turned and saw who'd caught him,

he let out a howl of terror. Halan stopped dead, the sound chilling her to the bone. She didn't know much about little boys, but she knew real fear when she heard it.

"Please, let me go," the boy whimpered.

"What's that in your hand, boy?" the guard growled.

"I'm sorry I stole it," the boy begged. "I've got two baby sisters and they need milk. My mother's sick. Please, don't—!" he broke off, cringing as the guard raised a fist in the air.

Hearing those words, Halan felt her anger dissolve. She could tell from his face that the boy wasn't lying.

"This is unacceptable," Halan said, and started forward. She pulled her cloak tight around her and drew her scarf up around her face like a veil.

"My lady," Soren muttered, rushing to stay at her side. "This is extremely unwise."

"Just follow my lead," Halan hissed back. "This guard is out of line and you know it. Excuse me!" she called out to the guard.

The guard looked up and an expression of deep confusion passed over his face. "My . . . lady?" he hazarded. His gaze fell on Soren, with his noble's bearing and fashionable robes, and he seemed to think, *Yes, these are nobles.* He straightened up, still holding the boy in an iron grip. "My lady. Your lordship. What can I do for you?"

"You can tell me what will be done with the boy," Halan said. "That's my brooch. As far as I'm concerned, once it's returned, I have no further business with him."

"In that case, he will be sternly reprimanded and sent home to his parents, my lady," said the guard smoothly.

Halan nodded, but then she met the boy's eyes. They were brimming with tears. He shook his head, very slightly.

*What does he mean?* Halan hesitated, frowning up at the guard. She was about to say more, but then she felt Soren take her elbow. "Thank you, sir," he said. "If you return our property to us, we will leave you to discharge your duties and return this child to his home."

"Here you are, my lady," said the guard, taking the brooch from the unresisting hand of the boy and giving it back to Halan.

"Let's go, *Amalia*. Father will be looking for us," said Soren, steering Halan gently but firmly away. Halan thought of digging in her heels, refusing to go until she knew for certain that the boy would be released. But Soren threw her a serious look, and she let him lead her back the way they had come. "Your Highness, what were you thinking? Do you *want* to get caught?" he whispered fiercely, once they were around the corner and out of earshot of the guard.

"I'm worried about that boy," Halan said honestly, turning the brooch between her fingers. "Do you—do you think he'll really be sent home?"

Soren hesitated, looking down at her with a frown that seemed strangely calculating. "You're the princess. Do *you*?"

Halan felt stung by his question. Was she supposed to know how criminals were punished in her kingdom? It had never come up in her lessons—but then again, useful things often didn't. Perhaps she'd have to bring it up with Lord Helavi. If she was going to be queen, she'd need to know everything. But for now, she had to admit that maybe Soren knew more than she did.

Swallowing her pride, she asked, "How will he be punished, Soren?"

"Princess," said Soren, with a creeping weariness that looked very wrong on his youthful, handsome face. "Tell me something—do you *really* want to know?"

Halan felt her skin prickle. She felt that if she went down this road, she might not be able to turn back. "Yes," she said, barreling on. "I do."

"Sometimes, Your Highness, the world is not as pretty as it looks from your palace window," Soren went on. For the first time that night, she felt something other than affection radiating from him. This was something . . . *colder.* Something sharper-edged.

Then he sighed, and his expression softened. He tried to smile. "C'mon, let's forget about all this. I wouldn't want to end your first visit to the city on such a sour note."

"Yes . . . Yes, you're right," said Halan. He *was* right. What did she expect, for the whole world to be as well mannered and safe as the palace? And as for the punishment, she assured herself that whatever it was would be equal to the crime. The boy had stolen from her, and he would have to face the consequences. Her kingdom was just, her father had made certain of that. Doubting the king's guard, she admonished herself, was akin to doubting the king himself.

Halan comforted herself with these thoughts, and then turned her attention back to the city around her.

By the time they came back to the bazaar, it was closing down for the night. The square was nearly empty. The crowds of customers had moved on. As Halan surveyed the stalls and tents, the only people left seemed to be guards, exhausted merchants packing up their wares, and a few rowdy, argumentative drunks. The guards moved from group to group, hurrying people along. The drunks put up some token resistance and then stumbled away.

At the sight of the guards, Halan put up her hood and drew the cloak tight around her again. She was glad she had seen her city, but now she was beginning to tire, and she found herself imagining what would happen in the palace if she was found missing—her mother's fury, her father's panic. What if Pedram and Ester somehow got in trouble for it?

What would happen to them?

She lifted her chin and turned to Soren. "It's late. We should go back."

Soren gave a curt nod. "Of course, Your Highness. But if you'll permit me, there is one more thing I'd like to show you."

Halan frowned. "Will it take long? I'm getting tired."

Soren smiled at her with the same slow, mischievous smile that had every young lady at court clamoring to dance with him. "That doesn't sound like the girl who escaped the castle and nearly told off a city guard," he teased her. "You know as well as I do, my lady, that *we nobles hardly ever get to have any fun*."

Halan laughed. "Oh, it's like that, is it? Fine, then. Lead on, my lord!"

She offered him her arm, and he took it with a chuckle.

He led her past the bazaar, farther away from the post where he'd tied up his horse. They followed the wide road for a little while, passing large houses with Thauma lamps burning bright under the archways, lighting up the brilliantly colored mosaics that depicted figures and animals moving as if alive. Halan looked, but not too long—these were probably the houses of nobles and rich merchants, and if she was unlucky one might emerge and recognize her.

Then Soren turned off that road and they walked on. The sounds of the bazaar had long died away, and most of the buildings were now dark and silent. Their way was lit by the stars and the moon, which seemed brighter than Halan had ever seen them before. She could almost have believed that they were what Soren had brought her here to see—but he simply smiled when she looked up at them, and kept walking.

"Will we be there soon?" Halan asked.

"It's not much farther," said Soren.

"It's so quiet," Halan said, feeling compelled to whisper as Soren led her through a courtyard where a dried-up fountain stood, full of sand and a few persistent weeds. "Doesn't anybody in the city walk around at night? The palace is always busy, even in the small hours of the morning."

"It's after curfew," said Soren.

"Curfew?" Halan asked, frowning haughtily to cover her annoyance that she didn't already know.

"It's a rule that states that no citizens can be on the streets after half past eleven or before five in the morning. Your father made that rule to impose *order*." He said the last word as if it left a bad taste in his mouth. "He was afraid that if the people could meet and organize in the dark, they might rise up against him. Anyone caught out on the streets after curfew is thrown in the dungeons. Some are never seen again." Soren looked at her, his handsome face made leaner and more serious by the shadows. "Did you know that, Princess?"

"That can't be right," Halan retorted. "Just for being outside?" It didn't sound like the father she knew. More like the rebel propaganda she'd heard the nobles complaining about. "You sound like that *Ironside*! With his lies and exaggerations. It's ridiculous, every word of it." She tried to laugh, but it came out as a nervous cough. "Aren't *you* afraid to be out at night, if it's so dangerous? If we're caught, won't we be clapped in irons?" She was trying to lighten the mood, to go back to their teasing tone, but it sounded hollow to her ears.

Soren laughed, but it was a long way from his normal, carefree chuckle. There was something dark and thorny in it.

Halan turned to look at him, but he was looking at something ahead in the dark. *Why is he acting this way?* "Where are we going, anyway?"

"Just down here," said Soren. He turned down another street—though this was more of an alley. The ground wasn't neatly laid with flagstones, it was just packed sand. The buildings here were low, rough, without glass or even shutters in the windows. There were no Thauma lamps here—merely candles that flickered in the breeze. Halan shivered, suddenly feeling the cold desert air creeping under her cloak. *How poor would one have to be to live in a home like this?*

She suppressed a gasp as they drew level with a doorway and what she had thought was a pile of black cloth suddenly stirred and turned toward them.

"Careful, lady," croaked an elderly voice. "It's far too late for a young girl like you to be outside."

The woman wrapped in the cloth looked up at Halan, and Halan struggled not to recoil. The woman's face was almost completely covered in puckered scars. One eye was white and crusted with a drying yellow substance. Her lips didn't align; they'd been twisted out of shape by whatever had done this to her face.

Halan looked down and saw that there was a bowl at the woman's feet, with a single copper coin at the bottom. How could this woman be living in such squalor in her beautiful kingdom? Halan felt dizzy and confused.

She fished in the pocket of her tunic and pulled out a handful of silvers, each one worth a hundred of the copper. She dropped all of them into the woman's bowl.

The woman's one good eye went wide. "My lady!" she breathed. "You are very generous."

"Will it help you?" asked Halan.

"Very much," said the woman quietly.

Halan nodded. She took Soren's arm and hurried away, feeling self-conscious. When they were out of earshot, she looked up at him. "That poor woman. What could have happened to her face?"

"She was burned by the Dust," said Soren. "The scars are unmistakable."

Halan felt her stomach twist. The Dust? But everyone in the palace always praised the Dust, how it was such an effective tool against criminals. Halan had never really stopped to think about how it worked. "The Dust is only used on violent criminals," Halan said, trying to sound confident. "That woman . . . she must have been rioting! I feel a little sorry for her, but she must have brought it on herself."

“Do you think my father brought it on himself?” Soren asked. His tone was so light that Halan almost didn’t understand his question, and she let out a nervous chuckle.

“What? Your father?” Suddenly Halan remembered. Last year, Lord Ferro, Soren’s father, had been killed when he tried to stop a mob from attacking the city grain stores. They’d been plotting to poison the palace’s food supply. David Ferro had been hailed as a hero for giving his life to protect the king. She remembered sitting by her father’s side as he received Soren’s pledge of allegiance to the throne as the new Lord Ferro.

What did any of that have to do with Dust?

Soren looked down at her, his tone still eerily casual. “Dust is Thauma metalwork. Quite brilliant, actually. Bits of iron ground to powder and magically heated, so that it burns any skin it comes into contact with. It is, as you say, used on rioters. But any guard, patrolling the city with a pocket full of Dust, is free to use it whenever he or she sees fit.”

Halan’s frown deepened. She knew what he was trying to say, but she couldn’t believe it. The guards were good men and women; they were only trying to protect the kingdom, protect *her.*

“Well, they wouldn’t use it if they weren’t afraid for their lives,” she said, as firmly as she could. “If the rebels weren’t using Wild Thauma and working with traitors like Ironside, the guards wouldn’t need the Dust!” She watched his face, hoping that the nobles at the banquet had been right. He nodded, and she allowed herself to feel slightly smug. *See, I do know some things that are going on in this city.*

"That's very true, they only use Dust when they feel threatened. But it seems that all sorts of things make guards feel threatened. Poor people. Crowds. Loud noises. Being questioned in any way." He counted them off on his fingers.

Halan wanted to tell him to stop, that these must be lies, but something made her keep quiet. Soren's voice was still light—he could have been talking about a new play he'd just seen—but something else simmered just beneath the surface. Something dangerous.

"Not many of the Thauma nobles in this kingdom care how their weapons are really used to oppress people," Soren continued. "But my father did. He resisted, passively at first, refusing to let the king manufacture his Dust in our family's workshops. But when he came across a guard about to mutilate an innocent man at the grain store—"

"*Innocent?*" Halan interrupted, shocked out of her silence. Her voice seemed to echo around the empty street, and she took a deep breath and lowered her voice before she went on. "They were *poisoning* the grain store!"

"They were starving," said Soren, as if it was as obvious as the sun being hot or the Sand Sea being wide. "They went to the warehouses to ask to be allowed to work, to earn enough for a few loaves of bread. There weren't a hundred of them, and they weren't armed. It was twenty desperate people asking for food. People who stood peacefully at the door and wouldn't leave until their voices were heard. They were no threat at all to a company of the king's guards. But the guards felt *threatened*, so out came the Dust." He paused, looking up at the bright stars. "My father shouldn't even have been there. He just happened to be passing by. He saw that one guard was about to attack a man with Dust, and he stood in the way. The guard struck him down."

Halan, stumbling in her shock, stopped walking. "Soren, that's terrible, but . . . are you sure this is *true*?"

A look of intense grief twisted Soren's features for just a moment—then was gone, replaced once more by that maddeningly calm smile. "I'm quite sure, Princess. One of the 'mob' told me. She came to me and told me my father was a true hero."

"And you believed her?" Halan asked. Soren listened to commoners above her own father, the king?

"Her name was Neema Sadeghi. Do you recognize the name?"

The name did ring a bell—something mentioned once in one of Lord Helavi's lessons, but Halan was too upset to think of it further. Her hands closed into fists, anger rising. How dare he lead her all the way out here to tell lies about the guards and slander her father's good name? Did he forget who he was talking to? "And what if it does?" she asked.

"I'm the princess. What has she to do with me?"

"The Sadeghi family used to be one of the greatest Thauma fabricworker families in the kingdom," Soren answered, his own anger rising to meet hers. "They were a good, proud family. But they became enemies of the king's father for speaking out against his treatment of nonmagical folk. They were forbidden to work. They lost everything. Their daughter Neema was reduced to begging for work at the grain store that day while the king's court feasted and complained about the heat." He took a deep, steadying breath. "So, *yes*, my dear Princess, I believed her."

Halan, unsure of *what* to believe, squinted at the young noble. "If this is so, then I have no idea why you've kept this information to yourself—or why you've brought me all the way out here to tell me! We'll return to the palace this instant and tell my father as soon as the sun rises. If the guards truly are abusing their power, he will know what to do about it."

She turned back the way they'd come, but then stumbled to a halt, her heart pounding.

The street wasn't empty anymore. A row of figures dressed in black stood silently across the road, blocking her way. Their faces were in shadow, but the starlight glinted off shards of metal—small, jagged lightning bolts through each one's ears.

Halan's blood turned to ice in her veins. She looked back at Soren, suddenly afraid of what she would see.

She'd chosen Soren to help her because of the cunning she sensed hidden in his charming, friendly manner. She thought he'd only been hiding a sense of mischief—something they had in common. But looking at him now, she could see it was much more than that. He seemed much taller than she remembered. And the shadows that the moon cast across his face made him look older, too.

The boy she knew was gone. All that was left was the hunter.

Halan's heart leaped into her throat. *What is happening? Who are these people? Why is Soren doing this?* But as sheltered as she had been, she knew this wasn't the time to ask questions.

It was time to run.

She dashed back the way they'd come, flying through the dark. The gate at the end of the street was padlocked shut. She rattled the cold metal bars, whimpering, a prisoner in her own kingdom. She darted from one door to the next, tugging and pounding and screaming out loud into the silent street.

But there was no way out.

That was why Soren had brought her here.

The line of figures watched her, unmoving. After trying every door, Halan let out a breath and tried to calm her racing heart. She was trapped.

Throwing back her shoulders, she assumed the bearing of a princess and turned slowly to face Soren.

"I command you to return me to the palace immediately," she said, gritting her teeth.

"But your people wish to spend some time with you, Your Highness," Soren replied, his face a deadpan mask of respect. "People who are working toward bettering this kingdom of yours."

"*Rebels,*" Halan whispered to herself. "And what about you, Soren? What's your role in all of this?"

"Me?" Soren asked, almost coyly. "I am doing this because these people need a champion. Someone to get them the justice they deserve. And after what happened to my father . . . let's just say that I was more than willing to assist. When you asked me for that dance the other day, you delivered yourself into the service of your people too, Princess. And for that I must thank you. It was quite generous of you to walk into our hands so willingly."

A chill ran along Halan's spine as the pieces fell into place. "You're *him*—the noble that's been working with the rebels. You're Ironside!"

Soren executed a crisp bow. "One and the same, my lady. I'm sorry that I had to lie to you tonight. But mice don't usually scurry into their traps without a little cheese."

Halan had the horrifying thought that her mother had been right—the world outside the palace *was* dangerous. In ways Halan hadn't even imagined. Halan's cheeks burned with shame.

She had been trying so hard to show she wasn't the

naive, useless princess people thought she was.

*But I guess they were right about me all along.*

Halan pushed those punishing thoughts aside—she could wallow in self-pity later. Right now, she needed to get herself out of this mess. "Holding me against my will is an act of treason," Halan said, but even she could hear her voice quavering. "The consequences will be on your own heads! It's not too late to let me go. My father will be merciful if you do."

"Thank you for the warning," said Soren quietly. "But I must decline. I'm glad you were sick of the palace, my lady, because you won't be going back anytime soon."

Halan's scream was swallowed up by the night as the rebels closed in, her mother's words echoing in her head.

*Without power, you're defenseless.*

# Part Two
## Into the Mirror

# Chapter Nine

## Nalah

*When the Thauma War ended, the chaos began.*

*A year of storms, of fire, of death. A year of famine and drought. The waters boiled and shrank away from the city. The Sand Sea was left behind, its dunes littered with dead and dying fishes, and the hulls of sunken ships.*

*Those who had power discovered that they were stronger than they ever knew. They used their talents to keep themselves and their families safe, until the quakes and gales that battered the land ceased.*

*Then the first of the deep wells were sunk, deeper and deeper, until water was found that didn't ebb away. Roads were cleared. Houses rebuilt. We learned what would grow, and what would not, and traveled to the Delta Lake to establish new farmlands there.*

*We Thauma took control of our fate, and through our guidance led the common folk who had survived back to civilization. And slowly and painfully the Magi Kingdom rose from the ashes of the old world.*

**Prince Nestor Tam, The History of the Magi Kingdom**

Nalah felt as if she were staring directly into the sun. She wanted to raise her hand and shield her eyes from the blinding golden light, but for a moment after she stepped through the mirror, it felt like she didn't *have* hands—or any physical body at all. She felt herself hanging, suspended in an in-between place, wonderstruck and trembling with fear.

Then she fell forward, and her very real body struck a solid stone floor, face-first. She groaned, and then quickly rolled out of the way as Marcus tumbled after her, landing just where she'd been.

Nalah sat up slowly, blinking. She was in a dim room, surrounded by soft, flickering light.

"Ugh," Marcus groaned. "I shouldn't have eaten those kebabs right before we left. I think I'm going to be sick."

"Not on me, you're not," Nalah said, shifting away from him. She got to her feet and scanned her surroundings. "Where are we?"

They were in a cavernous chamber lit only by burning candles in iron candelabra. A Transcendent Mirror stood behind her, glimmering in the shifting light. The incantation must have made a passageway between her mirror and this one. All around her there were shelves, many, *many* shelves, most of them filled with books. The stone floor and walls were covered in beautifully woven rugs and tapestries. A large desk, covered in papers, sat under a window.

Various objects stood on pedestals around the room—probably Thauma artifacts. It felt like Zachary Tam's study, except . . . different. There was something strange about it that Nalah couldn't quite put her finger on. It was old-fashioned, somehow, like a room stuck in time.

"Looks like a library," Marcus said, still clutching his stomach.

Nalah nodded. It was so quiet, she hardly dared to speak and disturb the still air. In New Hadar, even in the small hours of the morning, you couldn't escape the constant hum of motorcars and ships and people.

Not here.

She closed her eyes and listened. There was nothing but the buzzing of insects outside, and a soft rattling sound like someone clattering pots together a long way away.

She looked out the window at the cloudless black sky filled with stars. She tried to make out what lay below, but a courtyard wall blocked her view. *Why does this place feel so familiar, and yet so different?* she wondered.

Then something screeched, so loud and so close that Nalah whirled around, thinking it must be right behind her. But there was nothing there. She and Marcus were alone in the library.

The screech sounded again, a sound like glass edges vibrating against each other, and Nalah felt a strange prickling against her leg. She looked down.

Something inside her pocket was wriggling and twitching

underneath the fabric of her tunic. Nalah yelped and just barely resisted the urge to tear the tunic off. "What is it?" she said. "Get it out!"

Marcus shook his head vigoriously. "Nope! I'm good right here, thanks!"

"Coward," Nalah muttered, and tried to get hold of herself. Whatever the thing was, it was getting bigger by the second—she had to get it out before it ripped her tunic to shreds. She had terrible visions of a gigantic spider or rat that had somehow found its way into her clothing. With trembling fingers, Nalah reached down and gingerly pulled open the large pocket.

Something blue emerged and soared into the air, wings flapping. It flashed like a great jewel in the candlelight as it circled the room and came to rest on top of a bookcase.

Nalah gaped up at it, not believing what she was seeing. It was a bird. A living bird had flown out of her pocket. But this bird had no ordinary feathers. Its feathers glittered and shone as the bird moved, and Nalah realized it was because they were made of glass. Blue glass. The bird looked down at her, its head cocked in curiosity, and made a chirping noise like a wind chime blowing in a breeze. It preened its feathers, nuzzling its sharp beak into the slash of white at its breast.

*That white slash* . . . Suddenly it all made sense. Sort of.

"Marcus," she said slowly, not taking her eyes off the bird, "it's my glass falcon. It's come to life."

"But . . . but that's powerful Thauma magic," Marcus whispered. "I've never heard of anything like it outside of history books and fairy tales. How did you do it, Nalah?"

Nalah thought about the lucky turquoise and moonstone she'd used in making the falcon. Those small magics were nowhere near powerful enough to accomplish something like this. She remembered that strange moment when the bird had seemed to glow. But that was nothing, wasn't it? Anyway, the bird hadn't come to life until they got here.

"I don't know," Nalah finally replied, and took a tentative step toward the bird. The falcon ruffled its feathers once more, looked around as if it'd heard something that disturbed it, and then dropped from the bookcase and swooped right toward Nalah.

Nalah flinched, but the bird just landed lightly on her shoulder, its glass talons hooking into her tunic. It was heavy and warm, like a real animal. It chirped again and nuzzled her cheek with its hooked blue beak.

"What *is* this place?" Marcus asked, looking around as if he half expected more objects to come to life.

Nalah began pacing the room. "You know how when you look at things in the mirror," she said thoughtfully, "they always look a little bit different than they do in real life? This place . . . it's like that. There's something about it that reminds me of New Hadar. Everything feels the same, but different somehow."

"You're right," Marcus replied. "It almost feels like we

didn't go anywhere at all. It's weird." He paused, his eyes scanning the spines of the books. "A mirror world, huh? It's almost like a tale from one of those old storybooks we read when we were kids."

Gingerly, Nalah reached up a hand and ran her fingers over the smooth glass of the falcon's wing. The bird head-butted her palm like an affectionate cat and made an urgent cheeping sound.

She looked into its glass eye, and for a moment she saw herself reflected in a field of swirling dark blue. But then her face faded, and she saw something else, a different image reflected back from the bird's eye. A dark, stone room with iron bars; the crumpled shape of her father sitting on the floor, his clothes filthy, his face smeared with dirt.

"Papa!" she said. Then the bird blinked, and the image was gone. "Marcus," she exclaimed. "I saw where Papa is. The bird showed me! He's in some kind of dungeon. He looks terrible, but he's alive!"

The bird chirruped again and bobbed its head, almost as if it were saying, *Yes, that's right!* "Do you . . . do you understand what I'm saying?" she asked it.

The bird bobbed its head again and puffed out its chest feathers. As it did, the white stripe across its chest glinted in the candlelight. "Papa fixed you," Nalah whispered, touching the stripe. "Is it possible you have some kind of connection to him?" Another chirrup, another bob. She suddenly wanted to pull the bird close to her chest and hug it tight, as if she could send some of her love through it to her father.

"Well, I can't just keep calling you 'bird,' can I?" she said, "You need a name." She paused for a minute, thinking of the special blue glass she'd used to create the falcon in her father's workshop. "Cobalt," she said. "Do you like it?"

The falcon seemed to consider this. Then he closed his eyes and rubbed his beak against Nalah's cheek.

Nalah laughed, feeling slightly hysterical. Her heart was beating fast, and her fingers were tingling—but there was something different about the sensation now. At home, it felt like storm winds battering the shore, ready to sweep everything away. Here, it was more like the roar of the furnace fire, still potentially deadly, but steadier.

*Whatever was happening to me back home, it seems like it's happening faster here.* She looked at Cobalt—once so cold and still, now warm and alive. *Maybe what happened to him is happening to me too.*

She blinked and refocused on Marcus. *No time to think about that now.*

"We've got to find Papa's cell, quickly, and then get back to the mirror," she said. "We won't have long before Tam discovers we found a way through. I don't want to find out why he wants me here." She started toward the door, Cobalt still perched on her shoulder. But before she got there, she heard voices outside. Someone was coming.

"Too late," Marcus said.

She shrank back, putting her finger to her lips as she turned to Marcus. He nodded, pressing his lips together. They held their breath, listening as the people outside approached the door. Nalah let out a sigh of frustration as she realized that the people weren't moving on—they had stopped right outside the door. It didn't sound like they were coming in, but they weren't leaving, either.

Marcus poked her and whispered, "We should look around if we're stuck in here. See if we can work out anything about where we are."

Nalah hesitated, but couldn't think of a reason why they shouldn't. They would just have to keep their voices down. Slowly, trying to listen for footsteps moving away, she went over to one of the bookcases. Many of the book titles were about Thauma craft—history, practice, and theory. Other ones were simply titles she didn't recognize. There was *The Control of Water,* which was odd, and *Tales of the Outer Kingdom. . . .*

"Nalah," Marcus whispered. "Have a look at this."

Nalah spotted Marcus standing by one of the tapestries that hung on the wall between the bookcases. It was a picture of a city on fire. Under the beautiful, burning towers, soldiers wearing blue cloaks were fighting against ones clothed in red and black.

"That's strange," Nalah said. "This looks a lot like that engraving of the Thauma War in our history books at school."

"It does, doesn't it? The king's soldiers defending the city," Marcus agreed. "Buying the king time to get the weapon ready." He paused before continuing. "So, if the Thauma War happened here too, does that mean we're just in a different part of the country? But if that were true, why would Tam have needed a magical mirror to get here? It doesn't make sense!"

Nalah heard him, but she wasn't really listening. Her fingers itched to touch the tapestry, just like they had with the obsidian dagger, just like with the shard. It was calling out to her. She reached out, her fingers brushing the coarse threads, and—

*CRACK!* Nalah jumped as she heard something splinter. She felt hot air on her face, and smelled smoke. All around her was the sound of crackling flames. But there was no fire in the library.

*Another vision?* she thought. *But of what?*

But this was different from her experience with the dagger—she wasn't dropped into another place and time. Instead the tapestry in front of her was coming to life, as if every individual thread had a mind of its own. The threads flowed in and out of the stitches, colors bobbing and weaving, animating the scene. The flames licked around the roofs and windows of the buildings. Tiny people ran from the fires, clutching their children to their chests.

"What are you doing to it?" Marcus asked.

Nalah tore her gaze from the hypnotic movement of the

tapestry to frown over at Marcus. "What, you mean you can see it too?"

"And hear it." Marcus's eyes looked like they might fall out of his head. "How are you doing that?"

Nalah just shook her head. She could feel her blood flowing smooth and strong through her veins, into her fingertips. *How* am *I doing this?* she wondered.

As they watched, the scene in the tapestry suddenly changed, as if the frame of their view was zooming over the heads of the soldiers, up a tall sandstone tower, and in through a window to a dark room. A man in deep purple robes was standing alone in a stone chamber, raising a great glass orb over his head. The orb was filled with murky, swirling colors.

*"Forgive me,"* a voice whispered, and the figure dropped the orb. It fell to the floor and cracked open like an egg, falling into two jagged pieces.

A strange pulse seemed to shake the whole room. Marcus doubled over, and a purple-covered book on the shelf beside him fell to the floor. A roaring sound filled Nalah's ears as the colored whorls escaped the orb and filled the scene with their dancing colors. The sound was like fabric being ripped in two, but so loud and unsettling that she stepped away from the tapestry to throw her hands over her ears.

As soon as she wasn't touching the fabric, the noise stopped. When she looked up, the tapestry was back to normal, a still picture of a battle scene.

Nalah backed away from the tapestry, massaging her fingers, which were threatening to cramp up. She felt suddenly dizzy and exhausted. *What was all that? Was that the king? But what was the orb he was holding?*

"Do you think tapestries just *do* that here?" she asked Marcus.

Marcus shrugged and touched the tapestry. Nothing happened.

"I don't get it," he said. "If this is a Thauma tapestry that works by touch, I should be able to use it as well. So, why did it work for you, but not me? I'm the fabricworker!"

Nalah hadn't thought of that. She couldn't even begin to answer the question.

She looked around for the book that had fallen when the orb broke, but it wasn't on the floor where it had landed. Instead it was right there on the shelf, as if nothing had happened.

*That's strange*, she thought. She reached out and picked it up, afraid and a little excited that it might flip itself open and begin to read itself aloud to her. It didn't.

"*A History of the Magi Kingdom*," she read. She opened the book and skimmed the contents page. "Huh, I've never heard of this one." It was strange, because she'd always begged her father to find more stories about the fairy-tale kingdom. He'd always told her that there weren't any more.

"Nalah, we don't have time for bedtime stories," Marcus said.

"No, no, wait a second," Nalah insisted. "There's something odd about this."

Marcus shrugged. "There's something odd about everything," he said. "What is it now?"

"Maybe it's nothing," Nalah said. "It's just that this doesn't have any of the stories I know. It hasn't got 'The Singing Butterfly' or 'The Princess Who Stole the Stars,' or the one about the lovers and the dragon."

She ran her finger down the contents page and read out some of the chapter titles.

"'Administration of the New Farmlands in the Delta Region.' 'The Digging of the Great Wells.' 'Family Trees of the Great Thauma Households.' It all just sounds so—"

She broke off, uncertain if she could finish her sentence without sounding crazy.

*Real.* It sounded . . . *real.*

Nalah looked around at the room again—the stone floor, the candles, the proudly displayed Thauma artifacts.

"Marcus, if magic is more powerful here, and they're writing about the Magi Kingdom like it's a real place," she said slowly, "maybe this isn't our world, after all. Maybe this is the Magi Kingdom."

"What? The Magi Kingdom is a fairy tale! It doesn't really *exist,*" Marcus said. But he didn't sound so sure.

Nalah shrugged. "A man's evil twin kidnapped my father, I walked through a magical mirror into a different place, and a bird I made came to life," she said. "I don't know about you, but I'm feeling like what does and doesn't exist is a bit flexible right now."

Marcus whistled through his teeth. "So the tapestry wasn't about the Thauma War, after all? It was just about some battle that happened in the Magi Kingdom?"

Nalah frowned at the picture in the tapestry. The scene did look *exactly* like the ones she had seen pictures of back at home. The old-fashioned soldiers' uniforms were the same, the buildings they were fighting around were the same kind as the ones that New Hadar had been built over. Those buildings had crumbled into ruins when the last king used the Great Weapon to end the war.

"Wait a minute," Nalah said, her heart in her mouth. She opened *The History of the Magi Kingdom* again and turned to the very first chapter. It was called "The End of the War." She scanned the page for a moment and then read aloud: "'The king went to the highest tower room and used the Great Weapon, despite the warnings of his advisers, and of the Prophet of the Sands. Accounts state that at once the king's enemies were felled where they stood—but there was no time for the royal forces to celebrate, as the first great quake ran through the kingdom almost instantly.'"

"But that sounds like *our* history," Marcus said. "I mean, mostly. So that man in the tapestry, with the swirly orb thing—that was the king setting off the Great Weapon?"

Nalah nodded, reading on. "It's strange, though," she said. "In our history, the Great Weapon was said to have rid the world of powerful Thauma magic, so that no one could ever start a war like that again. That's why, once the battle was over, the Hokmet took control and started weeding out the last of the Thauma users, restricting magic more and more as the years went by. We had that big quake that destroyed the old city when the weapon was set off, but that was all. It seems like here, it was totally different. Here the weapon caused a *year* of storms and earthquakes."

"A *year*?" Marcus asked in disbelief. "How did anyone survive?"

"It sounds like a lot of people didn't," Nalah continued. "Many died during that year. The kingdom was rebuilt only after it all was done—by the Thauma. Instead of being weakened like they were in New Hadar, the Thauma here got stronger. A lot stronger."

Marcus stared at her, and Nalah could almost see the gears in his head turning. "So this place and New Hadar shared the same history, the same Thauma War. But then, after the war—after the Great Weapon was used—everything was different for us than it was for them."

Nalah nodded. "That's what it seems like. But I still don't understand how they're related." She skimmed more pages in the book. "They've still got kings and queens here, just like in the stories. Thaumas rule the kingdom. That might explain the tapestry and Cobalt." From his bookshelf perch overhead, Cobalt gave another chirrup.

"But if no one had ever traveled between the kingdoms

before Tam, how did we get those stories in the first place?" Marcus wondered.

Nalah shrugged. "I got a vision of this world from the mirror—some other Thaumas from the past might have gotten inklings as well. Maybe their stories ended up as fairy tales only because the Hokmet wanted to cover up the truth about the war."

A thrill of excitement passed through Nalah. She'd always wondered what it would be like to live in the Magi Kingdom, and now here it was—a real place, with a real history, just on the other side of a mirror from her own world! How many of the stories were true?

If only her father were free to enjoy it.

So, who was Tam? If he had her father locked up in a dungeon, then was this a palace? Maybe the royal palace? He must be a powerful man here too, then, just like his twin was.

Her train of thought was cut off as she heard a clank of metal and whispered voices outside the room.

"Ready?" said a gruff voice outside the door.

"Yes, Captain."

It was too late to hide or run. The door to the library flew open and nine people strode inside, all of them wearing black leather breastplates, with black metal helmets on their heads. *Guards*, Nalah thought. They looked like something out of a storybook, too—each of them had a curved scimitar hanging from his or her belt.

Cobalt took flight and landed on a candelabra, setting it swinging. Nalah threw up her hands, her heart hammering. Were these people working for Tam? *We can't get captured already—we've only just got here,* she thought. *I have to rescue Papa!*

The guards formed a line in front of Nalah and Marcus. All of them were staring straight at her. Nalah risked a glance at Marcus, then back at the guards. No, she was right—they were staring at *her*, not him.

Some of their faces were partly obscured by their helmets, but the woman closest to her wasn't wearing one, and there was an odd look on her face, an expression of intense wonder and curiosity.

It reminded Nalah of the look Tam had given her when she'd first seen him in the market.

*I guess they were expecting me.*

Up on the candelabra, Cobalt gave an angry screech, and the guard looked up and raised an eyebrow at him. She didn't seem particularly surprised that there was a living glass bird loose in the palace—he seemed more of a minor annoyance. The guard collected herself and addressed Nalah with a half bow.

"Greetings, lady, and young sir," she said. "Do not be alarmed. We are here to welcome you to the Kingdom of the Magi. Please, come with me and all will be explained. And bring your . . . pet, too, of course," she added, glancing up at Cobalt again.

Nalah and Marcus looked at each other in amazement. *It's true! This really* is *the Magi Kingdom!*

This woman seemed to be in charge—she must be the captain Nalah had heard speaking gruffly outside. The captain stepped aside and gestured for Nalah and Marcus to walk in front of her, between the guards, toward the open door.

Nalah looked at Marcus and saw her own worries reflected on his face—they both doubted that these guards' intentions were good, but they didn't have much of a choice. Nalah lifted her arm and Cobalt fluttered down to land on it. He turned his head almost fully around to stare balefully at the guards as Nalah walked past them.

Nalah and Marcus walked out into a long, dim corridor lit with burning torches and lined with more tapestries. It was built from the same thick sandstone slabs as the library. The guards accompanied them closely.

Despite the guards marching beside her, still sneaking her stunned glances when they thought she wasn't looking, it gave Nalah a thrill to know all of this was real. Swords and chain mail, living glass, a huge palace made of stone . . . It was just like all those tales had said it would be. All the stories were about the rise of the Thauma lords, or about princes and princesses who made amazing things or went on quests to retrieve rare crafting materials, or about young crafters whose creations got them into trouble. If all this was possible, maybe the stories were too.

They led her up a dim, tightly curving staircase, and at the top, Nalah found herself in a long corridor lined with windows. Marcus stepped forward to gaze out of one, and a guard drew his sword.

"Get back in formation, boy," snapped the guard.

"Armsman Khadem!" snapped the captain. She cleared her throat. "Our guests are children—let them look out of the window if they wish." She smiled at Marcus and then at Nalah, in a way that made Nalah think of the jackals that sometimes came into New Hadar and ate the trash from the market.

"Sorry, Captain," said Khadem, stepping back and sheathing his sword.

Gingerly, Nalah went over to the window to join Marcus, hoping that here, unlike in the library, their view would be unobstructed. She looked down, and gasped.

They were peering out from a high window of a magnificent palace, cloaked in night. Nalah could see golden-domed towers and, below, the tiny shapes of guards patrolling the top of a thick courtyard wall, passing in and out of flickering torchlight. Beyond the wall, there was a slope dotted with palm trees, flower beds, and walkways, and beyond that, a city. But not like her dull, soot-colored city, with its buzzing electric lamps and clanking motorcars. The roads of this place were lit up with torches of blue Thauma fire, like a maze of colored light. She could see a wide square, festooned with jewel-toned tents and filled with people, surrounded by tall buildings, each one decorated with shining mosaics and elegant arched windows, and low-lying, square, sand-colored buildings farther out, where the torchlight ended. It was a kaleidoscope of color and light.

The tingling sensation in Nalah's fingertips returned, and she laid them against the cool sandstone, almost imagining she could feel it pulsating in time with her heart. A flicker of wonder and awe filled her as she looked at the beautiful city, but it was quickly doused when she remembered the armed guards at her back.

"We've got to get away," Marcus whispered to her. "Out of this palace. These people are taking us to Tam, I can feel it."

"I know," Nalah breathed, trying to look like she was still just staring down at the city. It hurt to even think about leaving here without her father, but she knew Marcus was right. "If they throw us in the same prison as Papa, it'll all be over. We'll have to come back for him."

"I've got a plan. We need a distraction, though," said Marcus.

Nalah looked up at Cobalt, who was sitting on her shoulder. The bird leaned in, as if listening intently. He gave a quiet chirp.

Then he turned and leaped off Nalah's shoulder, flapping wildly, and flew right at the guards. He circled their heads, pecking and screeching. The guards ducked and yelped. Several of them drew their swords.

"Stay calm!" the captain yelled. "For Thauma's sake, it's just a *bird*!"

But Cobalt kept on swooping, snatching one guard's helmet right off his head. For a moment, Nalah just watched the whole spectacle, her stomach clenched with anxiety for her new pet. What would happen if they hit Cobalt with a sword? Would he shatter?

Then someone threw a cloak over her head. Or, rather, it seemed like a cloak, but instead of blocking her vision, it simply turned the world gray, as if she were looking through a veil of smoke. Marcus stood beside her; the veil was over both their heads. He put a finger to his lips and grabbed her arm with his free hand, guiding her away. They slipped silently by the shouting captain and hurried down the hall. More than one of the guards seemed to look directly at them as they passed, but didn't acknowledge them at all. *We're invisible*, Nalah thought in wonder.

They were at the end of the corridor when she heard the captain scream, "Where are they? You idiots, you let them escape! Forget the bird and find them—the king wants the tawam alive!"

*Tawam?*

Nalah had never heard that word in the stories. *Is that me? Am I the tawam?* She held on tight to Marcus's hand and they silently sped through the palace, looking for a way out. They rushed past ornate stained glass windows that radiated their own light, down hallways tiled with mosaics that changed like kaleidoscopes, and tiptoed past servants carrying baskets of fresh food and watchful guards dressed in black.

They finally made it out into a large outdoor courtyard, bordered by high, pale walls—perhaps the same ones that had blocked her view from the library. At one end was a large metal gate. A cold breeze slithered up underneath the cloak, chilling her ankles and smelling of Thauma smoke and horses.

Marcus nudged her. "Look, a wagon," he whispered. "It's going out of the gate. We should jump on!"

Nalah hesitated. "But what about Cobalt?" She looked back up at the palace.

"We've got to go," said Marcus. "This may be our only chance to escape!"

Nalah knew he was right, but she still didn't move. She just couldn't bring herself to leave another piece of her father behind. "Just wait. Just one more minute—"

A flash of bright blue shot out of an open window overhead, glinting in the torchlight. The falcon circled once, squawking, and then soared away over the wall and out toward the city. Nalah exhaled in relief.

"Now can we go?" Marcus asked.

"Yes!" Nalah said. They ran awkwardly, trying to keep their bodies under the cloak, and fumbled their way onto the back of a donkey-drawn cart full of empty sacks smelling of cardamom. The old man driving the cart turned around at the noise. They huddled together, hardly daring to breathe. Seeing nothing, he grumbled and went back to guiding the donkey out through the castle gate.

Nalah felt like she could breathe easier as soon as they'd passed the gate and were on the winding road down toward the city. They hadn't even seen Tam, but she felt as if he were watching them, even through the transparent cloak, even as tall palm trees passed between them and the bright windows of the palace. Her stomach was tying itself into knots at the thought that they were going farther and farther away from her father—but it had to be for the best.

*I'll be back*, she swore, as she watched the palace recede and become a bright, ghostly shape against the dark sky. *I'll find you, Papa, I promise.*

She and Marcus carefully arranged themselves so they were sitting side by side, the soft, velvety fabric of the magic cloak caressing their faces.

"What *is* this thing?" Nalah whispered.

"It's a shadow cloak," said Marcus. "It was my grandmother's, and *her* grandmother's before her. *Serious* Thauma. Totally illegal, of course."

"Not here, it's not," Nalah said with a grin.

The night sky was dotted with stars, and a full moon lit up the path ahead. The cart carried them down a long road paved with flagstones and past a guard post with a sleepy-looking guard leaning on a spear. They passed grand houses with domed roofs and archways, guarded by winged stone lions made fierce by the night's shadows. Beautiful red-and-gold flags fluttered above them, even though there was no wind. They turned down a quiet side road between smaller, flat-topped buildings, and finally pulled into a stable.

Carefully, Nalah and Marcus slipped off the cart and made their way to a dark alley where it was safe to take off the cloak. Nalah was very glad to be out from under it, but a moment after she'd shaken it off she shivered. "It's cold! Much colder than it is back home. It's strange. In the stories, the Magi Kingdom's always hot." Nalah's teeth started to chatter. "Cobalt," she whispered up into the air, "are you there?"

A soft *cheep* came from behind her. Nalah turned to see the falcon perched on a gutter, his head cocked in that funny, questioning way. She held out her arm, and Cobalt flew down to her.

"We'd better find somewhere to hide out until morning," Marcus said, stuffing the shadow cloak into his bag. "Then we can really get a good look around the place!"

"We're here for one thing, and one thing only," Nalah said, as much to herself as to Marcus. "And that's to get my father back. We can't let ourselves be distracted by the things we see here. As soon as dawn breaks, we need to start working on a plan."

Marcus looked at her, and Nalah tried not to let him see

how scared she was. How terrified that she was going to fail at this, the one thing in her life that ever really mattered. Maybe he saw all that, anyway, but what he said was: "As soon as dawn breaks."

They walked to the end of the street and found themselves in a wide square. It seemed that a busy market had been going on, but now the square was quiet, the stalls covered over with cloth, the air perfumed with the smells of smoke, sugar, and wine.

"I wonder what time it is," Marcus said. "Must be late. It's completely deserted, like a ghost town."

In that empty, open space, Nalah suddenly felt very exposed. It wouldn't be long before the guards realized they'd escaped the palace grounds and started searching the city for them. She picked up a tattered length of dark cloth from one of the covered stalls and wrapped it around her hair and face like a headscarf. "We don't want to be recognized," she told Marcus. "I suggest you take one to cover your head too," she added, gesturing to his sand-colored mop of hair. "You do stand out a bit."

Marcus shrugged and rummaged through several pieces of cloth before he found one he liked. "Grandma says when she was a girl and her parents had just moved to New Hadar, there were so few foreigners that it was like being the only pigeon in a city of crows." He wrapped the cloth around his head several times, for a makeshift turban. "So, which way now?" he asked.

Nalah gestured toward a winding street ahead. "I say, for tonight, we put as much distance between us and the palace as we can. Those guards will be looking for us, so we need to lay low for a while."

Marcus agreed, and they kept walking. They kept to the narrower, darker streets, but even there, Nalah felt as though silent eyes watched her. The buildings became low and simple. Gardens were choked with thorny weeds here, and the ground was crunchy with sand.

They started to see people on the streets, sleeping or leaning in doorways. Nalah kept her eyes down as they turned to watch her pass, but she couldn't help sneaking a glance at them from under her veil.

There were poor people in New Hadar. Nalah knew this from personal experience. But even the homeless in her world weren't *starving*. In New Hadar, the poor would have asked Nalah for money. Tried to offer her a good-luck charm or a bouquet of desert flowers in exchange for some food or coins.

These people stayed silent. They stared at her from their dusty doorways, their eyes huge inside faces hollowed out by hunger. It seemed like they had simply given up on everything, even charity.

A bell rang loudly somewhere behind Nalah, and she jumped and turned around. Her heart skipped a beat. Two guards stood at the end of the road, one of them ringing a handbell.

"All right, off the streets, all of you!" the other one yelled.

Nalah and Marcus shrank into the closest unoccupied doorway.

"Cloak!" Nalah hissed. "Get the cloak out, quick!" As the guards advanced along the street, Marcus began rummaging in his bag.

"And don't you scraps give us any trouble tonight," the guard was saying. Nalah couldn't imagine any of these people even raising their voices, much less making trouble for a couple of strapping young guards.

"Psst! Hey, you!" said a young voice, right behind them. Nalah spun around. The door they'd been hiding in front of had opened a crack. Nalah could just make out the glint of an eye peeking through. "Wanna get off the street?"

"Yes!" Nalah said.

"It'll cost you . . . "

Nalah glanced over her shoulder. The guards were advancing, pushing and kicking the homeless out of the way. Marcus still hadn't found the cloak.

"Whatever it is, we'll pay it!" Nalah whispered desperately. The guards were getting closer.

"Well, okay, then." The door opened, and Nalah grabbed Marcus's arm and slipped quickly through into the darkness beyond. There was no candle or torch inside, but the roof was cracked, and a shaft of starlight cast a strange glow across their faces.

Nalah heard the door close behind them, and a young

boy stepped into view. He was short, and wore nothing but overlarge pants and a threadbare vest over his skinny frame. His head was shaved almost bare—Nalah guessed in order to keep the fleas at bay. But unlike the people she saw on the street, this boy had a lively, mischievous look in his eyes.

They stood there in silence, waiting for the guards to pass, the boy looking at them both with obvious curiosity. Finally the noise of the bell receded into the distance, and the boy spoke. "Name's Darry," he said. "You two looked like you *really* didn't want to run into any guards. Tough luck, they're everywhere. What're you doing out after curfew? Bit of side business in the Storm Quarter? Dangerous work. I haven't seen you around here before. Where are you from?" He frowned at Marcus and peered under his makeshift hood.

Nalah threw Marcus an anxious look. What were they supposed to say? *We came through a magic mirror after a man who killed his own reflection?*

Seeing their discomfort, Darry laughed. "Don't worry, I'm just being nosy. You don't have to tell me your secrets."

Nalah smiled at him, relieved. "It's complicated, but . . . let's just say we're a little lost, and we need somewhere to stay for the night."

"Well, if you've got enough money, there are nice places near the bazaar. Chances are, you don't want to be out here in the Storm Quarter."

Nalah shook her head. "No money."

"Ah. Well, you'll fit right in, then." Darry chuckled. "Come with me, I'll show you some of the drop houses."

"I'm sorry about lying to you about paying," Nalah said. "We don't have money, but we'll find a way to repay you for your kindness, I promise."

Darry looked at her, and in the dim silver light, Nalah thought she saw a slight blush cross his cheeks. He rubbed the stubble on his head and grinned. "I would have done the same thing, money or no money. Nah, I couldn't let them guards get you, could I? Us common folk have to look out for each other, now more than ever. Come on."

Nalah and Marcus followed him into the dark, maze-like passages of the house.

"*He likes you*," Marcus hissed, and made a kissy noise. Nalah glared at him and stamped on his foot.

"So, why is this called the Storm Quarter?" Nalah asked, to change the subject.

Darry looked back. "Have you seen the desert yet?"

"Desert?" Nalah repeated, wondering what that had to do with it. She vaguely remembered that some of the stories of the Magi Kingdom talked about its being a desert country.

"You're in luck. It's best at night. Come on, I'll show you!" And with that, Darry took a sudden turn through an archway and out into a barren, starlit courtyard. Nalah hesitated for a second. Then she saw something flash overhead—blue glass reflecting the starlight. Cobalt landed on the roof above her and cawed into the night.

As they walked, Nalah was aware of Cobalt following them at a safe distance, staying out of Darry's line of sight. It worried her that he didn't completely trust the boy, but she felt safer knowing that the bird was with them. While she had Cobalt, she had a link to her father.

She started to notice that the streets were no longer paved with flagstones, or even with packed earth. It was only sand here. On the windows, piled up in little heaps against the buildings, and filling decrepit flowerpots.

They entered a crumbled ruin, and Nalah stopped dead in her tracks at the sight that greeted her through the broken-down wall.

Rolling dunes, as far as the eye could see, glowing silver in the moonlight. They crested and dipped, like an ocean frozen in time. Nalah had stood before the ocean back in New Hadar hundreds of times, and this felt similar, but not the same. It was quieter without the sound of the waves.

"The Sand Sea," Darry said proudly. "It's amazing, isn't it? There used to be a real sea here, they say, before the war. It's quiet tonight, but on stormy days the wind whips up the sand and batters the houses in this area of the city. That's why it's called the Storm Quarter. People only live here because they don't have a choice."

"How many of you are there?" Marcus asked.

"Maybe a thousand or two? It's hard to keep track."

"That many?" Nalah asked, surprised.

Darry sighed. "Yes."

"But why?" Nalah asked. "With all the magic and wonders here—how can so many people be poor?"

Darry raised his eyebrows. "You're really not from around here, are you? In this kingdom, if you're not a Thauma lord, you're nothing. Some nonmagical folk manage to get by working in a noble house or for one of the Thauma artisans, or selling bits of stuff at the bazaar, but those who can't end up in the Storm Quarter. Everything here is based on magic, and the nobles control the magic. A commoner can hardly get a drink of water without the say-so of one of the Thaumas. Believe me, living rough in the Storm Quarter is getting off *lightly*."

Marcus and Nalah exchanged glances.

*This wasn't in the stories*, Nalah thought.

"Not to mention I could be *disappeared* for saying any of this," Darry added, with a bitter smile. "King Tam is a bit touchy about unsatisfied citizens speaking their minds."

"King Tam?" Nalah exchanged a dismayed glance with Marcus. *It's worse than I imagined—Tam doesn't have connections to the king, he* is *the king!*

"The one and only," Darry said. "His Majesty, King Asa Tam, our great and benevolent overlord." Sarcasm dripped from his voice.

*Asa and Zachary*, Nalah thought. *The same, and yet different. Just like this place.* She'd thought they were twins, but now that didn't seem quite right.

She turned to look back at the city, her mind awhirl with confused and anxious thoughts. From here she could see the palace, lights burning brightly, up on its hill.

The back of her neck prickled. *Why did this view look so familiar?*

She took a few steps backward, adjusting her perspective.

"What're you doing?" Marcus asked.

There was something about standing here, in this spot, with a breeze at her back and the city laid out in front of her, the huge house on a hill crowning it all—

"Oh my god," Nalah breathed. "It's New Hadar!"

"*What?*"

"Stand right here." Nalah took his arm and placed him right where she'd been. She glanced at Darry and then pointed over Marcus's shoulder and whispered so that Darry wouldn't hear them. "We're standing on the beach! The promenade runs along there, right? Look up at the palace, it's exactly where Zachary Tam's mansion is! Over there is Market Street—see how the line of buildings is the same?" She turned and stared out at the Sand Sea again, her heart thundering in her chest. "The Hadar Sea should be here, but it's . . . *gone.* All the water's gone, there aren't even any clouds. That's why it's so cold!"

Suddenly pieces of the puzzle began falling into place. How the Magi Kingdom and New Hadar could seem so similar and yet so different. "Darry," Nalah called out. "Can I ask you something?"

The boy turned to her.

"Can you tell me what happened after the Great Weapon was used during the war?"

Darry raised an eyebrow at the strange question. "Amateur historian, are you?" he asked.

"Please, it's important," Nalah urged him.

Darry shrugged. "Well, the weapon was made by a foolish king, who thought he could stop the war by ridding the world of all its Thauma magic," he said.

Nalah nodded. *That much, at least, was the same. But in New Hadar, the king was revered, not despised, for creating the weapon.*

"But the king didn't realize that in setting off the weapon," Darry continued, "he was literally splitting the world into two pieces, like the weapon itself." Nalah remembered the vision in the tapestry, of the Great Weapon cracking like an egg. "Each world exactly like the other in every way—except one. One world was left barren, cold, and empty of Thauma magic, and in the other"—Darry gestured toward the land all around him—"the Thauma magic intensified tenfold. The initial shock of all that magic caused the Year of Storms. But even with that, this world fared better than its twin."

Marcus blinked in shock at this revelation. "Why?" he asked. "What happened to the other world? The one without magic?"

Darry blew out his cheeks to make a whooshing sound and spread his hands wide. "Gone," he said. "Destroyed. A world cannot survive without magic. Like I said, we got the better end of the deal."

Nalah breathed deeply, letting it all sink in. "Thanks, Darry," she said. "That's very helpful. Will you give us a minute?" Darry nodded and went off to explore some of the ruins nearby.

"It's just as I thought," Nalah whispered to Marcus. "The Magi Kingdom and New Hadar were once the same place—until the Great Weapon split them apart. We lost most of our Thauma magic, they got more. We heard stories of this world, but thought it was a make-believe fairy-tale land, and they believed our world was destroyed. All this time, each world was ignorant of the other—until Tam was able to cross over to New Hadar with the Transcendent Mirror."

Marcus shook his head in wonder. "If it didn't make so much sense, I'd say you were crazy," he said. "But Tam must have known that New Hadar still existed. Because he used the mirror to get there. But why? Why come to New Hadar and kill this other Tam, and try to kidnap you?"

Nalah shrugged. "That, I still don't know."

"Hey!" Darry's voice rang out, and then came a cascade of muffled shouts. Nalah turned to see the boy being dragged through a dark doorway, into one of the ruined buildings at the edge of the desert.

"Darry!" she shouted, and dashed after him, her feet kicking up sand and Marcus's footsteps crunching after her. Had one of the guards been following them? It was their fault Darry was in this mess at all. She couldn't allow him to be punished for it.

Nalah threw herself through the doorway, only to run right into something hard that stank of grease and smoke. Strong hands grabbed her by the shoulders. In the dark, she heard Marcus and Darry yelp. Marcus cursed the person who'd grabbed him, but Darry shushed him.

"Heard you coming," said a gruff male voice from above Nalah's head. "What're you three kids doing out in the dark? Didn't your mummies and daddies tell you what happens to scrappers who are out after curfew?"

Nalah was dragged outside, onto the starlit street. The man who'd seized her was a guard, dressed in black and with a scimitar at his belt. Two more guards emerged from the building, holding Marcus and Darry by the scruff of their necks.

"What's this?" said one of the other guards. His hand had sneaked into Marcus's bag, and he was pulling out the shadow cloak. Darry saw it and his eyes went wide. "How did a guttersnipe foreigner like you get your hands on something like *this*?" the guard snarled, shaking the delicate fabric in front of Marcus's face.

"Hey!" Marcus snapped. "Be careful with it, would you? That's a family heirloom!"

Nalah's heart seized in her chest as she saw the guard's face turn purple with rage. These guards reminded her of Hokmet enforcers—cruel, vicious, easily provoked. Because Marcus's family was rich, he'd never had to worry about being picked on by an enforcer.

But they weren't in New Hadar anymore.

The guard threw Marcus to the ground like a rag doll. "How dare you speak to me that way, mongrel!" he growled. He tossed the cloak to the guard holding Darry and drew his sword. "I'll teach you to disrespect a king's guard. Hold out one of his hands!"

Marcus screamed, digging his heels into the sandy ground, trying to get away from the moonlit blade.

As Nalah watched, time seemed to slow.

*No!* something inside her said, righteous, defiant. *You will not hurt him.*

She wrenched her body around in her captor's hands, and when he held her tighter, she stamped down hard on his foot. He let out a yelp, and his grip loosened. Pulling free, Nalah threw herself at the guard who held Marcus's arm, and she grabbed for his sword. Her gloved fingers closed around the dull side of the blade.

"Stop!" she shouted, and there was a sound in her voice like that of a hammer striking an anvil. Her blood felt like lightning in her veins, and suddenly the sword bent under her hands like it was made of clay. She yelped in shock, but didn't let go of the blade. It folded almost in two and began to glow red, as if her fingers were as hot as a furnace.

The guard screamed—his hand smoking—and dropped the sword, which fell in a twisted heap onto the sand. He released Marcus, who scrambled to Nalah's side, panting. Nalah staggered back and stared at her hands, the sudden courage she'd felt rushing away in a wave of fear. What was happening?

"Impossible," whispered the third guard, backing away. "What kind of magic is this? Are they Thaumas?"

"Of course not. Look at them—they're street rats. Anyway, stop standing there gawping," the burned guard shouted back, gripping his ruined hand. "This could be some Wild Thauma trick—they're probably working with the rebels. Kill them!"

The third guard drew his sword and approached them warily. Nalah and Marcus began backing away, looking for an escape. "Whatever you did, can you do it again?" Marcus whispered.

Nalah swallowed hard. "I don't know," she said, trying to control her shaking voice. "I'm afraid to find out."

Luckily, she didn't have to. Just as the guard was closing in on them, a flash of blue came out of the sky like a streak of lightning. Nalah and Marcus ducked out of the way when the guard looked up in confusion, and Cobalt plunged down and sank his glass claws into the man's shoulder. The man yelled in pain and flailed at the bird, but Cobalt held fast. In his panic, the guard smacked his sword into his own ear, then dropped the sword with a string of wild curses.

Darry wriggled out of his captor's grip, snatched the shadow cloak out of his hands, and danced out of his reach.

"Come on!" he cried, and Nalah and Marcus took off after him down the street. The guards tried to follow them, but they were sluggish with pain and confusion. Darry darted in through a doorway and led them down a sandy flight of stairs, through two basements, and out across an overgrown garden. Nalah's thudding heart started to feel tight in her chest and she could hear Marcus's breath rasping in his throat, but they couldn't stop. Not until they knew they were safe. Finally Darry held up a hand and they all collapsed onto the ground, gasping for breath, listening for sounds of pursuit.

There were none.

"Okay, that's it," panted Darry. "I'm taking you to Ironside."

"Where's that?" Nalah asked.

"It's not a place. It's a person. He's the leader of the rebels."

"Rebels? Like the ones the guard mentioned?" Nalah said. She glanced at Marcus. This place was definitely turning out to be more complicated than it was in the stories. "Who are they?"

"They're people who want to make things better around here, for everybody," Darry said, with feeling. "That dumb guard was right about one thing—I'm one of them."

Nalah bit her lip, still uncertain.

Darry noticed. "It's okay, Ironside will help you," he said reassuringly. "After what I saw you do, he may be the only one who can."

"I don't know what happened." Nalah wrapped her arms around herself, suddenly cold again. "I've always had problems with breaking things that I touch, but only glass things." Then she remembered the embroidered flower blooming at her touch at the market. "Well, at least until recently. I don't know. It doesn't make any sense."

"But you've always been different," Marcus said. "I think you've got to face it, Nalah . . ."

He paused.

"What?" Nalah demanded.

"You're a *massive weirdo,*" Marcus said, his face a deadpan mask of concern. Nalah let out a slightly hysterical laugh and slapped him on the arm, and his mask cracked into a grin.

"You know I said you didn't have to tell me your secrets?" Darry said, crossing his arms. "I take it back. Where are you two really from, and what are you doing here?"

Nalah took a deep breath. "Are you sure you want to know?" she asked.

"Very sure," Darry answered.

*Ironside, leader of the rebels,* she thought. *That certainly sounds like someone who's opposed to King Tam. Maybe he can help us.*

Right now, he was her only hope.

"All right. My name is Nalah Bardak, and this is Marcus Cutter. You know that other world that everyone thought was destroyed after the war? The one with no magic? That's where we're from. We came here through a magic mirror to rescue my father from the king's dungeons."

Darry stared at her silently for a long moment with his mouth open. "You're right," he finally said. "I'm sorry I asked." He blew out his cheeks and waved them on. "Well, come on, then. You need to see Ironside right away. I have a feeling this is going to be a very, very long night."

# Chapter Ten

## Halan

*Many men and women of my class are happy to ignore the plight of the poor in our kingdom, and instead to fill their minds with trifles and petty rivalries. But I believe that to look the other way while violence exists is the same as committing the violence yourself.*

***Letter from David Ferro to his son Soren***

Halan strained against the ropes holding her to the chair. She didn't care that there was a group of rebels watching her every move. She didn't care that her wrists and ankles were tied hopelessly tight, or that her skin was starting to feel raw from pulling on her bonds. She didn't care that even if she somehow got free, she would have no idea how to get back to the palace because she'd been brought here with a sack over her head. None of that mattered. She had to *try*.

The room was dark and dusty, lit by a couple of weak candles in a sconce by the door. The flickering light illuminated the lean, hungry faces of the rebels as they watched her, as a group of mice might watch a cat inside a cage. The rebels whispered to each other in the dim light, making certain not to let her hear what they were saying. There were four of them, two girls and two boys. They all looked like they were under eighteen. Every rebel she'd gotten a good look at seemed surprisingly young, which didn't exactly mesh with the hardened, violent rebels of her imagination.

*Maybe it's all some strange game,* she thought. *Maybe they don't know what danger they're really in, keeping me here.*

Soren was in the next room, talking with one of the others. Then they parted, and the young lord entered the room where Halan was being held. "My apologies," he said, still irritatingly polite, "but I must leave you in the able hands of my friends here. I have some urgent business to attend to." And with a crisp bow, he was gone.

Halan slumped in her chair. She still couldn't believe it. *How can Soren Ferro be Ironside? I never see him talking politics or even showing off his family's Thauma weapons—he's always seemed more interested in flirting with girls than in the kingdom's economic problems.*

Her heart sank as she realized that was the whole point. He'd presented himself as a frivolous boy, avoiding the other nobles and doing nothing to draw attention to himself. That was how he got away with arming the rebels like this. Misdirection.

Halan tried to twist her elbows around, thinking if she could get just the right angle she could work her fingers free.

"Why are you still struggling?" jeered one of the rebels, a girl of about sixteen who wore her thick, dark hair in a severe braid.

The other rebels tried to pull the girl back. "We're not supposed to talk to her!" one of the boys hissed.

But the girl ignored him. "We could take away the ropes, you know," she continued. "It wouldn't make any difference. You couldn't get away from here even if we gave you a ten-minute head start. Take away your fancy clothes and your guards, Princess, and what are you? Nothing. No better than a common street rat."

Halan's cheeks turned red-hot. She was used to nobles whispering behind her back about her being powerless, but she'd never been insulted to her face before. Rage and indignation bubbled up inside her. "I'm your future queen, that's who I am! Not a thief and a murderer like you and your filthy little friends!" she snapped.

"Murderer?" said a boy, younger than she, who was sitting in the corner picking his teeth with a short knife. "Who've you murdered, Felis?"

The older girl—Felis—glared at him, and then stepped closer to Halan. "I'm no murderer. It's your father who's the murderer, *Your Highness*." She bowed to Halan, with a mocking flourish. "We steal food. We steal to keep warm. Because your father's given us no other choice."

"Yeah," said the other girl, adjusting her headscarf. "You think you know us, but you don't. We go out on the streets every day and stop nobles like you and your precious guards from oppressing the good people of this city."

*Like that boy thief* . . . , Halan thought, and she couldn't help wondering where he was now, what was happening to him. But she shook the thought off.

"I'm not oppressing anyone," Halan said. "And if some of the guards are acting too harshly, then kidnapping me is not the way to solve it! Let me go. Let me tell my father about your grievances, and he will root out the problem. I promise you!"

"My brother was taken," said the boy. He stood up, a dark look on his face. "He was taken away two months ago. Nobody's seen him since. Where is he, Princess, do you know? Because if he's in the dungeons, then your father knows about it, and if not . . ."

Halan flushed even more. It wasn't her fault that his brother was a criminal, was it? Why were they behaving as if it was? The girl in the headscarf put a supportive hand on the boy's shoulder, and Halan fought against the urge to say she was sorry.

*I didn't do anything to you!*

Halan looked at the other boy in the room, the only one who hadn't spoken. At a guess, she'd say he was only about eight years old. He was sitting against the wall, in front of a rack piled high with weapons. It was a lethal-looking mess—swords and axes with glowing blades were stacked up together, next to a bucket full of arrows and crossbow bolts. Glass jars were lined up against the wall, each one filled with swirling smoke that Halan guessed must make them some kind of bomb.

"If you're all so peaceful, why have you stolen those weapons?" she demanded.

"We have to protect ourselves," said Felis haughtily. "We wouldn't last long against your butchers otherwise."

"And they're not stolen," said the girl in the headscarf. "Ironside forged them. He makes them Wild, so anyone can pick them up and use them, even a non-Thauma. He's brilliant. *And* he's been inside the palace, gathering information right under your nose! With him on our side, we can't lose."

Halan doubted that. She doubted that any of the rebels except Soren had any idea just how well protected the palace was, how many soldiers protected the royal family.

But, Soren *had* been inside the palace, within striking distance of the king and queen. He had *danced* with Halan. Who knew how many more spies he had?

The skin on Halan's arms prickled.

*My mother was right. I was in danger this whole time.*

Her stomach twisted as she thought of Queen Rani up in the palace, probably sleeping peacefully. All this time she had been so concerned for Halan's safety, and now . . .

It wouldn't take very many guards stepping away from their posts in the middle of the night to let a whole host of rebels into or out of the palace. Halan knew this very well.

The rebels would be armed with Wild Thauma weapons. Halan pictured them rushing through the halls, cutting down nobles and servants alike. The guards would fight. The battle would be bloody on both sides.

If the rebels reached her mother and her father, would they execute them right then and there?

The door opened, and a boy of about ten stuck his head inside. "Felis, Masou—come and see what Ironside's got!"

"We're watching the prisoner, Baga." The headscarf girl rolled her eyes.

"No, but it's crazy," said Baga. "Darry got caught by a guard, but he was with this girl and she *melted a sword* just by *touching* it!"

*That's ridiculous,* Halan thought. *That's not how Thauma magic works.* She should know—she'd had to sit through years of Lord Helavi's lectures about it. She'd heard that one passage so many times, she remembered it verbatim: "*Thauma magic is created through the process of craft, using ingredients with magical properties, closely guarded techniques, and ancient incantations.*" No, she thought. *Thaumas can't just* touch *something and make it magical.*

"That's impossible!" said the youngest boy, echoing her thoughts. "No one has that kind of power. Darry's always telling stories."

"Well, there's a girl here, and a boy foreigner, and she's got a live bird made out of glass! Ironside's talking to her now. I'm going," Baga said, shrugging. "You can miss out if you like. I want to see if she can do anything else."

Halan doubted it.

"Well, *she's* probably not going anywhere, is she?" Felis said slowly, jabbing a thumb at Halan.

Halan tried not to look excited.

*Yes, go. Check out that amazing magical girl. You should all go. You said I could never get out of here alone, anyway. Why not?*

She tugged ineffectually on her ropes again, and it seemed to do the trick.

Felis smirked. "Sure, we can leave her here. Masou, you stay and watch her."

The small boy looked up from where he'd been drawing in the dirt and groaned. "Awww, why me?"

"Because I said so," said Felis, and the three older rebels left the room.

*Not ideal, but it'll do.* Even though she'd never been in a fight in her whole life, Halan was pretty sure she could overpower one skinny eight-year-old boy. She just had to get out of this chair.

*I'll show them. I'm not nothing. I'm not useless while I have my wits.*

"That was mean of them," she said. "I wish I could see

this girl. Melting swords, and a glass bird that flies around after her? It sounds amazing."

"Ugh," groaned Masou. "Don't remind me!"

"It's not fair. Felis should have let you go instead of her," Halan pressed. "It's not—" She stopped abruptly, making her eyes bulge. She started to choke, coughing and spluttering, shaking her head. She threw her weight to the side, and the chair tipped over. Halan flinched as she hit the ground, and lay there twitching, coughing as hard as she could.

"What's the matter?" the boy exclaimed. "Oh no! Princess? Don't die, hang on!" He ran around to the back of her chair and untied the rope. Halan's arm was set free, and she let it fall limp and twitching across her face.

Halan felt almost guilty for how easy it was. Little Masou clearly didn't share the same ruthlessness as the older rebels. As he was coming to untie her ankles, she brought her arm around in a wild swing, and her balled fist struck him hard in the side of the head. He reeled, and she reached up and grabbed his shirt, pulling him down to the floor so his head hit the stone with a horrifying *thunk*. He lay still.

"Oh god!" Halan gasped, feeling sick. She knew she had to escape, but she'd never hurt anyone before. Not intentionally. She quickly fumbled out of the rest of her ropes and then knelt at the boy's side. She pressed her fingers to his wrist and bent over his face, and then sat back, relieved. She didn't know anything about medicine or head injuries, but he was breathing, he had a pulse, and he wasn't bleeding. It would have to be good enough.

"I'm sorry," she whispered to the boy's still form. Then she staggered to her feet and out through the door.

She could hear faint voices, some distance away—she imagined it was the sound of a crowd of young people gathered around a magical metal-melting girl. She felt the tension in her chest loosen and she smiled a little, grateful to this girl, whoever she was, for the distraction.

There was a corridor that ran straight on, and one to the right. She took the right, guessing and hoping that it would lead away from the sounds.

She reached a flight of steps and scrambled up them. It was dark up here, but the air felt slightly fresher. She ran, keeping one hand on the wall and another out in front of her, uncertain what kind of a place she was in or what else the rebels might be keeping there.

Behind her, she heard a yell. "Ironside, it's Masou! And the princess, she's gone!"

"Find her!" Soren shouted, an edge of desperation in his voice. "Split up and search everywhere!"

Halan burst into high speed, turned a corner, and saw light up ahead. There was a flickering torch illuminating the crumbling plaster on the walls and the cracked tiles on the floor. She sprinted toward it and swung around another bend.

"Ow!" someone yelled, as she crashed right into them. It

was a girl. Halan felt herself slipping on the tiles and made a grab for anything to keep herself upright, but all her fingers found were the edges of the girl's headscarf. The two of them went down in a heap.

A loud, glassy squawk rang out from above them, and Halan, dazed, looked up and saw a blue bird made entirely of glass giving her an angry stare from a windowsill. *Maybe this is all a dream*, she thought numbly, her head still spinning.

"There she is!" yelled someone else. Halan peered down the hall, and her heart sank. That torchlight she'd seen was growing brighter because torches were being carried toward her by half a dozen rebels.

She tried to get to her feet, but then she looked at the face of the girl she'd run into, and she fell back against the wall in shock.

The girl was *her*.

# Chapter Eleven

## Nalah

*When you look into a mirror, who is that person you see looking back? They have your face, they wear your clothes. But are they truly you?*

*Your tawam is a reflection of your inner being. Some reflections are warped, others are true. They may seem very different, but always, in them, you will see some part of yourself.*

*From* Legends of the Magi

Of all the strange things to happen since Nalah had arrived in the Magi Kingdom, this was by far the strangest.

The girl staring back at her, eyes wide with shock that probably mimicked Nalah's own, could have been her twin. It was like looking in a mirror—a very flattering mirror. Like everything else in this world, this girl was similar, and yet *so* different. She and Nalah had the same eyes, the same large mouth and aquiline nose, the same thick, black hair. But this girl's hair shone in the dim light, as though it was given a thousand strokes a day with a horsehair brush. Her skin was smooth and unmarred by glassworking scars and blemishes.

Nalah had never thought of herself as beautiful. Never looked at her own reflection very much, really—she didn't have the time or the luxury for such things. But looking at this girl, Nalah began to wonder if she'd been looking hard enough at herself.

*This is the girl from my vision,* Nalah realized. *The one I saw in the Transcendent Mirror. She's wearing different clothes, but it's definitely her. Tam had a twin in this world; maybe she's mine.* She'd never even considered the possibility until now.

After a moment of stunned silence, the girl spoke, a torrent of questions spilling from her mouth. "Who are you?" she asked. "A relation of my mother's? Some distant cousin? How did you get here? Are you working for the rebels?"

Nalah took a deep breath. The girl's voice was *her* voice. It was so eerie, hearing the words but not being the one speaking them. "Not a cousin," Nalah answered carefully. "I think it's a little more complicated than that."

At that moment, the young man who the rebels called Ironside stepped between the two girls, looking warily back and forth between them. Darry had said that he was actually a young noble who'd been working for the rebellion undercover, supplying the rebels with inside information and weapons. Seeing Nalah without the headscarf for the first time, Ironside took in the unmistakable resemblance between her and this other girl, and his eyes widened. "Everyone go back to the hideout," he said to the rebels. "Bring the boy and these two . . . girls with you." He looked at Nalah meaningfully. "When we get there, I think that will be a good time for you to explain."

As they made their way through the passage, Nalah cast a glance back at Marcus, who was surrounded by young rebels. He looked as surprised as she by the appearance of her twin, but at her questioning look, he shrugged as if to say, *Go ahead. What have we got to lose?*

Nalah reached up to her shoulder where Cobalt was perched, silently taking in his new surroundings. She caressed his warm, smooth glass feathers and felt just a little bit calmer.

After a few minutes, they came to a small, shabby sitting room with a few moldy cushions and a cold fireplace. There, Nalah told them the truth. Not everything, not about Tam—but she told them how she and Marcus came through the mirror from another world. A world created when the Great Weapon was used. A world with almost no magic.

When she finished, everyone in the room fell silent. Nalah only had eyes for her twin, who had listened intently to her story. Nalah noticed that the rebels were still holding the girl's arms as one would a prisoner's, though they left Nalah alone. Looking at the ground, Nalah noticed a pile of loose ropes around a chair that had fallen on its side.

*Were those for her? What was going on here?*

"I've told you who I am," Nalah finally said to Ironside. "Now it's your turn to answer some questions. Who is she? Why are you holding her here against her will?"

Ironside smiled. "Of course you wouldn't know," he said. "This is Her Highness, Princess Halan. And we are holding her in order to demand the release of our people from the king's dungeons."

Just then, a tall boy with a scar down one side of his neck spoke up. "Ironside," he said, "I need to speak to you for a minute. I have an idea."

Ironside nodded and, followed by several other rebels, went into the next room. Marcus stayed to talk with the others, showing off his shadow cloak. With everyone otherwise occupied, Nalah turned to the princess.

"Are you all right?" she asked quietly. "Did they hurt you or anything?"

Halan shook her head. "No. You?"

"No. I'm not a prisoner. At least . . . I don't think I am," she added, her heart sinking.

"Hah. Well, I didn't start out as one, either. I'd keep an eye on Soren—er, Ironside—if I were you." Halan met Nalah's eyes. "I didn't believe it, when they said someone bent a sword with their bare hands," she breathed. "Did you actually do it?"

Nalah nodded. "Yes. Although I'm not sure how," she admitted.

"And this story about another world. It's really true?"

Halan looked her up and down, as if trying to understand how it could be possible.

Nalah nodded again. "Things are very different there, though," she added quickly. "I'm not a princess like you. I'm not anybody important at all. I mean, I'm a Thauma—a glassworker. But that's not considered a good thing, where I'm from."

The princess's expression changed. Her eyes widened and she suddenly looked slightly sad. "You . . . you're a Thauma, you have powers?"

"Well, yes," Nalah said. "I made Cobalt! Well, he was just a glass figurine when I made him—infused with a little bit of luck. But when I came through the mirror, he came to life." Hearing his name, Cobalt rubbed his head against Nalah's cheek and chirruped.

Halan looked at the glass falcon with wonder in her eyes. "Can I touch him?"

"Sure, if he doesn't mind."

Wondering how he would react, Nalah watched Cobalt carefully as Halan reached up to touch him. He was hers, and her father's. They were all linked. So, would he like Halan as much as he liked Nalah? And if he didn't, if he screeched or pecked at Halan, would that be a clue that Halan was a bad person?

But Cobalt preened happily as Halan's fingers stroked the smooth feathers at his neck. He leaned in to her touch and closed his eyes, trusting and blissful.

"He's so beautiful," said Halan, looking back at Nalah with a wistful expression. "I still don't understand, though. Even if you are from another world, why do you look just like me?"

Nalah thought about everything she'd heard, everything she'd learned, and one word stuck out in her mind.

*Tawam.*

She whispered it to herself, and the princess heard. "Did you say 'tawam'?" she asked, her eyes lighting up.

"Yes!" Nalah answered. "Why? Do you know what it means?"

Halan nodded. "I guess Lord Helavi's lessons aren't so useless, after all. There's an urban legend that says everyone has a twin who lives on the other side of mirrors—I've heard that if you look in a mirror too long, you might be replaced by your tawam. Or if you meet your tawam on the street, you should pretend not to have seen her in case she, well—kills you." She paused. "Those parts are probably just superstition, but the mirror thing makes sense, doesn't it?"

Nalah nodded agreement, though she couldn't help thinking of Tam and the knife he had plunged into Zachary's back. *Some of those stories are truer than you think.*

"Do you think everyone in this world has a tawam in mine?" Nalah asked.

Halan thought for a moment and then shook her head. "I doubt it. A lot of people died during the Year of Storms. So even if both worlds started out with the same people, not all of them survived in ours."

Nalah nodded. It made sense. Once the two histories diverged, people in the two worlds would have gone on to have totally different lives, different relationships, different children. "So I guess it must be pretty rare to have a tawam," she said.

"I guess so," Halan replied. The princess was studying her with interest, almost smiling. "It's like finding out you have a sister you never knew about," she said. "I bet you'd fit in all of my clothes."

Despite herself, Nalah smiled back. After her mother died, she'd spent many nights wishing she had a sibling to keep her company. Never once did she think that it would happen. And certainly not like this.

But she couldn't deny this feeling in her heart when she looked at the princess. It was like meeting someone for the first time, and after just a few minutes, knowing that they would always be a part of your life.

Their conversation was interrupted by Ironside, returning with the tall boy with the scar. "Change of plans, everyone," he said. "Princess Halan stays here, as backup. But now that we have our own princess—and a Thauma one at that—we can send *her* back to the palace in Halan's place. Except she'll be working for us."

"Hang on," Nalah said, holding up her hands. "I'm not *yours* and I'm no princess! I'm not interested in becoming part of your rebellion. All I want is to get my father back."

"I know that," said Ironside quickly. "But, Nalah, please—you have to understand, we rebels stand against the terror that King Tam has inflicted on his citizens. Many of our friends and families are being held in the palace dungeons, probably right alongside your father. We were going to hold Halan hostage and use her as a bargaining chip, to persuade the king to set them free. But now, you can help us instead. You can help us free them all!"

Nalah bit her lip. It sounded reasonable, and Ironside's face was very sincere. She could get into the palace dungeons and free her father—and wasn't that what she wanted, more than anything?

Still, she couldn't help but feel like she was being manipulated. This plan sounded very convenient for Ironside, but was it something she could do?

*I don't know half of what's going on here. I* can't *pretend to be a princess. Can I?*

The real princess interrupted her thoughts. "Nalah, don't listen to him," she said. "He's a liar! He hasn't tried to fix this the right way. I can get my father to listen, if they'd just—"

*Your father?*

A prickle of fear crawled across the back of Nalah's neck. She had been so caught up with talking to her twin, her tawam, she hadn't put two and two together.

*If she's the princess, her father is the king. King Tam, the man who kidnapped my father. The murderer.*

That realization was upsetting enough. But then another thought came to her. If she and the princess were tawams, wouldn't that mean their fathers were tawams too? After all, how could they have ended up looking exactly the same if they didn't have the same parents? But her father wasn't the king's tawam. . . . Zachary Tam was.

*Zachary Tam, who my father never liked. Who had been such close friends with my mother* . . . Nalah suddenly felt ill. But she was jolted off that disturbing train of thought as Halan threw herself forward. Nalah yelped and dived aside. What was she doing?

Then she realized that the princess was aiming for a gap between the rebels. They were caught off guard, and she might have made it—but at the last minute, a tall girl grabbed her shirt and swung her back around into the room.

"Not so fast, Princess!" the girl said. "We're not finished with you yet."

"Unhand me!" Halan yelled. "You don't know what you're doing! None of this needs to happen!"

Nalah couldn't help being impressed by the princess's determination. Even in a room full of armed rebels, she was just waiting for her moment to try to escape.

The boy with the scar shook his head. "I told you, Soren. You wouldn't listen. She's more trouble than she's worth. Now that we've got Nalah, what do we need the real princess for? She'll only make trouble if we let her live."

Suddenly there was a knife glinting in his hand.

Nalah felt an icy panic well up inside her, as visceral and intense as if the boy were pointing the knife at *her*. Without thinking about it, she leaped in front of Halan and heard her own voice shouting: "If you kill her you'll have to kill me too. Then you won't have *any* princesses!"

Halan glanced at her in shock.

Nalah was a little surprised herself, but then she realized that there was no other way. The princess might be the daughter of a villain, but that didn't mean she was a villain too. She would never have let them kill *her*. The bond Nalah felt with Halan was unlike any she'd felt before.

"Seyed, put that away," said Ironside evenly. "We don't murder people, remember? We're better than that. The princess will stay here, safe and sound. If everything goes well, perhaps we'll let her go home. If not, we'll think of something else to do with her."

Seyed snorted with derision. Nalah stood in front of her tawam, giving the boy what she hoped was a believable version of Halan's imperious stare. *The princess is in my protection now. No one hurts her while I'm around.* She wasn't about to help any organization that murdered defenseless girls, either. She could find her own way to get her father out of prison.

Finally Seyed put the knife away, and Nalah let herself exhale and step aside.

"You don't have to do this for them," Halan told her.

"You said your father was imprisoned in the palace. If I could just talk to my father, the king—"

Marcus sidled up to Nalah. "If her father is the king," he whispered, "then he must be—"

"Yes, Marcus, I know!" Nalah hissed.

There was that prickle of unease again—it was impossible. How could they be tawams of each other, but have different fathers? Perhaps Halan was secretly adopted? Nalah wanted to ask the princess for details, but she still wasn't sure if she could trust her completely.

"Nalah, when her father *kidnapped* yours, did you get the impression he could be persuaded to give him back, just like that?" Ironside asked smoothly.

Nalah swallowed hard. "Who told you it was the king who kidnapped my father?"

From the back of the room, Darry raised his hand. "You told me, remember? Why, was I supposed to keep that a secret?"

Nalah looked over at Halan, who was taking in this new information. "You think *my father* kidnapped yours?" she asked Nalah. She almost sounded hurt, as if Nalah's accusation had betrayed some kind of sacred trust. And, weirdly, Nalah almost felt bad. Almost.

"I'm sorry," Nalah told her, "but he did. That's why we came through the mirror. To get him back."

The princess shook her head. "I'm sure there's an explanation," she said. "For this—for everything. Don't you believe me?"

Nalah thought about all of her interactions with the king—Asa Tam. She shook her head. The princess was her *tawam*, and Nalah wanted to be loyal to her, but she knew she couldn't trust that man.

And she was here to save her father. Not to make friends.

"We can help you save him," said Ironside. "Get him out of the dungeon. Let you both escape to wherever you'd like to escape to."

Nalah thought longingly of their shabby little house in New Hadar. Had she really been in this world for only a few hours?

Soren stepped toward her, lifting her chin so that their eyes met. "But we desperately need your help in return."

"The prisoners we're trying to free," said the tall girl who was still holding Halan, "they're our parents and our brothers and sisters and our friends. We love them as much as you love your father. And their lives are at stake."

Halan suddenly stamped her foot, bringing Nalah's attention back to her. "They're all *lying* to you!" Halan snarled. "Don't you see? All of those people must have done something to get locked up. They're criminals!"

Nalah wanted to believe her—but she wasn't so sure. New Hadar and the Magi Kingdom were very different, but some things felt very much alike. How many people had been taken away for questioning by the Hokmet—and how many had never come back?

"Halan," Nalah said, gently touching her tawam on the arm. "I'm very sorry. But I came here with one goal: I've got to free my father. And Ironside's right—you don't know what these people did, any more than I do! If they are innocent, wouldn't you agree that they should be free?"

Halan looked confused. "If they really *were* innocent, of course I would agree—but I don't see any reason to believe that," she said. "In case you've forgotten, before you got here I was tied to a chair."

Nalah took a deep breath and turned to Ironside. He was looking at her with those sincere brown eyes again.

*Why would a teenage lord want to free a prisonful of hardened criminals, and why would he gather this gang of street urchins who are mostly even younger than he is?*

And just like that, her decision was made. Halan might still be right—Ironside might be a liar, and a traitor to the throne—but with King Tam in charge, Nalah would have to be a traitor too. She *had* to get her father out of there. Every moment that went by without him felt like an eternity.

"You must promise me that Halan won't be harmed," she said to Ironside. "And after we release the prisoners, you'll let her go. Those are my conditions for helping you."

She heard Halan let out a gasp of surprise, but couldn't look at her just yet.

Ironside hesitated, raising an elegant eyebrow at her, as if he was impressed that she would negotiate. But finally he nodded. "That's reasonable. Yes, I promise."

Nalah thrust out her hand. Ironside looked at it with a

curious smile, then shook it.

"Then it's a deal," Nalah said. She cast a look back at Halan. The princess looked quite disappointed, and a little worried, but when she caught Nalah's eye she gave a tiny, very wary nod.

"And when she's in there, if a guard gives her any trouble, she can just melt their swords!" said a young, excited voice. It was Darry. Nalah flushed. He'd just been getting to that when they'd discovered Halan had escaped. Ironside folded his arms.

"That's right," he said, "What *did* happen out on the street? Darry said something about turning a sword red-hot!"

"Well, that's what happened," said Nalah. "But I don't know *why* it happened. I've never even heard of anyone doing that in my world, and I've read all the Magi Kingdom stories hundreds of times, and no one in this world seemed to be able to do it, either."

"Nalah's always been different," said Marcus. Nalah glared at him, but he shrugged. "You have, though. Sure, you're like a bull in a china shop when it comes to Thauma, but clumsy or not—you've got power."

Nalah tried to pretend she wasn't blushing. "Thanks a lot, Marcus," she said. She turned back to Ironside. "Ever since I was little, I was always breaking things. My father made me wear gloves so I wouldn't accidentally lose control in public. Anytime I was scared or upset, or even really happy, things would shatter. But it used to be just glass! And then recently, it started happening with other things too. Metal, fabric . . . I don't know how to make it happen, it's like it has a mind of its own."

The rebels all stared at her.

*Have I said too much?* she wondered. She had never in her life spoken this openly about her power, about her *problem*. She imagined them all shrinking back from her, starting to look at her as if *she* was the more dangerous tawam. . . .

But they weren't shrinking back. They were staring; their eyes were full of wonder instead of fear.

"I told you," Darry whispered. "It was amazing. She bent the metal, just like that!"

"I can't believe it," said Ironside quietly. "It's like something out of a fairy tale."

Nalah laughed. "That's what I thought about your whole world!" she said. "Where I'm from, there are hardly any Thaumas left, and even the ones who are still around can't produce anything like the objects I've seen here. Magic is illegal in New Hadar; we feared for our lives every day. It's dangerous to be magical at all, let alone to have the power to shatter glass with just a touch."

Halan let out a sigh. "Try being *unmagical* in a world where everyone expects you to be magical," she said.

Nalah stared at her. "What do you mean?" she asked

Halan's expression turned stony. "I have no powers. The

royal line are all powerful Thaumas, every single one of them—except me."

Nalah flushed, feeling strangely guilty. Why would she get so much power, while her tawam got none? If anything, it would have made more sense for Halan—a royal princess in a magical world—to be the Thauma, not her.

"Well, that's going to be another problem with me pretending to be the princess," she pointed out to Ironside. "If I get scared or panicky and I . . . *do* something, they'll know I'm an imposter! They'll put me in prison with my father!"

Ironside stroked his chin. "I think I'd like to see this power of yours myself. If what you say is true, we'll need to figure out a way to help you control it. Who has something glass with them?"

There was a general rummaging as the rebels fished in their pockets, and finally, after some whispering and elbowing, one of the youngest reluctantly held out a little red marble. She was tiny, with deep brown skin and curly black hair that cascaded down to the small of her back. The yellow tunic she wore was so overlong that it brushed the sandy floor as she moved.

"Don't break it," she said as she handed it over to Nalah.

Nalah smiled at her. "I'll try not to." She held the marble in the palm of her hand and looked at it. Nothing happened.

"Well?" said Ironside.

"I don't know!" Nalah sputtered. "It's always happened

by accident. I've never tried to do it intentionally—I've spent my whole life trying *not* to do it!"

"What's usually going on when it happens?" he asked.

Nalah shrugged. "Usually it's when I'm really excited, or upset, I guess."

"I see," Ironside mused. And without another word, he walked over to Nalah and planted a kiss right on her cheek.

Nalah's entire head seemed to blush. Out of the corner of her eye she saw both Darry and Marcus—Marcus?—throw daggers at the young lord with their eyes.

"So?" Ironside asked rakishly. "Are you excited or upset?"

"Look at the marble!" one of the rebels shouted.

Nalah looked. The little red marble was melting into a pool of liquid glass in her hand, and then reforming, like soft taffy, into a long, wicked point.

Everyone looked at the thin red glass knife that had formed in her hand.

"Ah," Ironside quipped, "upset, I see."

The little girl rebel folded her arms. "You broke it," she whined.

"No, I didn't," Nalah said. She stared at the glass knife and concentrated. She willed herself to bring back that feeling—the strong pull from her belly, the quickening of her heart—and it *worked*. She could feel the blood flowing around her body, every vein and nerve pulsating. She raised the glass to her lips, thought for a moment, and whispered: "*Little glass world, light the way in darkness.*"

The words came to her out of her memory, as if someone had whispered them to her a long time ago and she was simply repeating them. She heard the glassy chime in her voice, and from the way the rebels looked at each other and drew back slightly, she knew they'd heard it too. The glass in her hand glowed and melted, rolling back into a perfectly smooth marble. She knew it should have been agonizingly hot, but just like with the sword, she didn't feel anything but a gentle warmth and the power in her fingers.

The marble turned hard and cool. Then it began to glow, not from heat, but with a shifting, dancing light that shone from her hand into the darkest corners of the room. She leaned down and handed the marble back to the little girl, who took it with glee.

"It's so pretty," she whispered. "Thank you."

"Here," said Darry, picking up a piece of old wood from the fireplace. "Try something with this!"

Nalah hesitated. "But wood's not my element," she said. "I wouldn't even know where to start."

"Metal isn't either, is it?" Ironside said. "Why not give it a try?"

Nalah began to protest, but then she held the wood in her hands, and was silent. She ran her fingers over the grain and she could feel the sap that had once flowed through it, the pulse of life. She thought hard about the wooden chests she'd seen being sold in the market, held the image of them in her mind: solid, square, polished things.

Nalah let her mind wander, and once again the words floated up from the depths of memory. "*Keep safe my treasures*," she whispered, and there was a sound like the creaking of ancient branches in it. She brought her hands together, and the wood folded as easily as paper, the edges slotting together to form a rough box about the size of her palm, with a lid that fitted perfectly.

"No," said a voice, choked with emotion.

Nalah turned to look at the princess.

She was standing, staring at Nalah. Her face was a mask of sorrow.

"What is it?" Nalah asked her.

Halan sniffed, and stared at her hands, seemingly not wanting to meet Nalah's eyes. "Because I had no skill as a Thauma, my parents sent me for lessons every day with a boring old lord in his dusty tower in the palace. Whenever I wanted to get away, there was one story, an old forgotten legend that I knew I could ask him about. 'The Legend of the Fifth Clan.' Most people don't know about it, but I found it when I was skimming through his library one day. It's about a mythical clan of Thaumas who could work with any material—glass, wood, fabric, or metal—just by touching it. Everyone has always thought it was just a story . . ." Halan smiled at her, but her eyes glistened with tears. "But now, here you are."

Nalah said nothing, her mind spinning with this news.

*I'm a Fifth Clan Thauma?*

Meanwhile, the rebels were abuzz with this new revelation.

"Try it with metal next! Make me a new helmet!"

"No, fabric. Get her to make something out of fabric!"

"Get her to do stone!"

"Don't be ridiculous, nobody can do stone!"

Nalah still wondered about one thing. "Why did you ask your teacher about that story?"

Halan chuckled. "Because he would always end up saying how amazing it would feel to have those powers, and I—Halan the Weak, Halan the Powerless—could pretend to be terribly hurt. He would apologize and flee, and I'd have the rest of the afternoon to myself."

"But you weren't pretending, were you?" Nalah murmured.

Halan stared at her.

Several of the rebels were offering up random objects from their pockets now—but Ironside rose and commanded them to be quiet.

"There's no time for this. Nalah, do you think you can control this power? It's a great gift, but as you said, if you lost control of it in the palace, all would be lost." His eyes bored into Nalah's.

Nalah bit her lip. *How can I know for sure? I've lost control so many times before, why not now?* She thought for a moment before the answer came. *Your father's life never depended on it before.* "I'll control it," Nalah finally said.

"And I'll keep my gloves on as much as I can, just to be safe."

"That's good." With a grim smile, Ironside squeezed her shoulder. "Because you should know—the king won't care if you're Fifth Clan. Magic makes our lives here possible, but in truth, it doesn't matter how good you are, only what family you're from, and how much trouble you make."

"Well . . . there's a bit of that in our world too," said Marcus quietly. Nalah nodded, thinking of the poor Thauma woman begging on the street, and the Hokmet enforcers patrolling the market looking for contraband. "I'll do my best, I truly will, but there's more to taking Halan's place than just not using magic," she pointed out. "How can I learn to be a princess so quickly?"

"Princess Halan," Ironside said, turning to Nalah's tawam, who gave him an angry stare. "This is your opportunity to prove to us that you're as innocent and well-meaning as you claim. I can promise your captivity will be much more pleasant if you do as I ask. Will you help her?"

"Fall in a furnace, Soren," Halan sneered. "I'll never help you deceive my father."

Ironside shook his head sadly. "I hope you won't regret that decision. Well, *we'll* help you, Nalah. I'll tell you as much as I can. And I'll be in the palace to watch over you—nobody there knows I'm a rebel, and they won't be surprised to see me with the princess, especially after our little dance at the feast." He waggled his eyebrows meaningfully at Halan.

"Humph!" said the princess.

*Is that it?* Nalah wondered. *That's the plan?*

She turned to look at Halan. The princess's lips pursed, but Nalah caught a flicker of worry crossing her face.

"Please, Halan," Nalah said. *I have to do this, but I won't make it without you.*

Halan seemed to be searching Nalah's face. Nalah felt the same strange pang of connection she'd felt before—as if an invisible thread tied her and Halan together. Still, she had no idea what her twin was thinking. She tried to look honest and good, but it was hard to do when her own eyes were staring right back at her, challengingly.

Halan sighed. "Fine. But I will only talk to Nalah. The rest of you get out. That includes you, Soren. And no more ropes."

Nalah let out a breath she wasn't aware she'd been holding. *One step closer to Papa.*

Ironside bowed. "As Your Highness desires," he said, with a hint of mockery.

When they were finally left alone, Nalah suddenly felt awkward. She studied Halan's face—it was her face, but without the little scars that Nalah had stopped seeing even when she looked in a mirror. Halan's skin was a tiny bit paler—she must almost never go outside, whereas Nalah spent hours each day at the market under the blazing sun.

*Aside from my Thauma powers, we're the same person,*

Nalah said to herself, *who led two different lives. I don't think I could ever be a bad person, no matter what happened to me. So she couldn't, either, right?* It made her wonder about Zachary Tam. She'd remembered him being a nice man when she was a child. Her mother had seemed to think so too. But somewhere in his heart, was there the potential for the same kind of evil that was in his tawam, the king?

Papa had never liked him. Maybe he was right all along.

"Well, I'm going to sit down," said Halan, and she sank down onto the pile of cushions. She scraped her hair back from her face. "I don't suppose you have a ribbon or something?"

"Um—no," said Nalah. Then she remembered that her own hair was braided, and was tied with a bit of string from the workshop.

She sat down in front of Halan, pulled her hair free, and handed the string over. "Here. I won't need it anymore. I need to look like you."

"Thanks." Halan braided her hair and tied it up with Nalah's string, while Nalah combed her fingers through hers and tried to get some of the tangles out. "Nalah," Halan said, in a businesslike, regal sort of voice, "I need you to know that I don't believe the king would go to your world and kidnap your father without a *very* good reason. This may all be just a misunderstanding. It's like all of Soren's talk of injustice and oppression—I know my father, and I don't believe that he could do something like that."

Nalah looked at her twin, feeling a tug at her heart. Part of her wanted to shake the princess. To tell her what she saw Asa Tam do with her own eyes. But she knew that alienating Halan would be a mistake, and besides, Halan must love the king very much to believe in him so strongly.

Probably as much as Nalah loved her father.

She tried to imagine what she would do if someone accused *her* father of doing something terrible. *Well* . . . , a tiny voice in the back of her mind needled, *if he really* is *your father.*

Nalah shook her head, trying to dismiss the thought. *You have to focus!* She needed Halan on her side right now. So she changed the subject. "So, what's it like being a princess?"

"Boring," said Halan. She looked around at the dusty old room. "On a normal day, anyway."

"It can't be *that* boring," said Nalah. "Didn't Ironside say something about a feast and dancing?"

"Even those things can be boring," Halan said. "I know that must sound spoiled, but it's how I've always felt. Everyone tells me what to wear and how to behave and who to talk to and even where to sit. I have no freedom. No life of my own. Though now that I've been in the city and seen how some people here live . . ." She looked down at the floor, fingering the fine fabric of her tunic. "I never really appreciated how *beautiful* everything is at the palace," she continued. "Every room is full of Thauma artifacts and colors and sunlight. There's always something delicious to eat, and something cool to drink, and everybody there—"

She broke off, sounding slightly choked, and Nalah felt her chest tighten in sympathy. Whatever their differences, Nalah knew what it was like to be taken far from home and shown an entirely new world. It changed everything you thought you knew about the old one.

"Everybody there wants the best for me," said Halan, shaking off her emotion. "And they think they know better than I do! They want to keep me safe because I don't have any powers. The problem is, they all think that protecting means keeping me locked away where nothing can ever happen to me at all! There are people watching my every move, all day—I had to trick my way out of the palace tonight. I guess it didn't do me much good, but I felt like I *had* to do it, because they were never going to let me leave the tiny world they'd made for me. Every day it's exactly the same. I get up, and Lilah, my handmaiden, dresses me. I take breakfast with my mother in the Sun Garden most days. We don't talk."

"Your mother?" Nalah whispered. She suddenly felt like she couldn't breathe. *Your mother is alive! Is she my mother's tawam?*

"Queen Rani," said Halan, and Nalah's stomach turned over at the sound of the name. *Rani and Rina—reflections of the same name.* That couldn't be a coincidence. Now that she thought about it, the names Nalah and Halan were reflections of each other too. *What a strange world this is.*

"Sometimes I don't think she likes me much," said Halan casually, as if it wasn't a desperately sad thing to say. "Don't expect any hugs, I'll put it that way."

Nalah swallowed, stunned by this. "That's terrible. My mother died," she whispered. "Her name was Rina. She was killed in a fire in my father's workshop, making something to cure an illness I had."

Halan paled. "Oh," she said. "I'm so sorry."

They sat together in silence for a moment. Nalah guessed that Halan was wondering the same thing as she: Which was worse, to have a living, breathing mother who didn't love you? Or to have lost a mother who did?

*Dead is worse*, Nalah thought, a painful flicker of jealousy in her heart.

"What do you do then?" she asked. "After breakfast?"

Halan seemed to pull herself together. "Lessons, with Lord Helavi. History, geography, Thauma theory. *Very* boring. Although today was the first time it really came in handy! After that, it depends on the day. Sometimes I sit in with the noble fabric Thaumas and sew things, and everyone pretends that my sewing is great, even though it doesn't do anything magical."

"That must be hard," Nalah said.

"It's fine," snapped Halan. "I'm not—" She sighed. "Sorry. I know you meant well. It's just . . . sometimes it's like people think I'm stupid, or they treat me like a baby bird that's fallen out of its nest, just because I can't do magic. It's infuriating."

Nalah nodded, although she couldn't really understand. In her world, not being a Thauma would have made her life much simpler. "It's funny, you know," she said. "I *am* a Thauma, and my father is always trying to protect me from it. Maybe we were just born in the wrong worlds." She chuckled.

Halan gave a quiet laugh too. But Nalah couldn't help feeling that despite the beauty and plenty of the palace, she herself—with her doting father and the memory of her loving mother—was still the luckier of the two.

"Sometimes I sit in my room and read," Halan went on. "Sometimes I go for walks in the gardens with my mother, or the noble ladies who are supposed to be keeping an eye on me, and we *don't talk* some more. I get changed for dinner, I eat dinner, I go to bed. That's my whole life."

"That actually does sound quite dull," Nalah conceded.

"The good news for you is, they really don't expect you to *do* much. You're more like a piece of the furniture that everyone's afraid of breaking. Just try not to look surprised by things, and you'll probably be fine. Anyway, what about you?" Halan asked. "I know I'm not pretending to be you, but I want to know. What's your life like in the other world? Is it exciting?"

*Sometimes it can be a bit scary,* Nalah thought. *Is that the same as exciting?*

"I don't know, not really. Before all of this stuff with the mirror, I used to get up and have breakfast with Papa—porridge, usually." She made a face, and then she realized that Halan was making the same face.

"Yuck. I hate porridge."

"Me too!" Nalah grinned. "But we can afford it, so I don't tell him how much I hate it. Then I'd usually take the little glass trinkets that Papa made and go to sell them in the market."

"You *worked* in a bazaar? That must have been amazing!"

"It was hot, and kind of smelly. People would come up to the stall and look at the things Papa spent hours making and say, 'This rabbit has a funny ear' or 'I don't like this shade of red,' and I just had to smile. Otherwise, they wouldn't buy anything, and we wouldn't have money for porridge, or sand to make more trinkets."

"That sounds awful. You should tell them to pay up or leave you alone."

Nalah couldn't help but smirk at that advice. *Spoken like a real princess!* "It's not really a good idea for Thaumas to speak their minds like that in New Hadar," she said.

"And what about your friend with the blond hair?"

Nalah chuckled to herself. "Marcus's stall is next to ours. His family sells fabric crafts. He's kind of annoying, but at least I have someone to talk to."

"So, do you spend all day in the market?" Halan asked.

"Well, because of my . . . problem, I promised Papa I would always go straight home from the market. But sometimes I walk the long way, along the beach. In New Hadar, the Sand Sea is a real ocean, with water!"

"*What?*" Halan exclaimed.

"It's true. People go swimming and sailing. Trading boats and passenger boats arrive at the harbor from other countries all the time. And then I go home and talk to Papa and have dinner."

"I like it when I can talk to my father, but he's so busy," Halan said, a pensive expression twisting her lips for a moment. "Please, Nalah . . . I know you think Soren's right and my father's a bad man, but I *beg* you to give him a chance to explain himself. Please, promise me you'll try."

Nalah looked at her tawam. She couldn't ignore the pleading look in her eyes. "I promise I'll give him a chance," she said.

She ran a finger in nervous circles over the rough stone by her knee. When Halan learned the truth about her father, whatever that truth might be . . . would she be able to handle it?

For now, Nalah realized, Halan's blind faith in her father meant that she couldn't completely put her trust in Halan, as much as she wanted to. The princess might defend her father, even if it meant betraying her twin. After all, wasn't that what Nalah herself was doing, right now?

*It's time,* Nalah told herself. *She needs to have all the information about our fathers, just as much as you do. She told you everything you must know. Now you need to tell her.*

"I need to tell you something," said Nalah. "About your father and mine." She clasped her hands in her lap, afraid of Halan's reaction.

"Yes?" said Halan warily.

"They aren't the same person."

"What do you mean?" Halan asked. "You mean yours isn't the king in your world?"

"No, he's not. My father is a man named Amir Bardak. He's a glassworker. And he's not King Asa's tawam. Your father came into our world, and he . . . *killed* his tawam."

Halan's expression went cold. "You're mistaken. Why would he do that?"

"I'm not sure, but I saw it," Nalah said. Then she remembered—it was a vision. She was certain it happened, but she wasn't actually *there.*

"And if your father and my father aren't tawams . . . ," said Halan. Nalah bit her lip. She could see the conclusion dawning on Halan's face. "*We* shouldn't be. But we're identical. We're the same person! Shouldn't that mean we have the same parents?"

"Yes," Nalah whispered. "So one of us must be wrong about who her real father is."

"Well, it must be you," said Halan without hesitation. Nalah flinched. Her tawam sucked in a breath. "Oh . . . I'm sorry, I didn't mean— Well, but it must be. I don't know any Amir Bardak. And I'm a princess—if my father wasn't really my father, people would know it! Like, my mother, for a start. What about you? Did you know my father's tawam? Before . . . whatever happened?"

Nalah's heart had started to beat high and loud in her ears.

"I knew him. When I was younger." She didn't want to go on, she didn't like where this thought was leading. She felt sweat on the back of her neck, her body trying to panic, telling her to run—even though there was no running from the truth. She owed it to Halan to be honest, and to herself. "He used to visit a lot. Before my mother died. He and my mother were good friends. And my father hated him. . . ."

She didn't want to look up at Halan's face. She knew precisely the expression she'd find, because it was the same expression she would be wearing if their places were swapped. Pity, and *I told you so.*

*Could it be true? Could Zachary Tam have been my real father?*

*What if it was true? He was never around, except for a few visits. After Mama died, he stopped coming to see me. And either way, Amir Bardak is the man who's looked after me and loved me all these years.*

*I just wish I knew for sure.*

"I don't care," Nalah said aloud, tossing her loose hair back over her shoulder and suppressing the tears that prickled at the corners of her eyes. "I don't care if our true father is Bardak or Tam. Amir Bardak is my *papa*—he raised me and I love him and I'll stop at nothing to save him!"

"I feel that way about *my* papa," said Halan quietly. "Please try to remember that when you meet him. What you're doing could be dangerous—and not just for you."

Nalah nodded. "I understand that. And I won't let any harm come to him until we know the full story."

"Be careful," Halan said darkly, leaning forward on her knees. "Soren is a liar. Who knows what his true motives are?"

Nalah nodded, though she couldn't help thinking the same about King Tam. And it made her feel as if the thread tying her and Halan together was in danger of snapping.

"Yes," Nalah replied, trying to keep her face impassive while her mind spun with fear and worry. "Who knows?"

# Chapter Twelve

## Halan

*Legend has it that the Fifth Clan has had a major role in our kingdom's history from the earliest days. Though not kings or queens themselves, the Fifth Clan were there: from the Wise Ones who traveled with our first tribal kings on their nomadic journeys, to the Queen's Sword who drove back the invaders when war came to our shores for the first time. It has been said that they rarely seek out power for themselves, but fight and craft with undying loyalty for those they love.*

*From "The Legend of the Fifth Clan,"*
*in* Myths and Legends of the Magi

Halan awoke in darkness, a damp, moldy-smelling cushion under her head. Her heart sank in disappointment—she had hoped that her kidnapping by the rebels and her magical Thauma twin were all just part of a terrible dream.

But no, she was still here, in a room half underground. And it was all too real.

The last thing she remembered was that Nalah had left

her to speak to Soren. She must have fallen asleep on the floor sometime after that. A group of rebels had come in to watch her, but they were asleep too—three of them had brought in mats and blankets. The room was getting a little brighter now; she could begin to make out the windows, where a tiny sliver of pink dawn filtered through a crack in the wooden slats nailed across them.

Halan sighed in frustration. *If I had Nalah's powers, I could command the boards to fall off the windows*, she thought. *Or melt the nails out of the wall.*

She shook herself and sat up, rubbing her eyes. She wasn't going to think like that, not even now. She didn't *need* powers—she had her wits. She would find a way out of there.

She'd tried not to fall asleep, but it had been a very long night. After hours of walking, arguing, and being tied up, even the horrid cushions had seemed inviting. Still, it was foolish of her to let her guard down like that.

Halan shuddered, remembering Seyed's cool determination that she should be killed. He wasn't one of the rebels in the room, but who knew how many of them he had convinced while she was talking to Nalah?

*Nalah and Soren stopped him. But what will happen when they're gone?*

How long would it take for the rebels to decide that, with their leader gone, it was too much trouble to keep Halan alive?

Halan got to her feet carefully, holding her breath and watching her captors. They all seemed to be fast asleep. Halan slipped off her sandals and tiptoed to the door. It was slightly open—Halan bristled at the arrogance of it, as if they were so certain she couldn't escape they didn't even need to lock her in.

"*Incapacitate?* What does that mean?" she heard a voice say from down the hall, and Halan's skin crawled with the strangeness of it—it was her own voice, more or less. Nalah was speaking to Ironside. If Halan squinted, she could just make out a black, cloaked shape. They had swapped clothes—Nalah was dressed in Halan's escape outfit, and Halan was in Nalah's plain tunic.

"Just what it sounds like. Out of the way, where he can't interfere with our plans. You are a Fifth Clan Thauma, right?" Soren added. "I leave the methods up to you. You should be able to get to him easily—he'll never expect it from his beloved, powerless daughter. As soon as our friends are freed from the prison, you take Tam out. I will rouse the others, every rebel we have, and we'll take the palace."

Halan couldn't make out Nalah's expression from here, but her tawam didn't argue with him. She was silent.

Halan felt something break inside her. *My own tawam is working against me.*

That line of thinking hurt too much, though she wasn't sure why—she'd just met Nalah. But there was something comforting about the girl. *Because she's another side of me,*

Halan realized. *Whatever she does, it's almost like I'm doing it too.*

Pushing her hurt feelings away, Halan focused on Soren. *Liar, traitor, murderer! You think you're going to kill my father and steal my throne?*

*Well, not if I can help it.*

She was so angry and frightened she almost didn't hear Nalah say, "Soren, do you know why Tam would have kidnapped my father? Why he might want me? Do you think it has something to do with my being Halan's tawam?"

"I've no doubt he has his reasons. What they are, I can't say."

"It's just . . . Halan seemed so certain. She loves her father. She really seems to think that he's misunderstood." Nalah's voice sounded sad, almost pitying.

*I don't need your pity!* Halan thought angrily. *It's Ironside who you've misunderstood. He's using you as a weapon against my family. Can't you see that he's manipulating you?*

"You don't believe that, though, do you?" Soren said. "Ever since the Year of Storms, Tam's family and people like them have stopped at nothing to keep control over the kingdom. Asa Tam is no different. In fact, he's worse than the kings and queens before him ever were. I suspect he's up to something bigger than just squashing the people's rebellion. It's possible your world is somehow part of the plan. If we don't stop him for good . . ."

Halan waited for Nalah to protest, to say that she

wouldn't hurt anyone. To demand to know all the answers before she used her powers against the palace. But all she did was set her jaw, a look of steely determination on her face that Halan recognized. It was the face Halan saw in the mirror when she'd made up her mind.

"I won't let him hurt my family," Nalah said in a soft voice. Halan felt tears well up in her eyes.

*I thought you were my friend.* When she and Nalah were talking, Halan had thought they had more in common than just wearing the same face. She'd thought they shared the same fears, the same convictions about what was important.

She was wrong.

*I guess there's nothing she wouldn't do to save her father, even if it means killing mine.*

She took a step away from the door, looked around at the sleeping rebels, and wiped her eyes on the rough, grubby fabric of Nalah's tunic.

*Very well, then. I can't depend on anyone but myself. Everyone at the palace is in danger. I have to get out of here and warn them!*

She heard a chirruping sound close by, and looked through the crack in the door again.

Soren and Nalah were walking toward the boy named Marcus, who had appeared at the entrance to the stairs, with Cobalt the glass bird perched on one arm. He was with the young rebel, the one called Darry.

As Nalah came closer, Halan recoiled slightly. Her tawam looked just like her, in her black clothes and with her hair brushed out.

*Even my own mother won't know the difference,* Halan thought bitterly.

Still, she couldn't keep a lump from forming in her throat as she thought about Nalah's mother, Rina.

If Rina had been warm and loving to Nalah, what had happened to Queen Rani, to make her so cold to Halan?

A small voice, one that Halan worked very hard never to listen to, whispered an answer.

*Maybe it's me.*

Halan balled her fists and angrily swiped another tear from her eye. She wouldn't think like that, not now. All that was important was saving her family. Maybe if Halan did that, her mother would finally realize that her daughter was more than just something to protect. Maybe she would see her as someone to respect.

"I don't like it," Marcus was saying. "I should be coming with you." Halan swallowed the lump in her throat and refocused on their conversation.

"No," said Soren. "How would we explain you at the palace? Nalah needs to go alone. Darry, are you ready?"

"Yup," said the young rebel. "C'mon, Nalah. The princess has been missed, so there are guards everywhere. Let's go make sure one of them finds you!"

"Marcus," said Nalah, fiddling worriedly with the edge

of the black cloak. "Keep an eye on Halan? Make sure she stays safe."

"We'll keep our promise," Soren said smoothly. "No harm will come to her."

*And what are your promises worth, Soren Ferro?* Halan thought, her sadness sinking under a flood of fear and anger.

"*You* promised. Some of your friends don't seem so keen," said Nalah. "Marcus?"

"Yeah, of course," said Marcus, with a serious nod. "I won't let anything happen to her."

"All right. I'm ready," said Nalah, and she and Darry headed up the stairs.

Soren watched them go. Then he turned, and walked right toward Halan.

Panicking, Halan leaped across the room and threw herself down on the cushions, closing her eyes just as the door swung open and Soren walked in. She lay as still as she could, pretending to be asleep.

"Get up, Your Highness," said Soren. "I know you're awake."

Halan sat up as gracefully as she could and glared at him. Did he know that she'd been eavesdropping? "Are you really going to keep your promise, Lord Ferro?" she demanded. "Or now that my tawam's gone, are you going to kill me, after all?"

"I keep my promises," said Soren lightly. "But I'm afraid

Seyed is right that you could make trouble for us if you managed to escape. Which you've already managed to do once."

"Then what are you going to do to me?" Halan asked, getting to her feet and tilting her chin in what she hoped was a gesture of regal defiance.

"I have a plan," Soren said, with a slight smile. "Don't worry—it will only hurt a little."

He reached into a pocket in his robe and pulled out a piece of midnight-blue silk about as long as his hand, so fine it was almost transparent. It waved and undulated in the air as he unfurled it. The ends were sewn to a delicate silver chain.

Halan took a step back, not wanting to find out what kind of magic the silk contained. But Soren advanced with his hands held up, like an animal trainer approaching a caged tiger.

"What are you doing?" Marcus exclaimed, coming up from behind. Halan's gaze flickered from the silver chain to his face, and she found that it was full of genuine alarm. "I promised Nalah you wouldn't harm her!"

"Marcus, stay out of this," said Soren, not taking his gaze from Halan's face. "As I said, this won't injure her. It'll just make things simpler. Besides, it's no more than she deserves as a member of our esteemed royal family."

*Deserves? What do I deserve? To be tortured? To be mutilated?*

Halan felt a cold, icy fear like nothing she had felt before. She backed against the wall, her palms slick with sweat against the cold sandstone, her breath coming in ragged gasps. Soren closed in on her, the veil close enough to touch. She lashed out, batting his hands away, and tried to duck under his arm. But Soren was too fast. He caught her with one arm across her chest and held her still while he slipped the silver chain over her head. It rested behind her ears, and the midnight silk slowly settled over her face.

"What is this?" Halan snarled. "Get it off of me!"

Soren let her go, and Halan reached up to tear off the veil, but as soon as she dug her hands under her hair to push the chain off her head, it squeezed tight around her temples, her head filling with throbbing pain. Halan staggered, letting out a groan of agony, but she didn't stop tugging at the chain.

"Don't try to remove it," said Soren quietly. "It won't hurt if you leave it alone."

Reluctantly, Halan let go of the chain. The pain stopped, but her face felt strange, prickling and tingling all over. Her skin seeming to tighten and loosen, rippling over her skull.

"What—what have you done to me?" Halan cried, raising her fingers to her face. She was shocked to find she couldn't feel the fabric of the veil—it was as if it had cleaved completely to her face and melted into her skin. The midnight blue was a film across her vision for a moment longer, then everything turned back to its normal color.

Marcus, openmouthed and as white as a ghost, was staring at her. "What have you done?" he whispered, turning to Soren.

"It's called the Veil of Strangers," said Soren. "Nobody can remove it but me. Take a look," He went to the rack piled with weapons and brushed the dust off an old metal shield, holding it up so Halan could see herself.

But it wasn't herself she saw. The girl looking back at her had a face that was twisted and pitted with scars. Halan jerked away from the mirror in shock, and saw the girl do the same.

"Now, even if you did escape, your own father wouldn't recognize you," said Soren. "You can learn what it's like to be a victim of the Dust—to be looked on with pity and scorn."

Halan's eyes filled with tears and she tugged at the silver chain again, but only got another blast of searing pain at her temples.

"You said you wouldn't hurt her," Marcus admonished Soren, under his breath.

"I promised no ropes, and no killing," said Soren, putting down the shield. "I didn't say anything about pain."

He walked out of the room.

Halan sank down on the cushions and stared at her reflection in the shield.

*Does this really happen to innocent people?* she thought, running a hand along the pocked, uneven skin. *Does Father know?*

But then Halan dropped her hand. *I can't get distracted*

*by doubts, not now. What am I going to do? Father and Mother won't know me. I won't be able to get back into the palace. Even if I escape, how can a strange, scarred peasant ever get to the king?*

She clenched her fists, trying not to let panic overwhelm her, and then suddenly realized that Marcus was still there. He knelt down next to her, and she saw that his expression was full of the last emotion she would have expected: compassion.

"I'm sorry," he said. "I had no idea he'd do that. I'm sorry that they have to keep you here like this. If you're as much like Nalah on the inside as you are outside," he added, with a friendly smile, "you don't deserve any of this."

*I don't deserve any of this,* Halan repeated in her mind, though there was something hollow about the words. *I'm glad someone here believes that.* She stared at Marcus, who met her gaze evenly. He didn't seem disturbed by her horrible new face at all. He seemed as comfortable as if he was still looking at his best friend.

*Well,* she thought, a new plan forming in her mind. *Maybe this situation isn't hopeless, after all.*

# Chapter Thirteen

## Nalah

*Dearest,*

*I've been thinking about what you said at court last night. You are quite right, it is a disgrace. This is the Magi Kingdom, the land of the Thauma. We simply cannot have a queen with no powers! But what is to be done? Could the king be persuaded to adopt a more suitable heir?*

*—DB*

*My Lord,*

*I have burned your letter. Please never write such things again. The king prizes his daughter far above your life or mine and we all owe her our unwavering loyalty.*

*Let us continue our discussion of that other matter in person.*

*—RA*

*Letters between Lord Belah and Lady Alizadeh, copied and given to the palace by the messenger who delivered them*

Nalah stumbled down the still-empty street, illuminated by the early morning light. The sun was already beating down on her, and she felt too hot underneath Halan's thick black cloak. She saw the road up to the palace ahead of her, the guard post at the bottom surrounded by men wearing glinting helmets and carrying swords. In the daylight, the palace looked even more imposing. It seemed to rise forever into the clouds—a collection of sandstone buildings piled one on top of the other, punctuated by domed towers, its arched windows staring down like a hundred watchful eyes at the city below.

She'd rolled in the dust so that her clothes looked rumpled and dirty, and even gone as far as to tear the hem of her cloak. But she didn't have to fake feeling tired or scared. Her hands trembled all by themselves.

*Tam is up there.*

She was walking straight into her enemy's lair, and she still wasn't sure exactly what she was facing, or what she'd have to do to free the rebels and stop Tam. Everything in her was screaming to turn around and go back.

*You have to go on. Papa is up there too.*

So she forced herself to breathe evenly, and kept walking. Nalah found her resolve strengthening as she drew closer to the guard post. Soren might have his own agenda, but that didn't mean he was wrong. Nobody should live in the poverty that the poorest Magi subjects endured while the Thauma nobles lived in the lap of luxury. It reminded Nalah of the injustices in New Hadar, but sort of reversed.

And the Dust! The Hokmet enforcers were terrifying enough, without the threat that at any moment they could unleash a storm of burning-hot metal. This place was truly broken, and if Nalah could help the rebels take over and restore some peace, some balance, then maybe there was hope for her world someday as well.

*I'll do what I have to, to end the injustice and make sure Tam gets what he deserves,* she thought. *I just hope I can keep my promise to Halan and not have to hurt him.* The idea of betraying her tawam filled Nalah with dread.

A chime rang out above her, and Nalah looked up to see Cobalt swooping past, catching the morning sun on his feathers as he circled overhead. It steadied her to know he was up there. If anything happened to her father, Cobalt would make sure she knew about it. She took a deep breath.

*Well, here goes nothing.*

She stumbled forward, waving an arm. "Guards!" she yelled. "Help me!" She waited until she saw them look her way, then collapsed to the ground in a pretend faint.

She kept her eyes closed until the running footsteps reached her, then let herself groan and blink as someone strong scooped her up in his arms.

"Alert the king!" the guard shouted back to the others. "The princess has been found!"

✳✳✳

A little while later, Nalah sat on the couch in Halan's rooms, the warm breeze coming in through an open window, filling the huge space with the scents of jasmine and sun-baked stone. All together, the princess's bedroom, bathroom, and dressing area were nearly the same size as Nalah's entire house back in New Hadar. They were filled with exquisitely carved wooden furniture, soft silk upholstery, and the most impossibly large bed that Nalah could have ever imagined.

Halan had not been exaggerating the loveliness of her surroundings in the palace. The ceilings were vaulted and painted with a beautiful deep blue sky full of yellow stars. The floors were covered with rugs so deep that when she stood on them, Nalah lost sight of her toes. She ran her hand over the cushion beside her and suppressed a sigh. It was like sitting on a cloud. *I wouldn't want Halan's life,* she reminded herself. *Even the most wonderful cell is still a prison.*

While the guard was carrying her, she'd tearfully told him the story Soren gave her: that she'd been hit over the head and kidnapped, but escaped when a careless rebel was looking the other way.

The guard had escorted her straight to Halan's luxurious rooms, to be bathed and dressed by Lilah, the handmaiden. She'd stumbled through the polished, mirrored halls of the palace, led by the guard. People in plain cotton servants' clothes and others in elaborate, colorful robes had turned to watch her, and she had tried not to meet any of their eyes.

It had been a deeply strange experience, to have a girl help her off and on with even the simplest bits of clothing. She stayed silent the whole time, grateful that she'd worked being hit on the head into her story, so it wouldn't seem suspicious that she was a little dazed.

It was very unlikely to ever happen, but she wished she could go back to Halan's bath, sometime when she wasn't terrified of being exposed as an imposter. Her jittery nerves had meant she couldn't really enjoy the perfectly warm water, the lovely scented oils, or the soft towels.

Now she was wearing one of Halan's silver silk night-dresses, her feet tucked into a pair of white fur slippers, and the court doctor was looking her over. He had a bushy mustache and a bag full of little Thauma instruments—he pressed one to her throat, another to her heart. Nalah tried to breathe evenly and folded her hands in her lap.

*Don't panic. He can't tell you're not Halan. He can't tell you're a Thauma.*

"Your Highness, the king and queen," the servant announced.

Nalah didn't have time to be afraid. Tam strode through the door, dressed once more in elaborate robes and a golden turban like she'd seen in her vision. Despite his noble bearing, his shoulders were hunched with worry. Their eyes met, and Nalah did her best to smile at the man who had manipulated her, tried to kidnap her, and stolen her father away and locked him in a cold cell.

*He'll know I'm not her,* said a frightened voice in her head. *He's met us both, he'll know!*

But Tam didn't so much as blink. As soon as he locked eyes with Nalah, he exclaimed, "My daughter!" He dashed to her side and threw his arms around her. Nalah forced herself to hug him back and hold on tight.

Then, over his shoulder, she saw a woman enter the room.

It took every last ounce of self-control not to pull away from Tam and run into this stranger's arms.

Because the woman was her mother. And yet, she wasn't. The queen had Rina's pretty face, her long black hair and deep bronze skin. But of course she was older than Rina had been in the photograph that Nalah knew so well. The queen was dressed in a blue satin dress that dragged along the floor behind her. She didn't rush to Nalah's side. Instead she hovered in the doorway, her heavily kohl-ringed eyes watery and her fingers twisting nervously together.

Nalah's heart was filled with love, and fear.

King Tam pulled away from the embrace and held Nalah at arm's length. "My love, did they hurt you?"

"No, Father," Nalah said, her voice slightly choked. "That is—they thumped me on the head. But otherwise, I'm fine."

"Where did they take you?" Tam asked.

Nalah was prepared for this. "They blindfolded me, but I managed to get a glimpse of where I was. I think they have a secret hideout, in the old sewer tunnels underneath the woodcarving district."

This was an essential part of Soren's plan. The search for rebels in the sewers would be long, distracting, and fruitless.

Tam turned to the guard who stood at the door. "I want those tunnels searched," he snapped. "I want anyone you find there thrown in the dungeons. For questioning," he added, turning back to Nalah with a smile.

Nalah smiled back at him.

*I can see now. You really* do *love Halan. She's probably the only thing you love as much as your own power. You've never let her see your true colors.*

"You poor thing." Tam leaned in and kissed Nalah's forehead. Nalah forced herself not to recoil.

*Kidnapper. Murderer.*

Tam pulled away and looked at her, but the love in his eyes was gone. Instead, a cool, assessing look had come over his face. Nalah swallowed and tried to look pitiful. *Does he know? Does he suspect?* Maybe she'd stiffened too much when he'd hugged her. Maybe the thick makeup they'd applied to her face wasn't enough to disguise her tiny scars.

"I'll have some food sent up," he said. "You must be starving. You need a hearty breakfast—porridge and pomegranate, perhaps. What do you think?"

Relief flooded through Nalah and she pulled a face and tried to think how Halan would respond. "Oh, please, not porridge. I simply couldn't bear it."

Tam's intense gaze softened and he grinned. "Of course not. Anything but that." He cupped her cheek in his hand for a moment and then stood up. "I must go. But believe me, Halan, I'm going to hunt these rebels down and make them pay for doing this to you."

"Thank you, Father," said Nalah, still trying to channel Halan's intensity, her determination. Tam left the room.

"Doctor Shivar, Lilah, would you give us a moment?" said the queen. The doctor hurriedly packed away his things, and only a few seconds later Nalah was left alone with Halan's mother.

Nalah stared at her, strangely afraid that if she looked away the queen would vanish, but certain that if she didn't look away she would eventually burst into tears.

Was this what her mother might have looked like, if she'd lived?

Nalah longed to rush into her arms, but her memory of Halan's words stopped her. *Don't expect any hugs.* Could this woman really *dislike* her own daughter? Could she possibly be as villainous as her husband?

"How could you?" the queen said, her voice trembling. "How could you be so reckless? So *selfish*? I know that you left the palace of your own free will."

Nalah swallowed and tried not to move a muscle in her face. Was the queen really angry with Halan? Nalah had never seen anything like this expression on her own mother's face—it was wild, half fury and half panic.

*How would Halan respond?*

"I was *kidnapped*!" she retorted.

"You're still lying to me. You don't understand, Halan. You don't know—" Queen Rani stopped and pressed her lips together as if to stop the words from escaping. "If you had listened to me before the feast, none of this would have happened."

Nalah just stared at her. *But I was in danger*, she thought. *Doesn't it matter more that I'm here now? That I'm alive?* But this time she kept quiet. She suddenly understood the painful truth behind Halan's little jibes about not talking to her mother. *She's yelling at me for not listening—but she's not listening to me, either.*

Queen Rani looked like she was trying to compose herself, and failing. Her shoulders heaved in the satin dress, and she pressed her hand to her heart. "You just don't realize that your actions have consequences," she said. "I'm the one who has to deal with the consequences, Halan. You don't know how angry your father was. You don't know how close he came to . . . doing something *rash*. You're getting older, Halan. It's time you understood how dangerous your father can be to people who stand in his way."

Nalah's breath caught. *Does she know? About Tam? Is*

*she afraid of him too?*

The queen hesitated. She refocused on Nalah and took a deep breath.

"Never disobey me again, Halan, do you hear me?" she snapped. And with that she got up and left the room, slamming the door behind her.

Nalah sat very still in the wake of the queen's departure, her heart racing, her fists balled in her lap. She could feel her powers tingling inside of her like electricity, surging and waiting to get out. *Calm down*, she ordered herself. *Breathe.* If she didn't, she might twist the whole couch up into a ball of wood and fabric and nails, which would be pretty hard to explain.

After a few minutes, the tingling subsided, leaving behind a dull sense of sorrow.

*Not quite how I dreamed being reunited with Mama would go*, she thought, and although she'd been trying to make herself feel better, the thought seemed to trigger something within her. She let out a sob, and then another. Shock and exhaustion and frustration balled up in her chest and shook her like a rag doll.

"My lady?" said a voice. Nalah looked up in alarm and saw that Lilah, flanked by two other young women, was standing in the doorway.

"Go away," Nalah croaked, certain at least that Halan wouldn't want them watching her cry, either. "I'm tired, I need to sleep."

"Go," said Lilah softly, and the other servants went out at once.

Lilah paused in the doorway for a second, then came into the room. She arranged the bedclothes and added an extra pillow. "You'll be expected to attend the afternoon meal, my lady," Lilah said softly. "I'll come to collect you a few minutes before. Until then, rest." And with a small bow, she turned and left.

Nalah stumbled across the room to Halan's bed and let herself flop down among the silks and the soft blankets. She curled up around one of the huge, squashy pillows while the tears subsided.

They'd come on like a summer storm, and were gone just as quickly. She felt shaky as she sat up, but she rubbed her eyes and then looked down at her hands.

"I didn't break anything," she said to herself. "Maybe I really am learning to control it."

A chiming chirrup sounded from the windowsill, and Nalah looked up and grinned tearily at Cobalt. He fluttered across to her and rubbed his warm, smooth head against her hand.

"It's okay, boy. I'm fine." She tickled him under his chin. "Cobalt, can you still see Papa? Is he all right?"

Cobalt flapped up to her shoulder and leaned over so that she could look into his eye again.

This time, the darkness in the cell was a little less deep. The crumpled shape that was her father was moving fitfully. She could *feel* the chill and ache in his bones, the hunger in his belly. But he was alive.

"All right," she said, and she was back in Halan's room, surrounded by soft sheets and pillows. "We've got work to do, haven't we? The sooner we figure out how to reach the dungeons, the sooner we can save Papa and get out of this place."

She got up, passed a brush through her hair because she probably shouldn't put it up, and wrapped herself in a flowing golden robe, hoping that her princess's garb would protect her from too many questions about where she was about to go. Fatigue and hunger pulled at her like irons on her legs, begging her to return to the soft, welcoming bed. But instead she splashed a little cold water from the basin on her face and set her mind to the task at hand. *There's no time to be tired now.*

*Out into the corridor, around the corner, two doors down on the right.* Soren had made her repeat the instruction four times. Cobalt followed after her, flitting from sconce to sconce along the wall, turning as still as a statue at any sound of approach.

The room Soren had sent her to was dim, lit only by the sun filtering down from a single high window. It was cluttered with all sorts of random objects: dusty statues, rolled-up rugs and tapestries, ornate boxes, and broken furniture. She picked her way carefully through them, jumping as her presence set off a music box that began playing a tinny tune, and found the tapestry he'd been talking about. It was woven with a scene of tigers creeping through a nighttime forest. She pulled the tapestry aside, and just as Soren had said, a hidden passageway greeted her behind it.

The passage sloped steeply downward, and she followed it, holding Halan's golden dressing robe up so it didn't drag along the dusty floor. Soren had said that if she followed the passsage all the way to the end, it'd lead her right out of the palace and into the gardens. Very good to know—but not her goal right now. He had asked her to gather as much information as she could while she was in the palace, and said that this passageway was a good place for spying.

At regular intervals along the passage there were small recesses in the walls, easy to miss if you weren't looking out for them. Nalah wrapped her hand in the sleeve of the robe, and—with a muttered apology—used the sleeve to clear the cobwebs and dust out of the first recess so she could put her eye to the tiny pinprick of a hole at the back of it.

The room on the other side was a bedroom. A woman was sitting at a desk, writing a letter.

The next room Nalah peered into was a dark storeroom, empty apart from stacks of clean cloth in neatly color-coded rows. There were more bedrooms, and then a vaulted hall where a few nobles were whispering to each other.

Then she looked through a peephole and found herself

looking down into a room that was a bit like a workshop or a very grand study. A huge window spilled bright sunlight onto a wide space where four tables had been laid out with different materials—sand, metal ore, thread, and chopped logs. The floor was a kaleidoscope of different colored woods, inlaid in the shape of the sun.

"It is a miracle," said a voice. It was faintly familiar to Nalah, in a way that made her skin prickle, but she couldn't put her finger on who it sounded like. "I went back to my workshop last night, and— Your Majesty, it's a *miracle*."

"It's no miracle," came another voice.

*King Tam.*

Tam and three other people walked into Nalah's line of sight. She squinted to make out their faces, and then threw her hand over her mouth in surprise.

*I know these people. I know them all.*

The elderly woman who leaned on a twisted staff and wore elaborate wooden combs in her gray hair was Mrs. Kayyali, the wood Thauma who had vanished from the market on the day Nalah first saw Tam.

The other woman, dark-haired and wearing a deep purple robe draped with glass beads that jangled together as she moved, was Kiva Lang, the glassworker who'd vanished a week before that.

Nalah wasn't as sure of the third, a thin, bald man with small, dark eyes—but as she watched he went to the table of thread and ran his hands over the skeins. A name came to her then: *Malek*. The dead fabricworker Marcus had told her about, the one who'd had an "accident."

Presumably, these people were *Lady* Kayyali, *Lady* Lang, and *Lord* Malek. The tawams of the Thaumas Nalah had known back in New Hadar.

It was Lady Lang who had spoken. She went to the sand and ran her hands through it, shaking her head. "My powers have never been so strong, my lord. I have never felt so alive!"

"It is quite the marvel," said Lord Malek. He began to knot the threads together, chanting under his breath. Nalah saw the shape of a net begin to form between his hands. It started to glow and tremble, and then it seemed to vanish altogether. "The base material of a shadow cloak, in less than a minute," he said in awe, holding up the filmy net. "It would normally take half a day of weaving and incantations."

"If I'd known it was so easy to increase my powers," said Lady Kayyali, with a cold chuckle in her voice, "I would have done the deed decades ago."

"You speak as if you were the one who did it," the king muttered. "Believe me, it was not as 'easy' as you say."

"Of course, my lord," Lady Kayyali demurred. "I didn't mean to suggest otherwise."

Nalah leaned her forehead against the cool stone, trying to get her head around this. *Their tawams are dead. Mrs. Kayyali and Kiva Lang—they were killed, but not by the*

*Hokmet. They were killed by Asa Tam.*

*And because they're dead, these Thauma lords and ladies are more powerful? But why?*

"I know that you are all grateful for this gift," said Tam evenly, and Nalah could hear the implication in his voice: *You had better be grateful, or else.*

The three Thauma nobles sank to their knees at once. It took Lady Kayyali a little longer to get down, but once she was there she bent deeply and touched her forehead to the floor at Tam's feet. They groveled before their king. Nalah wondered whether any of them resented having to do it. She couldn't tell.

"We are not worthy, Your Majesty. We will use these gifts to serve you."

"Even a legion of rebels couldn't threaten us now," said Lord Malek.

"Respectfully, my lord," said Lady Lang, sitting up and brushing back her hair, "your guards still haven't had any success finding their hideout in the sewers. And Ironside, whoever he is, still goes free."

"We won't need to find them," said Tam, brushing some dust from the sleeves of his robe. "They are coming to us."

Nalah pressed her lips together, afraid she might make a noise that would let them know she was listening. *He knows!*

"I am not sure when, but it will be soon. I believe they have my daughter's tawam. I had hoped to catch her right when she crossed through the mirror, but those bumbling guards let her slip through their fingers. Their mistake, however, turned out in our favor. Two of my night guards came back to me with news that she had fallen in with a young boy known to be connected to the rebellion. She is working with the rebels—I'm certain of it. And when she brings them here to rescue her poor idiot father, we will slaughter them all."

Nalah sucked in her breath. Tam got a lot of it right—except one thing. He didn't know that she was already here, in the palace, listening.

"I will hang their bodies from the palace walls," Tam said. "No commoners will dare to make such a nuisance of themselves after that."

Nalah felt sick. *He says it so casually!* As if the death of hundreds of his subjects were nothing more than a minor inconvenience.

Soren was right about Tam. Nalah's instincts were right too.

*But poor Halan!* Nalah's heart squeezed with fear for the princess.

She couldn't imagine finding out something like this about her own father. If Halan told her that she had been listening in on Mr. Bardak's conversations, that he'd killed people and was planning the deaths of hundreds more, would Nalah believe her?

There was a good chance she wouldn't. No matter the

evidence. She knew her father, just like Halan thought she knew hers.

Nalah sighed heavily. Halan believed in her father's innocence, because she was innocent herself. She couldn't imagine him doing anything so terrible.

*I'm afraid she's going to lose that innocence, and soon.*

She backed away from the recess in the wall and leaned on the other side of the passage. She couldn't let Halan's world crumble around her like this. What would happen to the thread tying them together if her tawam was destroyed?

"Cobalt, we can't leave," she whispered, thinking aloud. The blue bird tilted his head at her in surprise. "We have to rescue Papa and the rebels. But we can't leave until I know they're going to be all right. Halan, Ironside, all of them."

She looked down at her hands.

"Maybe I've been wrong about my powers all this time," she said. "Maybe they're a gift, not a curse. And I can't waste it."

Nalah hurried back to Halan's rooms, aware that she'd lingered longer than she meant to in the passage—and learned far more than she'd expected. If she wasn't back when Lilah came to fetch her, the servants would probably raise the alarm.

She was only back in Halan's rooms for a few minutes when there was a soft knock on the door.

"Halan, may I come in?" said a voice.

It wasn't Lilah, though. It was Queen Rani.

"Um, y-yes, of course," Nalah stuttered. Cobalt fluttered out through the open window, and Nalah sat down on the bed, awkwardly folding her hands in her lap, trying to look meek. Then she remembered that it wasn't very *Halan* to sit meekly and wait to be yelled at—but it was too late now. The queen had opened the door and come inside.

She looked at Nalah, and Nalah's heart gave a painful squeeze. The queen looked somehow, subtly, even *more* like Rina than she had earlier. Her hair was looser in its braids, and her dress was open at the throat.

"Halan, I . . ." She sighed. Her dark brows twitched with frustration and sadness. "I'm no good at this. I've made myself hard, over the years. I know that. Earlier, I was very tough on you."

Nalah felt tears prickling at the corners of her eyes again. She didn't dare speak. Did Rani often apologize? What would Halan say?

What did *she* want to say? All at once, Nalah realized that she might never have this chance again. Queen Rani wasn't her mother—*and yet* . . .

If she could tell her mother anything, what would it be?

"I love you, Mother," she said, her voice choked with emotion.

Queen Rani's lip trembled and tears sprang to her eyes. "Oh, Halan, I love you too. All I want, in this world, is to keep you safe. I know that I seem to overreact, but one day—very soon, perhaps—you will know that everything I do is just because I couldn't bear it if you were hurt."

"I understand," said Nalah, and she meant it. Halan thought that the king was a good man, who would never intentionally hurt anybody, but something told Nalah that the queen knew a lot more than she was letting on. Her words were familiar to Nalah. *Stay inside, be careful; wear your gloves for now, darling.* They were the same kind of words her father used, when he was afraid for Nalah's life in New Hadar.

Before she could stop herself, Nalah ran to Queen Rani and threw her arms around her waist. Rani froze for a moment, clearly not used to being hugged. But a second later she wound her arms around Nalah and held her tight. She kissed the top of her head and stroked her hair.

This woman was not her mother, and Nalah knew it. But at that moment, she didn't care. Something opened up inside her and she felt a warmth spreading throughout her body that she hadn't felt since she was a tiny child.

It felt safe.

"Oh, you're warm," the queen said, releasing her. "After everything you went through, you probably haven't had enough to eat or drink. Here." She reached over to the bedside table and emptied a small bottle of fruit juice into a glass. "Drink this."

Nalah took a few sips and set the glass back down.

"Why don't I tell you a story before we go down for the meal," Rani asked. "I haven't done that in years, have I?"

Nalah nodded against her chest. Queen Rani even smelled like her mother—like jasmine and sandalwood. "I'd like that."

Rani climbed onto the bed and Nalah curled up next to her, feeling the warmth of her through her beautiful satin dress.

"Once, in a faraway land, there was a princess who loved a handsome knight," she said. "She gave her heart to this knight, without reservation, without caution or care." Nalah's heart gave another little jolt of recognition. This was a story she'd heard before, but not for so many years. This was a story Rina also had loved.

"But not all the nobles in the land approved of their love," said Rani, stroking Nalah's hair as she spoke. "One night, as the princess was working at her forge, she heard a great roar and looked out of her window. It was her knight, riding a steed made of pure iron that would carry them away from the princess's castle as fast as a shooting star crossing the sky."

Nalah's mind began to drift as she listened to the story. She found herself staring at the empty bottle and the glass full of juice, and thinking about herself and Halan. There was the bottle, elegant and beautiful like Halan—but empty. And the glass, plain but full of juice. That was Nalah. Why couldn't they both be full and content? Why did it have to be this way?

*Because there's only so much juice.*

Suddenly, something occurred to Nalah. *What if there's only a finite amount of power between the two worlds?*

When the split happened, most of the magic must have spilled into the Magi Kingdom, leaving only a little bit left in New Hadar, in the Thauma families there—most notably with the people who had tawams here. But what happens to that power if one of the tawams is killed?

In a kind of trance, Nalah picked up the glass and the bottle, and poured the juice back into the bottle. Now it was beautiful, elegant, *and* full.

*That's why the king killed Zachary Tam. That's why he killed them all.*

"Halan," the queen said, pausing her story to look at Nalah questioningly. "What's wrong?"

Nalah blinked. "Nothing," she lied, an icy chill running up her spine. "I'm just not thirsty anymore."

# Chapter Fourteen

## Halan

*The Wild Thauma trade must end. The freedom that unsecured Thauma magic grants is far outweighed by the danger of allowing untrained peasants to pick up and use magic intended for the hands of their betters.*

*For the security of the realm and in the interest of peace, I instruct you to lead a phalanx of officers to the city and deal with this threat. Any craftsman or trader found dealing in these black market goods, or any citizen found in possession of them, is to be held in prison until further notice.*

***His Royal Highness Asa Tam, Great Shah of the Magi Kingdom, Protector of the Delta and the Sand Sea***

There were rebels everywhere she turned. Most of them were young, but that made no difference to Halan. Any one of them could be on Seyed's side, willing to murder her at the first hint that she would cause them trouble. The boy Marcus spoke with them easily; he seemed to get along well with anyone, no matter who they were. An ability that might be useful to her later.

Soren had left orders that Halan's world could be opened up a little, since he'd bound her into the Veil of Strangers. He seemed to think that without her identity—her *royalty*—Halan would be lost and would give up on any thought of escape.

He was spectacularly wrong, and the thought that he'd underestimated her gave Halan more courage.

She was allowed to go into the dingy kitchen to get her own water to drink. She had to pump it manually from the well, and it tasted like rust. She was even allowed to use the dank basement bathroom by herself. She'd searched it from top to bottom, even briefly considering whether she could capture the scorpion that she found hiding under the mop and release it somewhere later as a distraction. She filed the idea away as something to consider if she ran out of other options.

She wasn't allowed into the room with the pile of weapons, or up the stairs, so she found herself making a slow circuit of the basement, moving from room to room and trying to overhear snatches of plans from the rebels.

It wasn't getting her anywhere, until she heard a familiar glassy *cheep* coming from the kitchen. She followed the sound, and found Marcus sitting on the creaky old table with the glass falcon in his lap. He was eating a piece of bread and offering the crumbs to Cobalt, who was eyeing them suspiciously.

They weren't alone—two of the younger rebels were pumping water into flasks, and Seyed and another older boy were sitting in a corner playing a game that involved spinning a smooth rock between them and betting on where it would land. Seyed looked up at Halan with undisguised loathing, and Halan almost fled—but she forced herself to stand her ground. She had a plan. All she needed was a moment alone with Marcus Cutter.

She came into the room and approached Marcus and Cobalt.

"Does he eat food?" she asked.

Marcus looked up and saw her, and smiled. "Don't know. I'm not sure he knows, either," he added, looking down at the bird pecking at the crumbs. "It must be a shock, mustn't it? To suddenly be alive, when you weren't before?"

"Yeah, it must be," said Halan, sitting down on a chair beside the table. With a sad smile, she reached out and stroked Cobalt's smooth blue feathers. "I thought he went to the palace with Nalah."

"He did. He just brought a message tied to his leg. It was for Soren. I don't know what it said," Marcus added hurriedly, looking a little sheepish. "Sorry."

Halan raised an eyebrow. "Would you tell me if you did?"

"I . . ." Marcus trailed off, glancing back at Seyed and his friend. "It depends."

Halan nodded and stroked Cobalt some more. He seemed a lot more interested in the affection than in the bread, and Halan wondered if he could tell the difference between her and Nalah—one of them had so much power she'd brought him to life, and the other had none at all. But maybe that didn't matter to him.

The young rebels left with their water. Now it was only Seyed and the other boy, and their game of spinning rocks.

Cobalt's interest in her was good—she could use it. She ruffled his feathers, talking to him and Marcus about nothing very much, until finally there was a smack as Seyed's friend slapped his hands down on the floor.

"That's it. You win. I've got almost nothing left to bet."

"Aw, just one more?" Seyed asked. "Winner takes all!"

"Ha! I don't think so," scoffed the other boy. "You've gotten me that way before."

Halan held her breath. Would they stay and talk? Would they play some other game?

They both got up, Seyed casting her a final cold look as they left the kitchen.

Halan was alone with Marcus.

*Yes.*

She stared into her splintered reflection in Cobalt's feathers and let all of the rage and fear inside her come bubbling to the surface. She thought of the worst things she could: her father and mother hacked to pieces in the palace by children with Wild Thauma weapons, her whole world crashing down, Nalah caught and hanged as an imposter. Her eyes filled with tears. She bit her lip, trying to look as if she were suppressing them.

"Halan, are you all right?" Marcus asked. Just as she hoped he would.

"It's Seyed," she whispered in a ragged voice. "But it's not just him, it's *all* of them. I overheard them saying they're going to kill me. As soon as Soren leaves to check on Nalah."

Marcus sat up straight. "No! Soren wouldn't let that happen and neither will I."

She took a deep, shuddery breath and threw him a bleak smile. "That's brave of you, Marcus. But there are so many of them, and you don't know them like I do." Halan reached out and clasped Marcus's hand in hers. "Please, I'm begging you. Help me get out of here!"

Marcus frowned. "You know I can't do that—" he began.

"It might be the only way to save Nalah," she blurted.

"*Save* her?" Marcus's eyes widened, a flicker of fear passing over his face. "What do you mean?"

"There's something I didn't mention," Halan said, leaning in as if telling him a dangerous secret. "There are objects in the palace, Thauma doors and other things, that will only work for members of the royal family."

She had to be careful. She could lose his sympathy. Indeed, Marcus's expression darkened and he jumped up from his perch on the table.

"Why didn't you tell her that before you let her go off alone? She swore to protect you. Don't you care if she's safe too?"

"I don't want her to be hurt," Halan said. "I know it was wrong of me, but I . . . I thought that if she was caught, my father would keep looking for me and he might get here before the rebels decide I'm no use to them anymore. But the longer this deception goes on, the angrier Father will be when he realizes that his supposed daughter is actually an imposter! If I can get back in time and take her place, we can still save her."

She held her breath. Marcus turned away from her, shaking his head.

"If we do nothing," Halan prompted, "both she and I could be killed. You're my only hope, Marcus. And maybe Nalah's, too."

Cobalt scratched the table with one claw and gave a worried squawk. Marcus looked back at the bird, and his shoulders slumped.

"All right. We have to save Nalah, so I'll help you," he said. "But you have to help us get Nalah's father back."

"Of course," said Halan, giving him a watery smile. She decided that as soon as she found out what glass falcons really did eat, she would order Lilah to bring Cobalt a bathtub full of it.

She'd known that Nalah's best friend would be a powerful ally, but she hadn't realized just *how* powerful. Marcus

Cutter had a shadow cloak. Normally, such Thauma objects wouldn't work for Halan—unless they were Wild, of course—but since she was using the cloak with Marcus, it slid over both of them easily.

"I thought magic was forbidden in your world," she whispered as she felt the slippery fabric fall around her. It was such an amazing feeling, to be a part of a magical object like this! Halan wondered if Thaumas ever got used to being able to do such wonders. *I know I wouldn't.*

"It's an heirloom," Marcus whispered back defensively.

It was absurdly easy to slip out of the rebels' hideout under cover of the cloak. They stepped lightly, but even when a floorboard creaked under Marcus's feet and the little girl with the glowing marble heard it, the girl turned and stared right at them for a moment before shrugging and walking away. Soon they were at the crumbling back door of the house, walking out into a sun-drenched alleyway.

Marcus led them through it out into the street, and Halan suddenly recognized where they were. This was the Storm Quarter, a few blocks away from where the rebels had originally caught her. The ground was sandy and the houses were crumbling, returning to the desert piece by piece.

"I think we can uncloak now," she said.

"Right. It's not as if anyone but the rebels will recognize you." Marcus looked around to make sure they weren't being watched, then pulled off the shadow cloak and turned to stuff it into his bag.

*I'm so sorry about this, Marcus,* Halan thought.

Not allowing herself time to hesitate, Halan bent, scooped up a chunk of sandstone, and clunked him on the back of the head.

Too stunned to shout, Marcus slumped to the ground with a groan. Above them, a shriek like nails being dragged down a glass window made Halan cringe. She looked up just in time to see Cobalt wheel away on the hot breeze.

"I'm sorry!" she called after him. "I truly am," she told Marcus at her feet.

He groaned again, let out a string of curses, but couldn't get up.

"I *will* help Nalah," Halan said, backing away. "But I have to do this myself. My father *will* listen to me." And then she ran.

Before yesterday, Halan had never so much as slapped someone. Now, her knockout count was up to two. What was she turning into?

As she drew nearer the bazaar, she started to notice not being noticed. It hadn't been too strange at first, when the people she passed were the poor and homeless, but as the streets grew more and more crowded, and she started to pass homes and workshops run by nobility, the skin on the back of her neck began to prickle.

Some of these people *should* know her. But the Veil of Strangers had turned her into just another Dust-scarred peasant, and even those who did notice turned away quickly and pretended not to have seen her.

*At least it clears a path to the palace,* she thought determinedly. *If I can just get to Father . . .*

*Then what?* The unwelcome thought barged into her head, demanding to be heard. With this face, even getting into the palace would be difficult—being allowed to see the king would be virtually impossible. But she quieted those thoughts for now. *I have outsmarted some of the most brilliant minds in this kingdom,* she told herself. *I did it before, and I can do it again.*

The bazaar was crowded and noisy, and Halan shuddered to think of the time she'd spent exploring it with Soren at her side. She weaved and elbowed her way through the crowd, still attracting almost no attention apart from a few angry curses. "Out of the way, Duster!" a well-dressed noble snapped. Halan's cheeks turned hot with anger and humiliation, but she kept on running until she turned a corner and almost ran into Lady Lang and her retinue. They were browsing a sand merchant's wares.

Halan skidded to a halt, her heart pounding.

"Lady Lang!" she exclaimed. The glassworker was a good friend and adviser of her father's; surely *she* would help her.

Lady Lang looked at the princess and pulled a face as if she were watching a dog do its business in the street. "Get out of my sight, peasant," she spat. An angry-looking middle-aged servant moved between her and Halan, glaring fiercely. Lady Lang turned back to inspect the jars of crushed ruby and heliothyst. Halan didn't move.

"But, Kavi," Halan began. "Please listen to my voice, I'm—"

"Don't you *dare* address me by my first name! And don't spin me your sob stories, either," Lady Lang said. She dug inside her purse and produced a single copper coin—worth almost nothing—and threw it at Halan's feet. "There. Now, don't let me see your face around here again, or I'll have you thrown in the dungeons for a night to teach you a lesson in manners!"

Halan stumbled back, shocked. Lady Lang had been a friend of King Tam's for years, always cheerful and attentive to the princess.

Was this how she treated people outside the palace?

Leaving the copper coin on the ground where it lay, Halan hurried away, feeling the Veil of Strangers against her face even though she couldn't see it. She longed to tear at it, but she remembered the piercing headache and left it alone.

The servants' entrance to the palace was along a rough cart track at the base of the hill, hidden from the main gate. Halan was strangely glad of that—if she couldn't trust the nobles or the guards to treat a poor nobody with kindness, surely the servants would have a better attitude. She approached the servants' gate, and the bored-looking guard standing there gave her a hard look.

"Don't know you. Here to ask for work?"

Halan nodded, not daring to speak.

"Well, go on in and ask for Mistress Ruba—but I'll tell you now, she doesn't like Dusters in the palace. Makes Their Highnesses uncomfortable."

Halan swallowed. *That's why I never knew what the Dust was—all my life, its effects have been hidden from me.*

"Thanks," she said, grateful for the warning. She *knew* Mistress Ruba—she was the palace's head cook and mistress of servants, and despite her tough exterior, Halan knew, she had a soft heart. Perhaps she wouldn't like the scars, but she wasn't a noble like Lady Lang. She was definitely persuadable.

Halan hurried across the small courtyard and knocked on a big wooden door.

"What?" snapped a woman's voice, and the door was opened by a middle-aged woman Halan vaguely recognized as another of the cooks.

"I'm here to see Mistress Ruba about a job," Halan said.

"We don't want any Dusters," the woman sniffed. "What did you do to get those scars, eh? You're a criminal, I bet—and you think you're worthy to even breathe the same air as the royal family? Get out of here!"

"It wasn't Dust!" Halan said. It wasn't exactly a lie, after all—it *wasn't* Dust, it was just an illusion. "I know it looks like it, but I was burned in a kitchen accident. I was a serving girl in Lady Artaz's house. Now I can't get a job because no one will give me a chance. Please, I'll prove my worth in no time!"

"Is that a girl looking for a job?" came another voice from within the dim kitchen. It was Mistress Ruba, large and covered in flour, as she always was. Halan's heart leaped.

"Yes, mistress," said the cook. "But she looks like a Duster to me."

"Let her in, for goodness' sakes. Let me look at her," commanded Mistress Ruba. The other woman stood aside, a suspicious look on her face, and Halan took her first step back inside the palace.

Mistress Ruba was standing at a giant marble worktop, her arms folded as she supervised a small army of young boys and girls, who were pounding at a huge ball of dough. Puffs of flour and red and yellow spice burst from its surface like ash from bubbling lava.

She gave Halan a hard stare. "Well, she's not exactly up to our normal standards. Still, we're down two maidservants and it'll be my head if everything doesn't get done before dinner. Send her up to help with the floors. And give her a scarf to wear over that face. And you—are you listening to me, girl?"

"Yes, mistress," said Halan quickly.

"If I hear you've so much as looked at something you shouldn't, you'll be out on the street so fast, your head will spin. Understood?"

It wasn't quite the warm, kindly welcome Halan had hoped for, but she bowed low, anyway.

"Yes, mistress. Thank you so much, mistress." She took the dark headscarf that the other cook handed her and wrapped it across her face, over the veil, without complaint.

*If it gets me into the palace, closer to Father, I will do anything.*

She was given a mop and a bucket of water and instructed to take the back stairs up to the second floor. She struggled up the steps slowly—the mop was awkward and the bucket was heavy, and she didn't dare spill a drop. When she emerged into a corridor she actually recognized, she allowed herself to grin behind her headscarf. There was another servant here, an elderly man with a huge bushy mustache who was mopping as if his life depended on it. If she could give him the slip, then she'd be able to run to her father's study only one floor up.

"At last!" the old man complained. "Come on, girl, get mopping. I'm never going to finish this by myself."

Halan had never mopped anything in her life, and after five minutes she decided that when this was all over, not only would she never mop anything again, but she would give all the cleaning servants a large pay raise. After only a few minutes, her arms and back began to ache. She'd assumed mopping would be straightforward, but somehow it wasn't—either she was using too much water or not enough, and if she wasn't missing bits she was going too slowly. The old man had already covered four times as much area as she had, in half the time. "Ach," he scolded her. "Why did they send me a snail for a maid? You're no help at all!"

A door opened along the hall, and a serving girl stepped out, carrying a pile of laundry.

"*Ester!*" Halan exclaimed, almost overturning her bucket of dirty water.

Ester turned, and Halan's cheeks went hot as she recognized her mistake.

"Um—hello," the laundry girl said. "Do I know you?"

"No," said Halan quickly. "No, you don't. I'm—I'm a friend of Pedram's. I'm new," she added.

Ester hesitated, looking deep into her eyes, and for a moment Halan wondered if her friend could see through the Veil of Strangers, truly see Halan for who she was.

"Oh, well, it's nice to—"

"Girl! You, girl!" shouted a lady's voice. It was Lady Amalia, the chaperone who Halan had spent so much time and effort trying to avoid. She stomped toward them, silk robes flying. "What are you doing?"

Halan backed away, pretending to be mopping.

Ester froze. "Nothing, my lady, I'm just taking these down to—"

"Nothing? I'll give you nothing!" shouted Lady Amalia, and she seized the pile of clothes from Ester's hands and threw them against the wall, scattering them across the floor. Halan gripped the handle of her mop, trying to keep her face impassive. How could her chaperone do something like that? What had Ester done to make her so angry?

"Pick those up!" Lady Amalia ordered, and Ester scrambled to scoop up the clothes.

*You threw them down!* Halan forced herself not to scream it back at her. She was just doing her job! Why was she treating her like this?

"And tell the laundry master if he ruins another one of my scarves with his clumsy washing, I shall tell the guards he was seen with the rebels and he'll be out on his ear! Tell him that," Lady Amalia snapped, and then stomped off down the corridor and was gone.

Halan dropped her mop and hurried over to help Ester pick up the rumpled laundry.

"I'm so sorry!" she said. "I wanted to say something, but—"

To Halan's surprise, Ester gave a bitter laugh. "Oh, that's sweet. You *are* new here, aren't you? Don't worry about me, just concentrate on keeping out of the nobles' way when you can. You'll see soon enough, unfortunately, they're pretty much all like that."

Halan had never heard Ester talk this way before. She'd hinted that life in the palace wasn't always happy, but she'd never told Halan that she was being mistreated.

"Are they really all like that?" Halan asked quietly. *Am I like that?*

"Oh, some are better. Some are much worse. You learn to read the signs and keep your head down when they're feeling volatile." She looked down at the soiled laundry in her hands and sighed. "Normally. The only one of the lot of them that's ever treated me like a human being is Princess Halan."

Halan's heart soared. "Wow, really?"

"Between you and me? The princess is actually nice. I'm so glad she's back safely! If she were in charge, maybe things would be different around here."

Halan was glad that she was wearing the headscarf, because now she was blushing.

*There are going to be some changes around here, that's for sure.* She wished she could tell Ester that. *I'm listening. And I've seen how some of the people I trusted treat their subjects.*

She couldn't believe her father was the evil man Soren made him out to be, but perhaps Soren did know a little more about the darker corners of her kingdom than she did.

Ester hurried off to her duties, and Halan went back to mopping, impatient for the job to be done. "Finally," the old man said when he'd reached the farthest corner of the hall. "I'll say you got the hang of it there at the end, girl."

"Thanks," Halan said with a grateful nod. She waited until he had disappeared down the back stairs, and then stowed the mop and bucket in a closet.

*Now's my chance.*

She ran for the upper floors, her heart pounding. She had to get to her father before the rebels made their move.

Thinking of the reaction she might get for barging into the king's private rooms, Halan opened the door from the stairwell just a crack and peered through to check that the coast was clear.

"As Your Majesty commands," a voice said, and Halan held her breath. That was Lord Malek, the fabricworker. Lady Kayyali was beside him, leaning on her wooden staff. They were speaking to her father at the door to his study, flanked by guards.

Halan carefully shut the door again. She knew that there was no chance her father would listen to her while he was surrounded by nobles. They might be like Lady Amalia, or worse. She would have to wait a few minutes and hope that they'd leave.

As she waited, Halan heard the echo of a whisper from the floor below. "I know what I said," a woman was saying. "I meant it. It's just so hard to lie to her."

Halan's gasped. It was her mother's voice!

"I know, my love," said a deeper voice.

*My love?*

A strange, cold feeling crept up Halan's spine. *My father is still in his study. So, who is Mother talking to?*

Very carefully, Halan crept to the side of the stairs and risked a look down.

There was her mother—recognizable to Halan despite the dark shawl she was wearing over her dress—with a man in black scale mail, an iron helmet held under his hand. She couldn't see his face. He had black, curly hair, and he was leaning in to her mother, his lips pressed to hers.

Halan's hands flew up to her mouth to hold in the shriek of confusion that threatened to fly out of her.

*What about Father?*

Perhaps the king and queen didn't get to spend much time together, but for her mother to be having an affair, to betray her royal duty! It was unthinkable. Halan's whole world seemed to spin out of control. She felt sick, but couldn't stop herself from listening as they pulled apart and spoke once more.

"We *will* be together soon," the queen murmured, a note of happiness in her voice that Halan hadn't heard in years. "I won't put you or Halan at risk, but I can't wait much longer."

"We've kept our secret this long," the man said. "I'll do anything to make sure you're safe, you know that."

His voice was familiar, and as he turned his head to glance up the stairwell, Halan finally got a good look at his face.

She felt lightheaded, as if she might faint and tumble down the stairs, hitting the two secret lovers on the way.

It was Captain Bardak.

*As in Nalah Bardak.*

She *had* heard the name before. It had flown from her mind when Nalah said it. Or maybe she just hadn't wanted to remember.

*Captain Omar Bardak. A member of the royal guard.*

Halan's mother was in love with him. Not with her father, the king, but a guard. *Which means . . .*

He said they'd kept their secret for "this long." *How long was that? A year? Five years? Or maybe more?*

She pressed herself against the wall, letting its cool solidness keep her steady.

*Who is my real father? Is it the king, or this man my mother loves?*

The truth of it hit her all at once—those two never were the same person, and some part of her had known it for years and years. The way the king and queen talked to each other, and to her. It was always *cordial.* It wasn't love. Not like what she'd just seen.

Was this why her mother had always been so cold? She'd been keeping a secret so huge it could swallow her whole life.

*And mine.*

She reached up and angrily wiped away a tear. Perhaps her mother loved this man, but what was it Nalah had said?

*I don't care if our true father is Bardak or Tam. My papa raised me and I love him.*

Halan wouldn't betray her mother, but there was more

at stake than this right now. She had to get to Father before Soren led the rebels into the palace, before even more of her life crumbled around her.

Before it was too late.

# Chapter Fifteen

## Nalah

*I have loved you carelessly, with all my heart, and no one will ever be able to take that from me. We have both made our choices. One day we will be together. Even in death, our love will live on. You are the best person I know. I see you fight like a tiger to protect her, every waking moment. If the time ever comes, know that I will do the same.*

*A letter from Omar Bardak to Queen Rani Tam*

*I'm coming, Papa.*

Nalah fought to keep her steps under control as she slipped through the darkened palace halls. She mustn't run, no matter how desperate she was to see her father again.

The route from the royal quarters to the dungeons was longer and more tortuous than the passage with the spy-holes. Soren had told Nalah how to get there, but every step Nalah took away from the relative safety of Halan's rooms felt like walking into the lion's den.

She'd hoped that Cobalt would be back with a reply from Soren before she set off, but she'd waited until well beyond sunset and still he hadn't returned. Soren hadn't been at dinner, either, and Nalah hadn't dared ask after him. It had just been her, the king and queen, and twenty other courtiers, including the three Tam had empowered by murdering their tawams. They'd promised that the rebels who kidnapped her would be caught, but when she asked what would happen to them, they all clammed up. Tam had spun a line about justice, and Nalah had pretended to believe him.

After about fifteen minutes of walking and hiding, avoiding guards and slipping through forgotten, dusty rooms, Nalah found herself at the top of a dark staircase. She leaned over the well and looked down, but the stairs were swallowed up by the gloom long before they reached the bottom.

Soren had said not to bring a light, because it could be seen by the guards, but as Nalah looked down into that darkness, almost every part of her was clamoring to turn back.

Perhaps she could compromise. She reached up and took off the earrings she had borrowed from Halan's incredible collection—they were simple multifaceted glass. Feeling a little guilty, she snapped the glass orbs off their metal settings and held them in her hand.

After spending all day long trying not to do any magic,

Nalah felt a rush of relief to release a bit of her pent-up tension into the two little orbs in her hand. *"Light my way in darkness,"* she whispered in that chiming voice. *"Light it only for me."*

The balls of glass fused together into a globe the size of a marble and began to glow with a weak, pale light. She held it aloft. It only illuminated a few steps in front of her, but it would be enough. Carefully, she began picking her way down the steps, keeping her free hand on the wall for guidance.

The farther she descended, the colder and damper the stone became. She counted the steps until she was certain she had reached the bottom floor of the palace. Just like Soren said, there was an arched doorway here, and a completely black passage leading away to some other secret entrance; but the stairs kept on going, and she followed them. They grew rougher, and the wall started to feel more like natural, crumbling rock instead of the sandstone bricks. She felt moss between the cracks in the wall, and she could hear water trickling somewhere nearby.

Eventually the musty smell of the stairwell was replaced by something else—a foul stench, like a combination of mold and sweaty, unwashed people—and soon after she smelled it, she finally came to the bottom of the stairs and found herself in a tiny alcove. The darkness beyond was so thick that Nalah's handful of light barely pierced it. She made out a corridor ahead, and decided that was the way to go.

There were sounds coming from the murk. Crying sounds, wails of pain and distress, the low chatter of angry voices, the odd rattle of chains or clang of metal against metal.

She'd never heard anything like it. In her worst nightmares about the Hokmet's cells, she had never imagined sounds that frightened her as much as these.

Nalah knew that she had to go toward the sounds, but she waited a moment longer, taking a steadying breath, before she stepped forward.

The glow from her glass light fell on the gray face of an old man with muscles on his forearms like taut ropes; he was wearing rough black leather armor. He held a bowl containing crumbs in his hands. *He must be one of the jailers, coming back from feeding the prisoners.* The haggard man looked directly at Nalah as he passed by, but his expression didn't change.

Nalah pressed herself against the wall and held her breath as the jailer went by, going right past her and her little well of light without looking up.

*Only I can see the light!*

Nalah stayed frozen in place as long as she dared, as the old man disappeared into the darkness. After all, she wasn't invisible—she was just, as far as the guard was concerned, standing in the pitch black.

When his footsteps had receded, she stepped away from the wall and walked to the door the man had come through. The room beyond was lit by torches, their light spilling through the cracks in the ancient wooden door. Nalah pocketed her glass light and tried the door. It was locked.

She put her hand to the heavy iron lock and shut her eyes. Her heart was pounding, and she channeled her creeping fear into it, using the shudder building up behind her shoulder blades to heat and twist the metal under her fingers. The wood around it splintered and the lock fell out of place. Nalah caught it before it could hit the stone floor and bring every guard in the dungeon running.

The door swung open slowly, and Nalah found herself at the end of a long room lit blue by long-burning Thauma torches on the walls. Lining the room on both sides were iron cages that reminded her of horse stalls in a stable.

But these cages held people. Dozens and dozens of people—men and women and even children.

They sat in filthy straw, holding each other or curled in the corners. Some of them were crying, others hunched over injuries that looked fresh and painful. She saw Dust burns on many of them—pockmarked, bleeding, infected.

*This may not be my world*, she thought, anger burning in her chest, *but I'll do as I promised Soren, and gladly.*

But none of these miserable people was her father. This wasn't where he was being kept. She'd seen it in Cobalt's eye—the dark, cold room; all alone.

"It's the princess!" someone called out. It was a woman,

her hair shorn so that she was almost completely bald, who bore a terrible Dust scar all the way down one arm, from shoulder to fingertips. A rumble of fear, excitement, and anger passed through the prisoners, and Nalah cringed and looked back at the broken door behind her.

"Shh!" she hissed, raising both hands to her lips. "Please, be quiet. I'm here to help you!"

Several of the prisoners scoffed, and she even heard a few peals of bitter laughter. Nalah turned to the woman who'd seen her, who was eyeing her with distrust, but fascination.

"Listen, I'm *not* the princess, I'm an imposter. It's too hard to explain now, but suffice it to say, Ironside sent me to get you out of here!"

At that, several more of the prisoners got to their feet, the adults shushing the children and each other.

"Why should we trust you? Anyone could say they were working for Ironside," said a woman in another cage. "Perhaps she's just here to manipulate us into telling her who he is."

"Never heard of the princess doing anything like that," said a young man with a Dust scar on his neck that kept his head twisted at an awkward angle. "Ironside said she was naive, not cruel."

"I say we listen to her," said an old man with one eye. He was so thin, it was as if he'd worn away to almost nothing. "What choice do we have?"

Nalah breathed a sigh of relief—she hadn't realized she might have to convince these people to *let* her rescue them! She hesitated before continuing—everything in her wanted to tell these people to wait, to run through the dungeons and find her father first. But as she looked at all of their hungry, haggard faces, Nalah knew that her father wouldn't have wanted her to leave them in those cages a second longer. Not for him. Not for anything in the world.

"There's a secret way out," she said. "Get everybody up. You'll have to climb a lot of stairs. Can you all do that?"

"Those who can't will be carried," said the bald woman firmly, flexing her shoulders. "We won't leave anyone behind."

"Good. Go out of this door. In the third alcove on the right, feel along the wall until you find a gap. There are stairs on the other side. Don't go all the way to the top—wait where the archway is, Ironside will come for you there."

She began to move along the line of cages, placing her hands on the metal bars and commanding the iron to melt away. The prisoners stared at her.

"Can't be the princess," said the old man. "Everyone knows she's got no powers."

"Who are you, girl?" the bald woman asked in amazement.

Nalah tried to ignore them. Despite the rebels' awe of her powers, opening the prison bars was hard work, and she started to feel weak after she'd opened only three cages.

It felt as if her blood was thinning. It became harder to remember her fear, her anger, any of the useful emotions that would normally make her heart pump hard enough to channel the magic.

*Papa. I have to do this, to get these people out, so I can get to Papa.* It renewed her strength, but only just enough. By the eighth cage, there was a crowd of young people around her, catching her when she wobbled on her toes, hooking the pieces of the other cages around the bars so they could help pry them away with brute strength once she had weakened them with magic.

Finally it was done. Nalah was surrounded by a milling crowd of prisoners stretching their arms and legs. She leaned against the cool rock wall to catch her breath.

"Aren't you coming with us?" asked a young boy with big, dark eyes.

"I have to find my father. He's here, somewhere. Please, can you tell me where to find him?" She was so tired, so desperate to see him again, that she felt like crying. But she held it in—she couldn't waste any energy right now.

"If he's important to the king," said the bald woman with a grim frown, "he'll have been taken to the Well. It's just beyond that door. I'll come with you."

"No," said Nalah. "You all need to get out, as fast as you can, before the guards realize what's happening. Ironside's waiting, and I'll be right behind you."

She made herself stand up straight, fighting the dizziness

and fatigue, and ran to find the Well.

The door swung open and the blue torchlight from the prison spilled down a short flight of steps into pitch darkness. Nalah brought out her glowing glass orb once more, holding it up as she stepped down into a smaller room, with a single cell. The glass light flickered on metal bars, and on a faint shape leaning its back on the wall.

There was a groan, and a sound like someone trying to clear his throat.

"Who's there? Tam?"

Her father's voice was croaky and weak, but she would have known it even if he'd been speaking through a mouthful of sand. She ran to the bars, hope rising up in her chest like a boat on the swell of the Hadar Sea.

"Papa!" Nalah whispered. "It's me!"

"Nalah?" There was a rustle of straw and a clink of chains. Nalah peered into the darkness, and as her eyes adjusted she saw her father struggling to get to his feet. His face was covered in a ragged beard and his eyes looked bloodshot. "By the stars . . . *Nalah!*"

"I'm here!" She reached for him, and he caught her hand and pressed it to his chest. Nalah felt sobs welling up and set her jaw against them. *There's no time to cry now.* "I'm here to get you out."

"Do you have the key?" her father asked.

"Not quite," she said. "Hold this." She passed him the glowing glass orb, and Mr. Bardak stared at it in wonder.

"Nalah, what's happening? How did you get here?"

Nalah knelt down and reached through the bars for the iron manacle around her father's leg. "I went to Tam's house and . . . Papa, it isn't Zachary! We're in the Magi Kingdom—just like the stories! It's some kind of mirror world, and there are people here that look just like people in New Hadar. Tam is the king, and he killed Zachary, and—"

"Nalah," her father croaked. "Slow down. What are you doing?"

"I'm trying to—" Nalah's hand closed around the chain between the manacle and the floor.

Her father cried, "*No!*" But he was too late. Nalah had grabbed it and pulled.

A searing pain ran up Nalah's hand and she recoiled, banging her elbow on the bars of the cell. Her father let out a cry of pain and crumpled to the floor. Nalah blinked and groaned, rubbing her hand.

"It's Thauma," Mr. Bardak sighed, when he'd caught his breath. "It burns you if you try to interfere with it." He twisted his foot and held the glass light over it. Nalah recoiled as she saw that her father's skin was blistered and weeping with burns.

"No . . ." Nalah shook her head, swallowing back tears. "No. I can solve this. Just give me a minute."

"It's all right, love," said her father, and reached out for her hand again. She reached back through the bars and they held on to each other. "We'll find a way out of this. Tell me what you were trying to say about Tam. I didn't see much when they were bringing me down here, but I know he pulled me through the mirror. Did you say that this is the Magi Kingdom? How is that possible?"

"It's just like the stories said," Nalah whispered, doing her best to feel reassured by his words, while her mind spun wildly in the background, trying to figure out what she could do about her father's manacles. "It's a desert kingdom where magic is strong." She sighed. "It's *real.* Well, it's not quite as nice as in the stories, as you can tell. Some people exist in both worlds, like twins—except they call them 'tawams.' I haven't seen your twin, but I've met mine. There's a mirror version of me living here. Her name is Halan, and she's—"

*She's Tam's daughter. A princess. But she has no powers.*

Nalah looked up at her father's face, and she couldn't bear to ask him the question. She'd meant what she said to Halan. She didn't *care* if he was her real father—but it was a conversation they would have to have.

Some other time.

She looked down at her hands. "Papa, have you ever heard of the Fifth Clan?"

"The Fifth Clan? No, it doesn't ring a bell. It's not in the Magi Kingdom stories, is it?"

"I hadn't heard of it before, but it means Thaumas who can make things magical with their hands, just by touch, instead of with tools and incantations and stuff. They can control all four materials. That is"—Nalah swallowed, strangely nervous, as if he might not believe her—"*I* can."

Mr. Bardak met Nalah's eyes, his own eyes widened with wonder. "Nalah, did you make this light?" he asked, holding the orb more gingerly in his palm.

"Yes. I made it just now, with nothing but my hands," Nalah blurted. "I've been melting metal, bringing tapestries to life. I realized, I've always had this power." It was frightening, but also strangely powerful, to say it out loud like this. Nalah spoke a little more slowly and clearly as she went on. "In New Hadar I couldn't control it—it came out and just broke things. But here, it's been different. I feel different. People aren't afraid of me, they admire me. And I've already done amazing things. . . . I took out the bars from the other prison cells; I melted a man's sword in his hand. I don't know why I have this power, but it's been with me the whole time."

"Oh," breathed her father, holding tight onto her hand. "I always knew you were destined for greatness, Nalah. Many people used to say your great-grandfather Xerxes had special powers. Maybe that's where you got it from."

Nalah nodded. "But I thought it was just a story," she said.

Mr. Bardak raised his hands to indicate the whole world around them. "Sometimes, stories turn out to be true." He shook his head sadly. "I'm so sorry I tried to hide you from the world," he said. "I was just so afraid for you."

A flood of love rushed through Nalah's heart, and it was almost too much for her. Her lips twisted and she bit back a sudden sob as she thought of all the times he had said that to her and she hadn't understood. "Papa, this is all my fault. If I'd listened to you in the first place, I wouldn't have let Tam flatter me into making that mirror, I wouldn't have assumed I knew everything, when I didn't know anything at all."

But her father shushed her. "No, Nalah. Listen to me. Nothing was ever going to be able to hide the light within you. Perhaps you were meant to come here, to discover your true destiny. No matter what happens, nothing will ever stop me from being proud of you."

She reached for him through the bars and he held both her hands against his heart.

*I'll get us out of here*, she thought. *I will. Just wait and see.*

# Chapter Sixteen

## Halan

*Despite what our government may want us to believe, Thauma magic is not evil or dangerous. The hand that wields the sword chooses how to use it—to kill, or to defend. The hand that crafts it chooses only to create.*

**·*Xerxes Bardak, in an opinion piece for the*
New Hadar Sentinel**

Halan spent the whole day trailing her father around the palace, hiding in cupboards and stairwells and with groups of servants, pretending she'd been sent to help them with their chores. All the time, she was trying to get close enough without being caught and thrown out or even killed by the guards before she could convince them of who she really was.

Her mother's words to Omar Bardak were still ringing in her ears, the sight of the two kissing seared into her mind. But she did her best to put them both out of her head for now. If they all survived, if the rebels didn't kill the king and take the palace for themselves, *then* she would confront her mother.

She caught a glimpse of Nalah, walking with the royal family and their hangers-on as they went down for dinner. She didn't try to talk to her—if Nalah knew Halan had escaped and was in the palace, she might do something unpredictable, and Halan wanted to talk to her father first. From her hiding place, Halan watched her tawam strolling along with her parents, wearing her clothes, and felt strangely like she was a ghost haunting these halls, carrying a dark omen that no one wanted to hear.

At last, as night was falling, King Tam returned to his study, and Halan scrambled to follow him. She crept up to the study door and looked in through the keyhole, just in case there were guards or nobles who'd waited inside for him. But he was alone, sitting at his desk and poring over a large book. She was terrified, but she knew it couldn't wait a moment longer—the rebels could be at their door!

She suddenly understood how the queen felt, knowing that there was danger around every corner.

With her heart in her mouth, Halan raised a hand and knocked.

A moment later, her father opened the door. He looked down at her, a sneer of disdain and suspicion on his lips.

"What do you want? How dare you disturb me in my private study?" he snapped.

Halan swallowed hard. "Please, listen to me," she

stammered. "I—I . . ."

*If I come out with it now, he'll think I'm mad. He'll slam the door in my face and call the guard.* She had to be clever about this. That's what her father would do.

"I'm sorry to come to you like this," she said, "but I have some information, Your Majesty. Something you need to hear, and you alone."

King Tam's eyebrows arched, his interest piqued by this mysterious offer.

"Come in, child," he said, and stepped aside. Halan hurried into his study, her heart pounding. Now all she had to do was convince him of the truth.

She turned and faced him, her hands clasped in front of her, her heart beating so hard she wondered if he could see the pulse in her neck.

"Well? Out with it, girl. Do not be afraid," said the king, shutting the door behind her.

"Your Majesty, I'm sorry I have to tell you this," Halan said, "but the girl you just had dinner with, the one you think is your daughter? She's an imposter. *I'm* the real Halan!"

Her father's expression turned cold, his eyes glinting with anger.

"Please," she went on. "Listen to my voice. It's me, Father! The other girl is my tawam, she's from the world beyond the mirror. Her name is Nalah. She came here to free her father, who she thinks you have locked up. She promised me that no harm would come to you or Mother, but I overheard the rebels planning to attack, and I had to escape to warn you."

"Why should I believe you?" Tam said, looking down his nose at her. "You look nothing like the princess."

Halan stuggled to speak over the loud pounding of her heart. "The rebels forced me to wear a Veil of Strangers, so you wouldn't recognize me. This isn't my true face!"

King Tam's expression suddenly turned stormy, his lips twisting in anger. He drew a bejeweled dagger from his belt and it glinted in the torchlight as he approached her. It clearly was imbued with powerful Thauma magic. "Hold still, girl."

Halan backed up against the study desk, panic taking hold of her.

*He would never hurt me. He wouldn't hurt some poor deluded peasant girl, either. He* wouldn't!

But Halan thought of the woman defaced by the Dust; she thought, unwillingly, of Soren Ferro and the story he'd told of his father's death. Her chest constricted and suddenly she found it hard to brcathc. She didn't recognize this man stalking toward her, raising his dagger. . . .

"Please, Father!" she begged him. "I'm not a peasant. . . . It's *me*!"

King Tam's hand gripped her shoulder, and Halan let out a terrified shriek. He brought the blade down slowly and pain gripped Halan—but then, all at once, it stopped.

Her lungs filled, and her head cleared.

The Veil of Strangers dropped off her face into the king's hands, its midnight silk slashed in two. Halan raised her hands to her face—he hadn't so much as grazed the skin beneath.

"Father?" she said, looking up at him.

Her father stared at her, but instead of the joy she thought she'd see, a dark shadow of fury passed across his face. Then, as quickly as it had appeared, it was gone, and he scooped her into a fierce, tight hug. "My daughter!" he said, his voice muffled with emotion. "How dare they do this to you! I swear, every single rebel will suffer for this, a hundred times over, for the pain they've caused you."

"I'm all right," Halan told him, hugging him back, her knees buckling with relief. *I knew I was right. I knew you wouldn't hurt me.* "They didn't harm me, apart from the veil."

"They kidnapped the princess and sent an imposter in her place," Tam snarled, pulling away, his face again dark with anger. "That is enough."

"Father, it's not just Nalah I needed to tell you about," Halan interrupted. She straightened up, and suddenly it was an effort to push out the words. *This is the right thing* . . . "You have to listen to me. You are in danger! It's Soren. Soren Ferro is Ironside!"

Halan saw her father's face clear at this revelation. "That foolish boy—*he* is the rebel leader? *He* is the traitor to the crown?"

Halan nodded. "He's not so foolish, Father—it's an act. He's been in the palace, spying on us, and making Wild Thauma weapons for the rebels—and they're planning to attack us, maybe tonight! Nalah's going to release the prisoners from the dungeon and they're going to come here and try to take the throne."

"Tonight," Tam mused. He let out a bitter laugh. "*Soren Ferro.* Well, I never would have thought. He is a clever boy. He must know . . ." He shook his head. "Never mind that. Don't worry, my love. I have more power than he could dream. We will crush them like the insects they are."

*But that's not what I want.* Halan's momentary relief turned to dread. "No, you can't," she said, shaking her head. Tam stared at her. Halan realized she'd never talked back to her father before in her life. But then again, never before did she have something so important to say.

"Please, Father. I've been in the city, and I've seen things. The consquences of the Dust. The way the nobles and the guards abuse our people. They are starving, Father. So many of our people are living a walking death—while we fcast in thc palacc in ignorance of their suffering!"

She paused to look at her father—who was staring impassively, his eyes betraying nothing. *Does he believe me?* Halan went on in a rush: "Father, the rebels are misguided, and some of them are dangerous—but locking them up is only making things worse. They blame you for all of their hardships, but they are wrong! Perhaps if we could speak to Soren, work together to make things better in the city . . ."

She trailed off. Her father's face had settled into an expression, and it was the same look he'd given her when she'd first told him Nalah was an imposter—a cold, calculating stillness.

"Thank you, my child," he said quietly. "You may have just saved our whole kingdom, as well as my life and your mother's. I promise you, I will only resort to violence if I have no other choice. Do you believe me?"

*Do I?* Halan wanted to say yes, but she felt chilled. There was something about her father's calm voice that made her think of the way a butcher might speak to a lamb as he took it out for slaughter. A reassuring tone that would keep the creature from fighting back against its coming demise.

She banished the thought. That was ridiculous. He was her *father* . . . wasn't he? She shook the image of her mother kissing the guard out of her head. "Of course I believe you."

"Now, you must go to your rooms, clean yourself up, and try to get some sleep. Do not worry. I will deal with everything."

Halan felt her heart sink. *Am I back to being useless?* "What?" She frowned. "Father, no. I can't just go to my rooms. I'm involved now, Soren's told me his plans—I need to help! If I come with you, Soren will be more willing to talk instead of fight."

"No, my love. This is all *for you*, Halan. Do you understand that? If you were to be hurt, everything I have done would be for nothing. I want you safe, out of the way. Bar the door and don't let anybody in but me or your mother. Promise me!"

Instinct told Halan to agree. *But I can't,* she realized. *I will no longer stay locked in my rooms while others decide the fate of my kingdom.*

She nodded. It was only the second time she'd ever lied to her father, and it felt almost as painful as being cut out of the veil. Halan walked to the study door to leave, but her hand stilled on the ancient wood. She couldn't leave. Not yet. Not without saying what she needed to say. She turned back to face her king.

"Father," she said. "I will go back to my rooms, but I can't go back to the way things were, not after everything I've seen. This kingdom will be mine to rule one day, and I can't continue to sit in ignorance while my people cry out in pain. I know I am not a Thauma, but that doesn't make me powerless. Please, don't shut me out. Let me be a part of this. It's my right."

Her father raised his eyebrows, but his expression didn't change. "Child," he said softly. "You have seen what that traitor Ferro wanted you to see. He manipulated you because he knew it was a perfect way to get to me. I have done what is necessary to give my family everything, and to keep my kingdom safe. All your life you have reaped the rewards of my rule, so do not question my methods. I *will* protect you, and you *will* obey me. You may be the heir to this throne, but I am still the king. Now go."

Halan stared at her father, who once again seemed like a stranger. Something was beginning to build in Halan's chest, a feeling like she was falling from a great height, not knowing what lay below. She wanted desperately to take solace in her father's words, to feel them around her like a warm, safe embrace. But instead they felt like an iron vise, cold and unforgiving. And suddenly, for the first time, she wondered if she'd done the right thing by telling him the truth.

Her father led her out of his study, strode to the end of the corridor, and rang the Thauma brass bell that hung by the doorway. It let out a sound that was muffled to Halan's ears, but barely five seconds later there was a clattering of armor and a phalanx of guards came up the stairs, led by Captain Alamar, her sword drawn.

"Your Majesty," she panted. "Are you all right?"

"Rouse the guards," said the king. "I need a company to come with me at once to the dungeons, and more to guard the tunnel exits and the road into the city. Nobody enters or leaves this palace. Send word, if anyone sees the young Lord Ferro, that he—" The king glanced back at Halan, and his expression changed, just a little. "He is to be apprehended and brought to me at once," he finished, speaking very deliberately.

Halan felt like she was falling faster and faster. Her skin crawled. *What would the order have been if I hadn't been here?*

"Now, back to your rooms, Halan," her father said.

Numbly, she walked past the captain and down the stairs, barely noticing the curious looks the guards were giving her peasant clothing. She reached the next floor and paused in the wide hall, hung with Thauma tapestries, that she would cross to reach the royal quarters and her own rooms. She leaned against the wall, trying to stop this sick feeling of wrongness from overwhelming her. She'd believed so strongly in her father's goodness, believed that all she'd seen and heard was just a mistake that could easily be corrected—that she never stopped to think about what would happen if she was wrong. What would they do to Soren once he was captured? To those raggedy children in the rebels' hideout? What would happen to *Nalah*? Her tawam was still in the palace somewhere, with no idea of what Halan had done.

Had she just condemned them all?

Halan felt sick.

She heard the rattle of mail and the echo of soldiers' voices coming her way and wondered where they were going. Then she knew. There was another door straight ahead. It led back to the grand staircase, the great hall, and, eventually, to the dungeons.

Staring at that door, Halan made a decision. She had to know, for certain, what kind of a man her father really was.

Against one of the walls there was a couch upholstered in Thauma silk that radiated a gentle warmth at night. She pulled it out from the wall, and crouched down behind it just as the guards—led by her father—stormed past and went through the door. When she was sure they had all passed, Halan crept out from her hiding place and followed.

She was afraid that her father would turn and spot her instantly, but she needn't have worried. He was too focused on leading his troops down to the dungeons, and the clatter and stomp of their passage down the wide sandstone steps and across the great domed, tiled hall was loud enough to mask any noise Halan made.

Captain Alamar barked instructions to guards that they passed, giving the king's order to close all the gates and stop anyone coming in or going out. Confusion and worry spread behind them like a dust cloud raised by a horse's hooves, and guards and servants swarmed in the corridors, hurrying to make sure the orders were carried out.

Despite all the chaos around her, Halan felt exposed. *If only I had Marcus's shadow cloak*, she thought. Instead she put the plain headscarf she'd been given back on. With it pulled across her face, she was nearly as invisible as she had been when she was wearing the Veil of Strangers.

She heard her father's voice as they passed through the hall.

"You, armsman. Send messengers to rouse Kayyali, Lang, and Malek. Tell them to bring everything they have ready."

"Yes, Your Majesty," said a young voice, and Halan heard

one of the guards peel off from the group and hurry away.

The descent to the dungeons felt interminable, but finally they were there. Halan had never been in a dungeon before. The first thing that hit her was the smell—the stink of sweat and grime and fear—so bad she was glad of the scarf to cover her face. And then there was the darkness and the silence. The eerie, terrible silence that was almost like a prison in itself.

As she entered a long tunnel and approached a door lit by blue torchlight, she realized that the stomping of the guards had stopped.

"Your Majesty," said a creaky, frightened voice. "I—I don't know what happened."

Halan slipped into the blue-lit room, keeping to the shadows. Rows of cages—filthy, horrible-looking cages—lined both sides of the room. All of them were empty. Their locks were twisted and melted off.

*Nalah was here*, Halan realized, and her heart lifted. She hadn't expected to feel glad that her tawam had helped the rebels to escape, but another glance at the cages and she was certain that nobody, not even real criminals, deserved to be left in here to rot.

In the center of the room, a bony old man in an ill-fitting leather vest, a bunch of keys lying at his feet, was bowing to the king, his hands pressed to his face in shame.

"Please, I beg you, show mercy, my lord," he said. "I was at the door the whole time, nobody came in or out. It must have been some Wild magic!"

"Take him away," the king growled, and two of the guards dragged the jailer back through the door. Tam turned to a door at the end of the room, strode toward it, and yanked it open—and then he let out a laugh that chilled Halan to her core.

"Well," he said. "My darling daughter. What a surprise."

*Nalah!*

Halan felt a squeezing in her gut as she crept closer. *What have I done to her?* None of the guards seemed to notice Halan—they were too busy either running back out into the darkness to try to find the escaped prisoners, or flanking her father as he stepped inside the dark room. Captain Alamar took up a torch from the wall of the prison and followed him in. The blue light filled the small room, and Halan approached the doorway, afraid of what she would see.

There was only one cell in the room. Its lock had been melted off too, but it still held two people. One of them was Nalah, and the other, kneeling protectively in front of her, was a man who looked like a gaunt, dirty version of Captain Bardak.

*Nalah's father.*

Halan stared at him, a thought rising from deep inside her. *When are you going to stop fooling yourself?*

This Bardak was really Nalah's father—and Halan was not truly the king's daughter.

"Leave us alone, you monster," Mr. Bardak snarled in a dry and cracked voice. "Whatever you want from me, you won't get it."

"Don't be ridiculous," said the king, but all the rage had gone out of his voice. He sounded . . . *happy.* "I want nothing at all from you, Amir. Nalah has come to me, as I expected—so I have no use for you."

The king struck like a snake, so fast Halan barely saw his hand move. A small metal ball, about the size of a plum, flew from inside his flowing sleeve and struck Nalah's father in the forehead. It stuck there, and immediately crackled with tiny fingers of white lightning, sending them climbing all across his body. Amir Bardak's eyes grew wide with surprise, and his arms and legs spasmed uncontrollably.

And then, the ball stopped crackling and floated back into the king's hand. Nalah's father went limp and fell forward, lifeless in the dirty straw.

It all happened in seconds—but it felt like an eternity.

"*Papa!*" Nalah screamed, shattering the shocked silence in the room. She grabbed her father's shirt and shook him. "No, please, no!"

Halan silently retched as she watched her twin grasp her father's body, crying and begging him to come back. And at that moment Halan truly felt that they shared the same heart, the same searing, terrible pain. Because Nalah's father was dead, but, in just as real a way, so was Halan's.

For the man who had just murdered Amir Bardak before her eyes was no longer the man she thought she knew. He wasn't her *papa*.

Soren Ferro had been right. Asa Tam, the king, was a cruel, heartless man. He was a murderer.

And Halan had been wrong about him all along.

She stopped retching and stood, feeling numb.

The king was standing before the cell, watching Nalah's grief with interest. "From the moment I saw you at the market in New Hadar, I knew," Tam said, his voice making Halan's skin crawl. "I saw your raw power and I knew that you, a filthy peasant from another world, you were the reason my daughter suffered."

*What?* Halan couldn't believe her ears.

"I thought that I could simply put you out of your misery once you'd completed making my mirror—another tawam to add to my list," the king went on. "But fate had other plans." He sighed, glancing at Amir Bardak's body. "I hate it when things get *messy*, but then again, your coming to this world turned out to be in my favor. If not for your involvement in the rebels' little plan, I wouldn't know the identity of their leader! And I am so very glad to have that tidbit of information."

*All this time*, Halan thought, her breath coming in great, ragged gasps, *I was worried about Nalah hurting my father, when he was the one out to hurt her.* One of the guards turned and saw Halan, and began to advance toward her.

*Let them. I won't run. I have to face him sooner or later.*

She stepped into the room, her head as high as she could hold it.

"Father, what have you done?" she demanded. "How could you kill an innocent man who you had at your mercy?" She glanced at Nalah. Her tawam was doubled up with sobbing, but she looked up and met Halan's eyes.

The king spun around and pinned Halan with a calculating stare. "Halan," he said in a low, warning tone, stepping between her and the cell. "I'm sorry you had to see this, but soon you will understand it was all necessary. You do not understand what's at stake here. The future of the kingdom, of our family. As you said in my study, you are to become queen when I am gone. But to rule the Magi Kingdom without any magic of your own? Such a thing would be impossible. You may not think so now, but you wouldn't have been able to keep control of the people without true power."

Halan stared at him, each word like a tiny dagger in her heart. He had always told her that she would make a great queen, Thauma or not. He'd always made it seem like he believed in her for who she was. Was all of that a lie, to keep her from knowing how little he really thought of her?

"This common girl is a powerful Thauma," Tam went on, while Halan stood speechless and Nalah cradled the body of her father in the blue darkness. "She's hoarding all the power that should have been shared between you.

But when she dies, all that power will flow into you! You will be the most magnificent queen this world has seen since the Thauma War! You will finally have the life you deserve."

*How could he think I would want that?*

She looked at Nalah, and she was suddenly consumed with guilt. She remembered how she'd felt in the rebels' hideout, watching Nalah make wonders with her hands. Envious. Full of anger and sadness that Nalah was so effortlessly able to do what she could not. She wanted the power—she always had.

*I thought maybe we could be friends, but you were brought here for me, as a sacrifice. Your father is dead because of me. I've already betrayed you, though I didn't realize it.*

*I won't let that happen again.*

"Nalah is not a common girl," said Halan, as softly and clearly as her father had spoken before. "And I won't let you hurt her."

The king blinked at her in confusion.

"Excuse me?"

Nalah looked up from her father's body, and her eyes locked on Halan's. It was like looking into a mirror and suddenly seeing something in herself that she never saw before.

There was so much that divided them. Halan had rank; Nalah had power. Halan's parents were alive, but they were strangers to her; Nalah's were gone, but she would have the loving memory of them forever.

But they both had heart. They had their wits.

And they would not falter, not when their family was at stake.

"She's my twin," Halan continued. "My other self. She shows me who I am, and who I am not. I pity you, Father, that you never gave your tawam the chance to show you that before you killed him." She paused, shaking her head. "I don't want power," she finished. "Not if that's the price."

Her father's face flushed dark with fury, and then turned cold and serious once again. "You cannot make this decision, Halan. You don't know what you're saying, you're too young. Too sheltered."

"That was not my choice!" Halan yelled, years and years of frustration boiling over.

"No, it was mine!" Tam snarled back. He stalked toward Halan and she forced herself to hold her ground, even as he loomed above her. "You are nothing but a danger to yourself and to me, without any powers to protect you. You understand nothing about what it means to be a leader. But you will, in time. With the power you will have, we will crush the pathetic rebellion and rule this land in peace, forever."

*Peace? How can there ever be peace, when these are the lengths you'll go to? This isn't about peace—it's about your own pride.*

"No." Halan stepped between her father and Nalah.

"Captain Alamar, take the princess to her rooms and lock the door. We will execute the tawam at noon, when my daughter has had time to calm down."

Halan felt her arms seized from behind, and she screamed, "Let me go! You can't do this!" But the guards ignored her. She writhed and kicked out at them as they dragged her away, but it was no use.

Captain Alamar followed, straight-backed and silent, and when they reached Halan's rooms she stood in the doorway with her sword drawn. Halan wheeled around and tried to walk past her.

"You wouldn't hurt me," she snapped. "My father would have your head!"

"Princess," said the captain with a weary sigh, "I have done much worse than this at your father's behest. Be glad he still loves you enough to lock you away."

And with that she slammed the door in Halan's face.

# Chapter Seventeen

## Nalah

*There is a strange story about a pair of tawams who met in the flesh one moonlit night. The one from the nation of steel and smoke related a story from his life, while the one from the kingdom of sand and magic listened. They realized that despite their very different worlds, they had both lived the same story, had both experienced the same joy and heartbreak.*

*Other stories tell of tawams whose connection becomes stronger and stronger, until they can sense each other's thoughts, share dreams, even speak across the void.*

—*From* Legends of the Magi

Nalah sat pressed into the corner of her father's cell, hugging her knees, staring through tear-blurred eyes at nothing.

Her father's body was still at her feet, and it was cooling even as she sat here in the dark. She had rolled him onto his side and closed his eyes. In a way it had only made things worse. Now he looked like he was sleeping—like, any minute now, she would see him breathing and know that everything was going to be all right, after all.

But nothing was ever going to be all right again.

Nalah should have leaped to her feet as soon as Tam struck, formed her glass light into a dagger and stabbed Tam through the heart. She should have gotten in front of her father, should have been the one to take the blow from Tam's Thauma sphere.

She should have done *something*.

She only distantly remembered the moments after Tam had found them. Tam and Halan had argued. *What was Halan doing there?* Nalah wasn't sure, but she suspected that Halan had been drawn toward the palace for the same reason she had been—to save her father.

Halan had succeeded. Nalah had failed.

But in the end Halan had stood up to her father, who she loved so much, for Nalah's sake.

*Forgive me, Halan. I misjudged you. I misjudged everything.*

Halan didn't want her to die, but Tam had said she would, at noon the next day.

She was vaguely aware that there were guards at the door, guards in the dungeons, to stop her from using her powers to escape the way the other prisoners had. But she hadn't tried to escape. There was no point anymore.

Would it be morning soon? Nalah hoped it would. At

least this long night would be over. Whatever came next, it would be better than waiting here, with her father's body, watching it and waiting for the breath that wouldn't come.

There was a noise, as if someone had opened the door to the Well and walked inside. Nalah squeezed her eyes shut and tears scorched down her cheeks.

"Nalah," hissed a voice.

*Marcus.*

She looked up, her eyes so used to the darkness that she could make out the movement of a scorpion on the far wall. But Marcus wasn't there.

For a moment, she thought she was imagining things. Why wouldn't she imagine Marcus's voice, when she'd been imagining her father's all night?

"Oh my god," Marcus breathed. "Mr. Bardak . . ."

Marcus's head appeared, followed by the rest of him. He bundled the shadow cloak in his hands. Cobalt leaped from his arm, hopped though the hole melted in the bars of the cell, and climbed into Nalah's lap. He pressed his smooth, warm glass head against the underside of her chin, and Nalah bit back another sob.

"Nalah, I'm so sorry," Marcus said, climbing in after the falcon. "I should have gotten here faster. Halan clocked me in the head. Cobalt had to fetch the rebels. By the time we . . ." He trailed off.

Nalah cradled Cobalt in her hands, stroking the glassy feathers at the base of his neck. She didn't feel it anymore—

the connection to her father. She didn't hear his voice in Cobalt's sad, quiet keening.

*He's gone. Forever.*

"Did they get out?" she whispered, her voice hoarse and cracked. "The prisoners, did they make it?"

"Yes," said Marcus. "Ironside got them out of the palace just in time. They're back at the hideout now, arming themselves. They're going to attack in the morning."

"Tam's having me killed at noon," Nalah said flatly.

Marcus stumbled back, the words like a blow. "We won't let that happen," he finally managed. "We'll get you out before then."

Nalah nodded. She couldn't seem to feel anything. She knew that Marcus's words should have given her hope, but all she felt was empty.

"Halan must have told her father about the rebels' plan," Nalah said, as the realization came to her. "That's how he knew I was here."

"I should never have trusted her," Marcus hissed. "She told me she was afraid the rebels would kill her, and if we didn't get here, her father would know you were an imposter. Then she smacked me with a rock. If it wasn't for me, if I hadn't been so naive, she wouldn't have been able to get back here and betray us, and—"

He was looking at her father's body. Nalah shook her head.

"It's not your fault. She's not a bad person, and you were

trying to help her." She swallowed. "You're a good friend. You came to this place with me even though you didn't have to. I'll never forget that."

"Of course I came, dummy," Marcus said, feigning his usual mocking tone. "You're always getting yourself into trouble when I'm not around."

Marcus reached for her hand, and she reached back.

"Don't worry, Nalah," Marcus whispered. "When I leave here, I'll go straight to Ironside and tell him about the impending execution. He'll know what to do. He'll rally the rebels and get you out before they can touch you. Okay?"

Before Nalah could answer, a clatter of footsteps sounded outside the door, and they both pulled their hands back quickly. Marcus threw the shadow cloak over himself, and Cobalt scurried underneath it.

The door opened again, spilling blue light down the steps. Tam strode in, with a pair of guards dragging a limp figure behind him.

"I've brought you some company, Nalah," Tam said. "Not only for your cell, but also for your execution."

Nalah refused to look afraid. She regarded Tam with cool hatred, and hoped that it made him angry.

The guards didn't bother to open the cell—they simply shoved their prisoner through the melted hole in the bars. Nalah twitched as he nearly landed right where Marcus had been sitting under the shadow cloak.

He was almost unrecognizable, his clothes torn and a black eye swelling up one side of his handsome face, but Nalah knew who it had to be.

*Ironside.*

Her last hope, the one person who could have saved her from her fate at Tam's hands, was going to be executed right alongside her.

Dawn might have been breaking outside the palace, but inside that cell, the darkness was complete.

# Chapter Eighteen

## Halan

*What our people need is a leader who uses their strength not to control and suppress them, but to lift them to greater heights than they ever imagined for themselves. Only with such a leader can our kingdom be truly powerful.*

*David Ferro, from his personal journals*

"I'm sorry about this," Halan said to the servant who she'd tied to a chair in her bedroom. The trayful of tea and orange cakes the girl had been carrying when she'd come to keep watch over Halan lay scattered across the floor. "I really am. I promise I'll make it up to you when this is all over. Two weeks' paid vacation, courtesy of the princess, okay?"

The girl nodded—as her mouth was gagged, it was the best she could do.

Halan sighed. First the little rebel boy, then Marcus, and now this. She was turning into a barbarian. But she had to get out of here and do something. The old Halan, the pampered princess who might have stayed locked in her high tower, ignoring the evidence of her eyes and her heart, who couldn't face the truth even when it was right in front of her . . . that Halan was gone forever.

*And good riddance. I don't need her anymore, I have work to do.*

Dressed in Nalah's plain peasant clothes, Halan sprinted back down the tunnel. She was lucky: very few people knew about this entrance; even Lord Helavi had been surprised when Halan found evidence of it in the old history books. There was nobody waiting for her in the dark, and nobody was watching the trapdoor into the gardens, either—though there were guards patrolling the paths between the palm trees and beds of flowers and succulents. Halan crept under a bush and waited for them to pass before slithering down the steep hill, keeping away from the road. She scaled the wall by climbing up a prickly palm tree with her hands wrapped tight in her headscarf. She dropped down the other side and slipped between two buildings, back into the city.

The sky was orange-pink with the light of dawn. Her father had said Nalah would die at noon. Halan still had time.

She just prayed it would be enough. She *had* to make this right—for the kingdom, for Nalah, and for herself, too.

The king had to be stopped.

The city was just waking up. It felt very different from

the bustling, exciting place Soren had shown her. She could see the tattered clothes and tired eyes of the people pushing carts along the road toward the bazaar. She heard the hungry cries of children as she passed one house, and a loud argument from another.

This was what the luxury of the Thauma lords cost. This was what her father thought of as a *peaceful city*.

She couldn't help wondering what exactly the king thought would be left for her to inherit when he was gone. She could see it, clear as the rays of sun that slanted between the buildings: he would crush this rebellion, and in another few years he would have to crush another. How would the kingdom go on if, one by one, he turned every baker and stonemason and trader against him? How long would it take him to turn every Thauma against him, too?

How did he think he would keep his throne, if their loyalty was built on nothing but fear?

Finally reaching the rebels' hideout, Halan checked the street for guards before entering the abandoned house and climbing down into the subterranean rooms. There she found herself faced with a crowd of people, all gathered in a disorganized huddle. More than half of them, she had never seen before. They looked thin and dirty, and very angry. They were already armed, a motley collection of Wild Thauma weapons glinting in their hands and at their sides.

She searched the crowd for Soren, and her heart sank. He wasn't there.

*Soren or not, this is all I can do to save Nalah. I didn't believe my subjects when they told me how they had been hurt—I need to make up for that now.*

Feeling a little like she might be sick, she stepped forward and threw back the headscarf.

"Citizens! Listen to me!"

Heads turned. A few of the rebels exclaimed in surprise. Darry and Felis pushed their way to the front of the crowd, as did—to Halan's dismay—Seyed.

"It's Nalah! She's back!" Darry called out.

"No, it's not," said a voice behind her. Halan turned around to see Marcus standing there, looking haggard, the shadow cloak slung around his shoulders. "It's the princess. I never forget the face of someone who's hit me on the head with a rock."

A roar of shock ran through the crowd of rebels. Seyed drew his sword. It glinted red in the slanting sunlight.

"It's true," Halan said. "I'm Princess Halan, and I've come back because I need you. Where is Ironside?"

"Your father has him," said Marcus, through gritted teeth. "He's going to be executed at noon, along with Nalah. I just came from the palace."

Halan swallowed. She hadn't even had a chance to warn him.

Her throat felt as dry as the Sand Sea.

"Listen, please!" she said. "So much of this is my fault. I couldn't believe my father was who you all said he was, but I've learned the truth, and I need your help to make this right."

"Here to offer your head, are you?" Seyed sneered. "Because that's all we need from you." He advanced on her, his sword drawn. Halan felt a prickle of panic in her chest.

"Get away from there, boy," snapped another voice. It was that of a grown woman, as tall as Seyed and with one burned arm. The axe she was carrying sang strange harmonics as it cut the air, and she stepped between Halan and Seyed without a hint of fear. "You're not the leader here, you don't get to decide what happens to the princess."

"You're not the leader, either, Rosa," Seyed snarled. But there was a hint of childish petulance in his voice, and Rosa didn't move.

"*Ironside* is the leader," said Darry.

"Ironside is in the dungeons," Felis pointed out. "Someone needs to decide what to do."

"We're wasting time!" Halan said. "We have to storm the palace immediately—or Soren and Nalah will both be executed!"

"What do you care?" Seyed spat.

"I care because I'm not like the king! Soren and Nalah are good people, I know that now. I won't let them die because I was too blind to listen to them."

"How will we get into the palace without Ironside?" said an old man with a bag full of glistening glass orbs. "He was our way in, he knew every secret passage. Without him, we're just a doomed rabble. The guards would cut us down before we even reached the gate, Thauma weapons or not."

There was a moment of silence, and then Marcus spoke up. "The princess knows the palace better than anyone. If she really wants to make this right, let her help us."

Halan's heart beat faster. Every one of the rebels was staring at her now. Most of them looked like they were considering Marcus's words carefully. She looked at Seyed and Rosa, and then a broken cart a few feet away caught her eye. She ran over and climbed onto it, so that she was looking down at the whole group of rebels.

*This is absurd. You can't do this.*

*No—it would be absurd* not *to do this. If I don't, nobody will, and Nalah and Soren will die, and the king . . . he'll keep on hurting people. Perhaps he was good once. Perhaps he really was the man he made sure I thought he was, a man who wanted what was best for everyone in this kingdom.*

*But fear changed him. The fear of being overthrown, the fear of handing his kingdom over to a powerless daughter. And that fear made him do terrible things.*

Halan was all too familiar with fear. She'd lived with it all her life, been told to be afraid of everyone and everything. But since the moment she stepped out into the world that night with Soren, and all her fears were realized, she'd changed too. She'd begun to understand that it wasn't her lack of Thauma skills that made her powerless, it was fear itself. The moment she stopped being afraid of the world was the same moment she began to feel powerful.

And right now, the people didn't need her to be a Thauma. They needed her to be a leader.

"Marcus is right, I know the palace like the back of my hand," she called out. "Three days ago, I was sitting in that palace, looking out of the window, dreaming of the magical kingdom I would rule someday and the happy, thriving city I was about to visit with Soren."

A few of the rebels scoffed. But Halan barreled on.

"I know! I was wrong. Actually I was wrong about nearly everything. But I've seen my kingdom now, I've seen my city, and I see you. All of you. I see that you're starving and freezing. I see that the king's way of ruling has been cruel and unjust."

"Yeah!" cried one of the younger rebels. "Down with the king!"

Halan tried not to look like she was shaking, though she could feel the tremble starting in her fingers.

"I've seen with my own eyes how some of the nobles treat the people in this kingdom, not with courtesy and respect, but with insults and violence. But I've also seen that there are good nobles like Soren, like his father, like my mother, who only want to end the injustice of my father's reign." The trembling in her hands felt like the beating of a drum, and she tried to use that feeling, to make her voice louder and her heart stronger. "They will flock to us, and we will free our kingdom together. My tawam is in that palace, and so is your leader. Will we leave them to their fate?"

A roar went up from the rebels, nearly all of them raising their weapons.

"No!" they cried as one.

Halan suddenly felt something that she'd never felt before in her whole life.

Powerful.

"Then let's go and get them," she said.

# Chapter Nineteen

## Nalah

*There have been rumors for many decades that members of some of the great houses were also Fifth Clan Thaumas. None are supported by much evidence, but the tale of Zarek Ali, the legendary metalworker, is one that bears repeating.*

*Ali was one of the king's advisers during the Thauma War. When the world as we knew it ended, the Ali family worked through the Year of Storms to save not just themselves, but any others who came to their house needing shelter, water, or food.*

*Ali was said to be able to work metal into any shape, to give it nearly any property, within one day. He was famed for what he was said to call his "little trick": given any lump of rock, no matter how base, he could vanish for a single night and return with some Thauma craft, whether it was a battle-axe or a single, tiny pin. This led many to speculate that in order to refine the ore and craft it so quickly, Ali must have been a Fifth Clan Thauma, shaping the material with his very hands. Others said that he cheated, using scraps from his workshop to impress the gullible.*

*It is said that Fifth Clan Thaumas appear in our history only at times of unrest, when the kingdom needs a hero of legend to intervene in great battles. This is, of course, merely superstition, but as they say—in all stories there is usually a grain of truth.*

**From "The Legend of the Fifth Clan,"**
***in* Myths and Legends of the Magi**

Nalah opened her eyes, waking from one nightmare straight into another.

In the darkness, she felt the dirty straw under her hands and Cobalt's warm and solid body against her chest.

Reality struck her like a blow. Her father was dead, she was about to be executed, and there was no hope for rescue.

Then she heard the sound that had woken her—footsteps and a rattle of scale mail, outside in the main dungeon.

On the other side of her cell, a figure stirred.

"Hide the bird," Soren slurred past a thick, bleeding lip. "They'll take him."

Nalah hurriedly set Cobalt down in the corner and shoved a pile of straw over him, catching a glimpse of the white stripe across his breast as it reflected the torchlight.

She had no more tears to shed—she had cried a whole ocean overnight. But she sighed to see the rift that her father had so carefully mended. She wondered if anyone would ever be able to mend the crack in her heart the way

Papa had fixed the falcon's.

"Don't lose hope," Soren whispered. "The rebels will come for us."

"Without you to lead them?" Nalah whispered back. "They wouldn't know how."

Soren was silent for a second. "They'll find a way," he said, not meeting her gaze. "The people will rise." Nalah couldn't tell whether he believed it or not.

The door opened, and the blue light from the dungeon flowed into the Well.

"Up," said a voice. "It's time to go."

Nalah looked up at the stern faces of the two guards in the doorway. They were holding two long ropes that glistened with an oil-slick sheen. Behind them, Nalah could see a whole troop of guards, their swords drawn, waiting.

"We know about you," said one of the guards in the doorway. "You're a Fifth Clan Thauma. So just in case you have any ideas about crafting something, be assured—this rope has been made to resist any attempt to escape, and if we so much as hear a whisper out of you, our orders are to cut you down."

"I thought the king wanted a public execution," snarled Soren.

"He'll settle for a private one, if necessary," said the guard simply. "And as for you, *Ironside*," the guard sneered. "If you think your little band of thieves is coming to save you, think again. The king has erected Thauma barriers on every gate into the courtyard—no Wild weaponry can pass through. Don't you worry, though, there will be plenty of peasants—unarmed ones, of course—to watch you die. His Majesty wants to make absolutely sure the rebellion dies with you."

Nalah saw Soren's resolve falter at those words. What hope did they have now?

Nalah got to her feet and climbed out through the melted bars, her limbs feeling heavy. She let the guard tie her hands, and resisted the urge to immediately try to grab the rope and use magic to unravel it. What was the point?

*If I'm about to die,* she thought, *I'd rather see the sky again before I go.*

She allowed herself to be led out of the dungeons, through dark corridors, and up narrow stairwells. Finally a door was thrown open, and Nalah was pushed out into a sea of light.

She blinked, trying to adjust to the noonday sun, which was searingly hot after the cool depths of the Well. The sky was as clear and shining as a perfect sheet of turquoise glass. A heron wheeled overhead and was gone. It felt wrong to Nalah that such a terrible day could be so beautiful.

She was standing on a wooden stage in the corner of the palace's courtyard. The guards led her stumbling across it, and tied her hands to a stake. Beyond that, she saw the gates thrown wide open, and a crowd standing in front of the stage. It was a rainbow of color—with the nobles in colorful Thauma robes, peasants in threadbare tunics the color of sand, and guards in black.

To one side, in a raised gallery, sat a small group. The highest nobility, Nalah guessed—as well as two people she recognized. A girl dressed all in gold, shining like the sun, and a woman in robes of royal purple.

Looking at them, Nalah felt a dizzying mixture of longing, sadness, and awe.

*Princess Halan and Queen Rani.*

The queen was staring at Nalah with a stunned grief, as if seeing a perfect double of her daughter was too much for her to properly comprehend. Nalah guessed she was feeling a lot like she herself had when she first met the queen and saw her lost mother's face looking back at her.

She met Halan's eyes. For a moment, Nalah felt the thread that connected her to Halam pulling her tight. It was as if there was nothing else in the world but the two tawams, connected by a bright passage of heat and light. Would Halan truly get her powers, once Nalah was dead? Nalah hoped so.

*Remember me when I'm gone,* Nalah thought. *Think of my death, and use my powers to avenge my father and me.*

An answer came back, more clearly than any voice she'd imagined from her mother's picture. *Be brave,* the voice said. *I've still got a couple of tricks up my sleeve. Don't give up just yet.*

A jeering cry went up from the nobles in the crowd, and

the rest of the world rushed back into Nalah's mind. Her heart in her mouth, she stared at Halan.

Had she imagined the princess's reply, or was it truly her voice in Nalah's head?

Nalah then saw why the crowd had made such an ugly sound. Soren had been brought up to the platform as well, his swollen, bleeding face looking even more painful in the sunlight. Some of the nobles in the front of the crowd looked ready to tear him limb from limb, their faces twisted with rage as they shouted, "Traitor!"

And then, there were footsteps on wood, and Nalah looked around to see another man ascending the stairs to join them on the platform.

It was King Tam. He was dressed in robes the color of blood.

He strode to the front of the stage, facing away from the prisoners, and raised his hands. The crowd immediately fell silent.

"This day," he announced, "marks the dawn of a new era in the Magi Kingdom. Behind me are two traitors who would bring chaos and ruin to our land. With their deaths, the violence of rebellion and dissent will end."

The nobles cheered—and some of the peasants did, too. Nalah stared, wondering if any of them truly believed the king's words, if they thought that maybe this time he would be right, this time there would be peace.

Or maybe they just knew that if they didn't cheer, he

would cut them down, too.

They deserved better than this. They all did.

She remembered that voice in her head. *Don't give up just yet.*

Her father would not have wanted her to go down without a fight. She thought about what he'd said, in the dark cell, his kind face illuminated by the silvery glow of the glass orb.

*Nothing was ever going to be able to hide the light within you. Perhaps you were meant to come here, to discover your true destiny.*

Tears sprang to Nalah's eyes, but certainty filled her heart. It began to thump in her chest, her blood pumping hot and fast. Her hands tingled.

"The Fifth Clan have long been thought to be a myth," Tam went on, "But at last we have proof that they truly exist. My daughter's tawam is one such Thauma. When she dies, the power of the Fifth Clan will be restored to the princess and the royal line, where it belongs."

He held out his hands, and a servant approached, carrying something long and thin wrapped in white silk. Nalah's ears began to ring at its approach. *What is that?* she wondered.

Tam reached into the folds and drew out a sword.

Its handle was long and made of dark, polished wood inlaid with a crisscrossing pattern of silver ribbon. One side of the blade was forged steel, and inlaid in the other was a pane of glass that glittered like a diamond as Tam turned the sword in his hand. Nalah couldn't seem to take her eyes off it. She felt that she *knew* it, but it was new at the same time—like seeing an old friend for the first time in years. Her whole body tingled and hummed, as if communing with the sword.

"This is the Sword of the Fifth Clan, an artifact that has been kept safe in the palace since the Year of Storms. What more fitting weapon to dispatch the Fifth Clan traitor?"

He raised the sword over his head in triumph, and the crowd roared. Nalah felt her hands unhooked from the stake. "Time to die," she heard Tam whisper.

*No,* Nalah thought. *No!*

Her heart was thundering in her ears. A wild, primal rage overtook her, and she thrashed against her bonds and against the grip of the guards, not caring about the sparks of pain that the Thauma ropes shot into her arms when she did. "You can't do this!" she screamed. "Liar! Murderer!"

She was shoved down on her knees. Tam handed the sword to a man in a black hood. Of course he wouldn't strike the blow himself.

"Be quiet, girl," the man in the hood said. "If you move, it will only be worse for you."

One of the guards pushed her head down onto a low wooden pedestal, brushing her hair aside to expose the back of her neck. Nalah felt light-headed as she knelt on the wooden planks, facing the gallery where Halan and Rani sat watching.

*I'm sorry, Papa. I'm sorry I couldn't save you. I couldn't even save myself.*

She was about to close her eyes—for the last time—when a glimmer of gold sparkled in her vision.

Princess Halan had risen from her seat. She had something in her hands, Nalah saw, a glass orb, swirling with purple smoke.

*What is she doing?*

Halan, her lips pressed into a hard line, looked directly at Nalah and threw the orb into the crowd. It shattered on the flagstones below, and an impossibly large cloud of purple smoke billowed out, filling the whole courtyard and blocking the sky.

"*Halan!*" Tam screamed his daughter's name across the smoke. Nalah saw his eyes dart back and forth as the clouds rose around him, his face pale with helpless rage. Halan and her mother had been swallowed up already, and Tam's fists clenched. "Halan," he screamed again. "*What have you done?*"

The king's words were drowned out by the cacophony coming from the crowd—screams of panic and confusion and the clattering of feet across the flagstones.

Nalah tried to sit up, and the black-hooded executioner didn't stop her. He was too busy peering into the purple fog. As the smoke cleared, she saw young people pouring through a portal that had opened in the center of the courtyard—one she hadn't noticed before. *Another secret passage?* Nalah wondered. And as they charged into the courtyard at the surprised guards and nobles, glowing Wild Thauma blades and shields in hand, she noticed that they all had little metal lightning bolts glinting in their ears. *The rebels! Halan must have shown them a way under the courtyard so they could bypass the Thauma barriers!*

"No!" King Tam screamed. He drew a long obsidian dagger, the twin of the one that he'd left behind in New Hadar, and leaped from the platform. "Guards, get the princess and the other prisoner inside! Crush the invaders!"

Nalah rolled aside as the executioner suddenly remembered she was there and made a grab for the scruff of her neck. He missed her by an inch, and Nalah scrambled back across the platform, trying to get up despite her hands being bound. But she wasn't fast enough. The executioner was upon her again in an instant, the Sword of the Fifth Clan raised above his head.

Suddenly she saw an old man behind him hurl another glass orb at the wooden platform. It burst right by the executioner's feet, sending out a plume of blue smoke that curled around his foot like the tentacle of a sea monster, dragging him off the stage and engulfing him in a pulsating cocoon of smoke.

He'd dropped the sword. It clanged right by Nalah's shoulder, and she twisted around to try to reach for it, thinking somehow that even with her hands tied, if she had a weapon she could get out of these ropes.

A rumble from below their feet made her stop and crouch down, wishing she could hold on to something for balance. The rebels backed away from a patch of flagstones. One of the guards advanced, sword drawn, and then fell face-first into a hole that opened up under his feet. A flood of people climbed out, weapons raised.

"Long live the queen!" yelled the woman in front—the same bald woman with the Dust-scarred arm who Nalah had freed from the prison. "Get this to Ironside," she commanded a younger boy, thrusting a thin, sparkling silver sword into his hand. The boy ran to where Ironside was standing and began releasing him from his bonds.

Someone gripped Nalah's shoulder, and she jumped, thinking it was another guard coming to cut her down.

But it was Halan. The princess had discarded the golden robe, and underneath she was wearing a shirt of silver chain mail that glittered like stars in the drifting purple smoke.

"Are you all right?" Halan asked, taking Nalah's hands and quickly untying the ropes.

Nalah shook out her hands and rubbed her wrists. "I am now," she said.

"I'm so sorry, Nalah, I was wrong," Halan said. "I can't undo what I did, or bring your father back, but—"

"You saved my life," Nalah said. She felt choked with emotion, standing there with her mirror self. Their eyes met, and Nalah reached out and pulled Halan into an embrace.

Nalah felt it again: the warmth spreading through her body that she hadn't felt since she was a young child. It nearly took her breath away.

*I'm home.*

Halan was staring at her, her eyes wet with emotion. "I haven't known you very long," Halan said, "but I think that we were destined to come together. To look out for each other. I don't want your power. I have my own. I just want to bring peace to my kingdom. *Real* peace."

"Then I'm with you, Your Highness," said Nalah solemnly.

A black-clad shape loomed out of the smoke, sword raised. Halan and Nalah pulled apart and dodged out of the way of his swing. Halan vanished in the smoke, but Nalah could make out the hulking form of the guard, raising his sword for another blow.

A glassy screech made him look up at the last minute. Cobalt flashed out of the purple cloud, talons outstretched, and raked them across the guard's face. Blinded and filled with rage, the guard made another wild stab that might have caught Nalah in the shoulder if a flash of silver hadn't come down across it, batting it out of the way as easily as a kitten batting at a piece of string.

Soren Ferro rolled his shoulders and grinned at Nalah.

"I told you the people would rise," he said. "Find a weapon. This palace is ripe for the taking!"

Nalah grinned back at him and cast her eyes around the platform.

Where was the sword?

The guard had dropped it, but perhaps someone else had already picked it up. As she searched the platform, another smoke bomb smashed against the palace wall behind them, releasing a dragon made of red-and-yellow smoke that crawled up and along the battlements, shooting fireballs at the guards before dissipating into the air.

Down in the courtyard, Nalah saw rebels tangling with more guards and the few nobles who had stayed to fight.

She shivered as she saw Lady Kayyali fighting alongside the others with a wooden staff that seemed to shrivel and sicken the flesh of the rebels where it struck. Another rebel went down, without any apparent blow at all—until Nalah realized that she could see a pair of feet and ankles, dressed in black stockings, hurrying away and vanishing. Lord Malek was here too, wearing his brand-new shadow cloak.

But then, in the doorway to the palace, Nalah saw the captain who had captured her and Marcus standing with a huge number of guards. They jostled behind her, poised to rush into the courtyard and back up the king's guards, ready to crush the rebels. Nalah sucked in a deep breath, to shout to Halan, or Soren, to be prepared for the fight of their lives—but the captain didn't move.

"Captain Alamar," said one of the younger armsmen. "Shouldn't we attack?"

The captain turned on him. "When I give the order, armsman, and not before! Listen to me, all of you. Do you want to be on the right side of history or not?"

Nalah's heart leaped. Not all of the guards were loyal to Tam, and perhaps they would back Halan if it looked like she was going to win the day! The princess must know—

But then she heard Halan scream. It was as if someone had reached into Nalah's own chest and squeezed her heart.

"My own daughter!" raged the voice of the king. He was dragging Halan up onto the platform by one arm, his dagger gripped in his other hand. "How could you do this?" Tam yelled. "Throw your life away by helping this rabble? I am your father! I only wanted to give you what you always wanted: *power, respect!*" He jabbed the air with the dagger.

"Asa!" Two more figures stormed up onto the platform. Queen Rani, her black hair loose and flying, sprinted toward her husband. Beside her was a guard in black, the top of his face masked by an iron helmet. "It's over. Let her go," the queen demanded.

"Over? *Over?*" Tam sneered. "My dear, it has only begun. After all these years, you would betray me too?" He turned to Halan. "I always knew you were your mother's daughter. Traitors, both." He pulled the princess close against his chest, holding the dagger dangerously close to her throat. "You never loved me, Rani, but I know that you love her. So step back, *now.*"

Queen Rani hesitated, her eyes riveted on Halan. She

reached out for the arm of the guard behind her, and he took off his helmet.

Nalah's heart gave a thunderous leap in her chest.

It was her father.

Except . . . it wasn't. He was clean-shaven, burlier, darker from the relentless Magi Kingdom sun. And he was alive.

"Bardak?" Tam gulped, as if he'd seen a ghost. "But you're *dead*." The hand holding the dagger sagged, and Halan wrenched herself out of his grip.

"Captain Omar Bardak," she said, standing tall before the king. "He's been in the palace all this time. One of your very own guards—one of the hundreds of people you never really see because they're not rich or noble enough. He's my real father, not you."

Tam stumbled back as if he had been struck. He stared at Rani and Omar, standing before him, and then looked to Halan, defiant.

"Halan," Rani said. "That's enough—comc away from him."

*Yes, please,* Nalah urged in her mind. *He's dangerous. You know what he's capable of now!*

But Halan wasn't finished. "That's the real reason Mother was always so afraid for me," she went on. "It wasn't because of the rebels, it was because of *you*."

The tension in the air made the hair on Nalah's arms stand up, and she knew she had to act quickly. *You already took one precious life, Tam,* she thought. *I'm not going to let you take another.* She quieted her mind and listened for the hum she'd heard when Tam had unsheathed the sword. It was calling to her, like all the powerful Thauma objects did. Then she heard it, across the platform. She darted toward it and spotted the Sword of the Fifth Clan, forgotten on the ground.

Her fingers brushed the silver-ribbon-crossed wooden handle, and she immediately felt an electric shiver coursing through her body. As she clasped the sword in her hand, she could almost feel the weapon melding with her, becoming one with her like an extension of her own arm.

*This*, she thought. *This is my destiny.*

The moment was broken by Tam's strangled cry.

"Your mother was right to be afraid," he said softly. "You are no daughter of mine. That's why you were born powerless, useless! I should have killed you at birth!" He raised the obsidian dagger and lurched toward Halan.

"*No!*" Nalah screamed. She rolled to her feet in a single movement, the sword in her hands. This was like the feeling when she'd broken the glass at the market, but instead of passing through her and out her hands, it just seemed to keep cycling through her, like an electric current humming in her veins.

Half a dozen armed guards leaped in between Nalah and where Tam held Halan, but Nalah didn't stop. Something possessed her, a righteous fury that overtook fear and doubt like a cleansing fire. Three of them charged at her, raining down killing blows with their swords, but Nalah batted them away like flies. The Sword of the Fifth Clan glowed with a fierce light, and every weapon that it met shattered on impact. Within seconds, the six guards had been disarmed, their weapons in ruin, their eyes watching Nalah with awe and fear.

Finally, with the path to Tam cleared, Nalah stood before them, power surging through her like lightning in her veins. She pointed the sword at the king and said, "*Let her go.*"

But the voice was not merely her own. And it contained more than just the simple chime of her earlier wonders. This voice, her voice, contained cracks of thunder, gusts of wind, and the crash of waves on the shore. It reverberated across the walls of the courtyard so that it felt as if she was everywhere at once.

Tam was about to speak, but then he screamed and doubled over his hand. The obsidian blade was melting over his fingers, its volcanic glass heated to thousands of degrees.

"*Leave this place,*" Nalah boomed. "*Take your followers and go!*"

She pointed with the sword, and the smoke around her swirled and followed her gesture, all the colored smoke in the courtyard flowing together to form a tunnel between the platform and the gate. A wind began to rush down the tunnel, tugging at Tam's robes as he stood cradling his burned hand.

"*Your rule over this place is ended.*"

The nobles Lang and Kayyali and Malek all rushed to the platform, wielding their Thauma weapons, the wind current tugging at their hair and clothes. Lady Lang threw a sharp glass dagger at Nalah, but Nalah parried it easily with the sword, and it fell and shattered on the platform at her feet.

*"Hear me, and be gone!"* Nalah commanded. The wood under Tam's feet cracked and tipped up, throwing him off the platform. The Thauma lords caught him and they began to back away. Tam tried to start back toward the platform one more time, and Nalah brought down the sword in a wide sweep. The smoke twisted around the arms of the nobles, pulling them away.

"I will be back and I will destroy you. I'll destroy you *both*!" Tam shouted, but his words were swallowed up by the roar of the wind. The four of them, and a small gang of guards, retreated out of the gate and were gone.

Nalah reached out. She could feel the cool metal of the gate under her hand, even though it was on the other side of the courtyard. She grabbed it and yanked it down. The iron gate slammed into place with a heavy *clang*.

Nalah took a deep breath, and then couldn't seem to let it go. She felt as if she had suddenly become as light as air, as if she might float away on the wind like the last of the dissipating colored smoke. The world turned around her and she felt the sword drop from her grip as the wooden platform came up to meet her.

"Nalah!" cried Halan's voice, from far away. Nalah lay facedown on the platform until a pair of hands turned her over and she looked up into the face of her tawam. Halan was going in and out of focus a bit, but she was smiling, tears streaking down her cheeks. "Nalah, you did it! You saved us all."

She helped Nalah sit up. Nalah looked around at the courtyard, weak and dazed, waiting for her head to stop spinning.

The fighting had ended. Guards and nobles were surrendering their weapons to the rebels. With a clatter of mail, Captain Alamar and her armsmen marched up to the front of the platform and presented their swords to Halan.

"We serve at your command, Princess," they chorused.

Halan looked back at her mother, the queen. Queen Rani was smiling, with tears in her eyes. "It is your time, my love," she said. "Go."

*I wouldn't completely trust the guards*, Nalah thought. *Especially Alamar. She turned on her king at a moment's notice.*

*Don't worry, I won't*, replied Halan.

Then they stared at each other, openmouthed.

Nalah broke into a stunned smile. "Your Majesty," she said to Halan. "You should say something, they're waiting for you."

Halan shook her head, with a small smile. "They're waiting for *us*."

She took Nalah's hand in hers, and before Nalah knew quite what was happening, Halan had raised them both over her head.

Starting with the guards, and then the rebels, and then the nobles, all the people in the courtyard sank to their knees. Soren Ferro swept a low and elaborate bow, and laid his silver sword on the ground. Marcus was the last one left standing. He grinned at Nalah, and then bowed low, as well.

Nalah looked out over the crowd and to the bright blue sky, where a flashing glass bird was circling above. Now, it really was a beautiful day.

*This all started with a shard of glass and a challenge. Little did I know that I wouldn't just make a mirror. I would help make something else. Something better.*

*Peace.*

# Chapter Twenty

## Sisters

*When the Great War is over, peace will finally be welcomed in the land. But peace is not a trophy to be won, not a prize to be placed on a pedestal. Like a fire, peace must be tended, must be fed with justice, understanding, and cooperation. There will come a time when this fire may go out—but never fear. With only a single bright ember—or two—the flame of peace can be rekindled.*

*Cyrus, Prophet of the Sands*

The great hall of the Magi Palace was thronged with people, all of them silent, all of them staring at Halan. She looked back at her subjects, her face a mask of calm—though inside she felt anything but.

It had been two days since the battle for the palace, but so much had happened that it seemed like only a blink of an eye. A blur of celebrations, political shuffling, and public pronouncements filled Halan's mind, threatening to distract her from the moment at hand. And what a moment it was. She forced herself to concentrate on Lord Helavi's wizened face, as her old teacher asked her a very important question.

"And do you, Halan Ali," her old teacher boomed, his voice magically amplified throughout the hall, "swear to defend the state and its people, through dust and storm, through drought and flood, against all enemies, for as long as you live?"

"I swear," Halan said. She looked at her mother, who smiled, her eyes twinkling with a pride Halan had gotten familiar with over the last few days.

Nearly all traces of the worry that had plagued her for twelve years were gone from Queen Rani's face as she lifted the light, simple golden circlet and placed it on top of Halan's head. Then she stepped aside, and Halan gazed down at the huge crowd of people as her mother spoke the final words of the coronation ceremony.

"Let the sun and the sands bear witness, let the mountains and the farmlands bear witness, as I present to you all: Queen Halan the First, ruler of the Magi Kingdom!"

As one, the crowd of nobles, guards, servants, and common people knelt down and bowed their heads. In the front row, Nalah swept a slightly wobbly bow, Cobalt perched on her shoulder. As Halan caught her eye, the same thought seemed to be coursing through both of their minds.

*I always wanted a real friend, someone I would trust, who would treat me as an equal.*

*I got something else entirely. I got a sister!*

Halan's heart was bursting with joy as she brushed down her flame-colored gown and stepped forward. "My people," she called out across the sea of bowed heads, "I take the throne at a time of great changes. King Tam called this a new era for the Magi Kingdom, and he was right. This is a new chapter for us, but it isn't the one he wanted to write. I hope—with the Queen Mother by my side—to bring true peace to this land, and I will need the help of each and every one of you to make that dream come true."

The crowd roared their approval.

The hall had been draped in banners depicting every Thauma house and every profession in the city. All the doors to the palace had been thrown open, so that even the poorest citizens could come to see their new queen crowned.

But many had not come. The captains had told her that they'd been sent away from some homes with curses ringing in their ears, and some doors hadn't been opened to them at all. Halan knew she would have to work hard to prove to those citizens that she was a better monarch than the man she'd always called father.

She couldn't wait to get started.

Beside her mother, shining in a suit of silver armor that Soren Ferro had made for him, was her real father—Omar Bardak. Halan met his eyes, and he gave her a smile and a wink back. Halan nodded, in a way she hoped seemed warm.

She didn't know this man. In the hectic aftermath of

the battle and the run-up to her coronation, they had tried to talk, but those rushed conversations had barely begun to breach the chasm between them. It would take time—and, luckily, they had plenty of that.

She only knew that Omar was a better man than Asa Tam, and that her mother loved him. Had always loved him, ever since they met when they were barely older than Halan. But as a woman of royal blood, she'd had little say with regard to her marriage, and Tam was never a man to take no for an answer.

It would have to do for now. Halan instinctively trusted Omar, for a very simple reason: the happiness of not having to hide her feelings or keep Halan's paternity a secret from her dangerous husband had changed Rani, so that she was almost unrecognizable. She remained the formal queen mother, but now her smiles reached her eyes. The false pretense of happiness had been replaced by something genuine.

Music began to play—a self-playing Thauma harp and dulcimer, and a low thunder roll of drums.

Halan sat down—*almost* without looking behind her—on a pile of gold-embroidered cushions nearly as tall as she was. People began to join a long line to present her with their allegiance and their gifts.

"It will be a long day, love," Rani said to Halan under her breath. "But protocol says if you need to take a break, they have to wait for you."

"Perhaps protocol isn't all that bad," Halan whispered back.

Right at the front of the line were Nalah, Marcus, and Soren Ferro. But as they approached, Halan saw that Nalah wasn't looking at her—she was staring up at Rani and Omar, the queen mother and her consort, a wistful smile on her lips and tears glistening in her eyes.

Both of Nalah's own parents were gone, and yet here they were—or here they appeared to be. Through their newfound connection, Halan could sense Nalah's bittersweet feelings of pain and love as she stared at the two people in front of her.

Nalah approached Halan and dipped another slightly clumsy curtsy. She was wearing a gown of the finest Thauma silk, the color of Cobalt's wings, with a white sash across her chest.

"Your Majesty," she said.

As Nalah straightened up, Rani—to Halan's surprise—stepped forward and gathered her into an embrace. Rani looked down at her daughter's twin, a confused sort of love in her eyes. "Nalah Bardak," she said. "For everything you have done, I promise you, you will always be welcome here in the Magi Kingdom."

Nalah's eyes blurred with tears. "Your Highness. Captain Bardak . . . ," she murmured, her voice cracking. "Thank you."

She looked at Halan, and they smiled at each other,

though Halan felt an icy shiver as she thought about Nalah's return to the other world. It had been decided: Marcus had family in New Hadar, and it was where he and Nalah both belonged. They would step back through the mirror into their own world after the coronation ceremony was over.

Part of Halan hoped the ceremony would never end.

She had a kingdom now, a people to look after, and there was plenty to do. But she had something else, something she had always wanted, and never quite expected to have. More than a double, or a sister. A true friend.

And she didn't want to say good-bye.

The Transcendent Mirror was a beautiful thing. Halan stared into its radiant depths, wondering what the world on the other side was really like. Was the sea as blue and limitless as the sky? Were the great steel engines as fast as they were in the stories? And what about the government—this "Hokmet"—would Marcus and Nalah be all right if they went back?

She tried to put such thoughts out of her head. She was certain that anything Nalah had to face, she could overcome.

Marcus and Nalah stood before the mirror, dressed in their peasant clothes.

"Good-bye, Your Majesty," said Marcus. "Try not to knock anyone out today." Nalah gave him a playful shove.

"Marcus, she's the queen now! She can knock out anyone she likes."

"I'll try not to," said Halan, with a chuckle. "And I'm sorry again for what I did."

"Apology accepted," Marcus said, and bowed to her. He looked at Nalah. "Time to go?"

"Yes," Nalah said. She looked down at her hands, and then turned to the young fabricworker. "It's time for you to go, Marcus."

Halan stared at Nalah in confusion. *What is she saying?*

"What?" Marcus frowned. "What do you mean, Nalah? We're both going home."

"*You* need to get home," Nalah said, the words coming out all in a rush, like a dam was breaking. "Your mother and father, your grandmother, they're all waiting for you in New Hadar. It's where you belong. But . . . there's nobody waiting for me. My parents are both gone, you're my only real friend there, and I'm a wanted criminal. Here, I can be myself, and be as powerful as I know I can be. Here, I . . . I have Halan." Nalah looked up at Halan, and Halan felt as if her heart was frozen, scared to beat in case it burst with happiness. "And what if Tam comes back, like he said he would? My fate is here, where I'm strongest, where I can do some good."

*She's staying!*

Halan felt like dancing around the room, and then she looked at Marcus's face and sagged. Her gain was Marcus's loss, and she could tell it was devastating. He stared at Nalah for a moment, and Halan saw his lip tremble, just a little. Then he sniffed and nodded. "Dunno what I'm going to do without you around to make me look good," he said.

"Well, don't be a clumsy idiot and break the mirror, and you can come back and visit," Nalah replied. "Besides . . . I'm not sure why, but I feel I haven't seen the last of New Hadar. We are mirror worlds, after all. Our fates are intertwined."

"I hope so." Marcus grinned and pulled Nalah into a hug, and held on for a long few seconds. When he pulled away, Halan noticed that his eyes were wet. He blinked a few times and then said, "Nalah, I know you think I only talked to you at the market out of pity, but that wasn't why."

Nalah had raised her hand to begin writing the Thauma symbols on the mirror's surface. Now she turned around. "It wasn't?" she asked, looking curiously into her friend's eyes.

Marcus shook his head. "It might be hard to believe, given my charming personality," he said wryly, "but I didn't have many friends, either. You were the only one who'd put up with me."

Nalah huffed at that.

Marcus wrung his hands. "No, but it was more than that. I wanted to talk to *you*. Everyone else may have thought you were dangerous or clumsy—but I knew better. I knew you were special. And I wanted to be part of that. You were—you *are* my best friend."

Nalah's face broke into a slow grin, and she rushed

forward to hug Marcus again. "And you're mine," she said over his shoulder, "even if you *are* a know-it-all."

Marcus grinned wryly and pulled away. "Seems like you kind of needed a know-it-all."

Shaking her head, Nalah raised her hand again and began sketching the symbols on the mirror, chanting under her breath.

*"Way of light, open the door to the kingdom of the many sands. Let me cross over the void."*

Marcus turned away and Halan saw him wipe his eyes on his sleeve, but she didn't say anything. Blue-white light and a pungent smell of smoke and salty air began to seep from the mirror's surface.

"See you soon," said Marcus simply, and waved to Halan. Then he stepped into the mirror. It rippled and let him pass through, and a moment later it hardened and the light vanished, and there was nothing there but the glass.

"Nalah," said Halan breathlessly. "Are you *sure?*"

Nalah grinned at Halan. "I've thought about it a lot over the last couple days. I want to be here. With you."

Before Halan's blush could fully heat up her cheeks, a creaking caw rang out from above them, and Cobalt fluttered down onto Nalah's shoulder and gave her a slightly insulted glare.

"And with Cobalt, obviously," Nalah corrected herself.

Halan smiled and reached up to pet the glass falcon's neck feathers. She ran her hand down his chest, tracing the white line that Nalah said had once been a crack, until Amir Bardak had mended it.

"You said that Cobalt had a link to your father," Halan said slowly, hoping that it was all right to ask. "Do you . . . feel anything from him now?"

"Not really," Nalah said. "He's gone. Far enough that I can't reach him, anyway. But when I look into Cobalt's eyes, I do feel something. I feel . . . warm. It's like the feeling of the furnace when it's all but gone out and there's only a couple of embers left burning."

They were silent for a moment. Halan felt a little sorry for asking, but not sorry that she'd heard the answer.

"Oh," said Nalah. "Listen, there's something else I wanted to show you. I've been doing a lot of reading. There are *so many books* in here—it's incredible! How can one person ever read them all in a lifetime and still get anything done?"

"I'll make sure to introduce you to Lord Helavi," Halan said, with a grin. "You'll probably get along. What did you find?"

"Well, I was wondering about the sword. The Sword of the Fifth Clan. Where did it come from? Why did it have that effect on me?" She led Halan over to the study desk, where the sword was lying beside a pile of open books. "As far as I can tell, it belonged to some Fifth Clan Thauma during the Great War, but it was, well, *appropriated* by the king's descendants during the Year of Storms."

"You can say stolen," Halan said.

"I found an old legend that said that way, *way* back, before the war, the person who wielded the sword was a Fifth Clan warrior who protected the monarch on the battlefield. She was called the Queen's Sword."

*"The Queen's Sword,"* Halan whispered. The words had a strange echo in her head, even though Nalah hadn't spoken them with her Fifth Clan voice. Halan had heard them before, but when? Was it some story her mother had told her?

"My father said something to me," Nalah went on. "He said perhaps I was always meant to come here, to discover my true place in the world."

Nalah lifted the sword, and its glass pane glinted in the bright sunshine. Halan thought she saw her tawam's eyes sparkle, but whether it was a reflection or the power coursing through her, she couldn't say. Nalah knelt at Halan's feet, and held out the sword.

"I think my place is beside you. As the Queen's Sword."

A smile spread over Halan's face, irresistible and unstoppable.

*Like the two of us.*

"Then consider your destiny fulfilled," said Halan solemnly. "Rise, Nalah Bardak, Queen's Sword."

Her tawam stood, and Halan saw her own smile reflected on Nalah's face.

Whatever came next, they would face it together.